THE AMERICAN INDIAN *IN* SHORT FICTION

an annotated bibliography

Peter G. Beidler
and Marion F. Egge

The Scarecrow Press, Inc.
Metuchen, N.J., & London 1979

Library of Congress Cataloging in Publication Data

Beidler, Peter G
    The American Indian in short fiction.

    Includes indexes.
    1. Short stories, American--Bibliography.
2. Indians of North America--Fiction--Bibliography.
3. Short stories, American--Stories, plots, etc.
I. Egge, Marion F., joint author. II. Title.
Z1231.F4B44 1980 [PS374.I49] 016.813'03   79-20158
ISBN 0-8108-1256-8

For

Anne and Richard

CONTENTS

Preface   vii

Annotated Bibliography   1

Indian Tribes Index   189

Subject Key Words Index   194

PREFACE

The attitudes of white Americans have shifted radically in the past century. After the Civil War, American military personnel found themselves occupied with another kind of civil war, the war with the Indians west of the Mississippi. Most white Americans at the time, however, thought of these wars not as civil wars between people fighting for the right to live on certain lands, but as righteous crusades by Christian knights against the pagan savages who insisted upon interfering with the "progress" of a great nation. As time went on, however, and as the infidels fell one by one before the superior military power of the white knights, attitudes changed. After 1890, when the battle at Wounded Knee marked the last of the major military confrontations between the two opposing forces, the American public found that it could afford to look more generously upon the situation of the Indian, and saw the desirability of absorbing the Indians into the melting pot. In the 1920s the Indians were all "given" citizenship in the United States by a special act of Congress. In the 1930s, by which time there was no further threat of military aggression from these Indians, Congress passed the Indian Reorganization Act, granting Indian tribes the right to set up their own tribal governments. And by the 1970s many white Americans found themselves in sympathy with militant Indians who were demanding recognition of their rights as Indians and of their status as human beings.

There have, then, been important and influential changes in the public view of the American Indian. Unfortunately, these changes have never been charted, primarily because there has been no means for doing so. This book is an attempt to begin to provide that means by making available to scholars--in anthropology, history, popular culture, and literature--an annotated and fully indexed bibliography of American short fiction about the American Indian.

The short story has had an extremely important influence on, and has been an important reflection of, public opinion about Indians. By the end of the nineteenth century the short story had come into its own as a literary form. Writers of stories were finding a ready and lucrative market for their work in the many popular magazines which were receiving wide distribution across America. The American Indian was an amazingly hardy standby in such fiction. Some Indian characters were stereotyped, some strikingly original; some were unattractive, some very attractive; some were unrealistic, some quite realistic. The point is that these "literary"

Indians were all that most Americans ever saw. The reservations were remote from the centers of population and, once the wars were over, the Indians were not making much news. They kept appearing in stories, however, and those stories were widely circulated and read. Later on there were movies and television, but written fiction was important first and for a much longer period of time in the dissemination of information about Indians and Indian life. And even when movies about Indians did become prevalent, they tended merely to make visual the stereotypes already familiar in popular fiction.

Despite the importance of the American short story in conveying information about Indians and in forming public opinion about Indians, virtually no analysis of the nature of short stories about Indians has been made--primarily because it has been almost impossible for scholars to locate the stories. To be sure, the Short Story Index (H. W. Wilson Co.) does list most of the stories about Indians which have appeared in published anthologies of short stories, but only a fraction of the published stories about Indians have ever been anthologized. Another problem with using the Short Story Index is that it does not give any indication of the plot of individual stories.

By providing plot summaries for almost 900 short stories which have appeared in both books and magazines, we are hoping to help fill the research needs of scholars in a number of disciplines. Students of American literature can use this bibliography as the basis for various kinds of thematic, narrative, character, and stylistic studies. Historians and political scientists can use it as the basis for studies of the effect of political trends on popular treatments of Indians. Anthropologists and culture historians can use it as the basis for studies of the relationship between factual and fictional treatments of Indians, and for studies of the causes and effects of shifting popular attitudes about Indians.

A few of the specific kinds of questions which researchers in various fields might now begin to answer are:

--What are the most prevalent Indian stereotypes or "repeating characters" in American fiction? Are there, for example, more fighters than lovers? Are Apaches stereotyped in different ways than Hopis are?

--Do different publications tend to convey or project different images of the Indian? That is, has Atlantic Monthly published a different kind of "Indian story" than other magazines have? Is there a "highbrow stereotype" which is different from the "lowbrow stereotype"?

--What have been the shifts in the popular conception of the Indian as represented in the short story?

--Is there a relationship between federal policy toward Indians and the shifting popular image of the Indian? For example, was the Indian Reorganization Act of 1934, which gave Indians a greater power to determine their own affairs and which marked a distinct increase in federal respect for the validity of tribal ways, preceded or followed by a significant grouping of stories showing a similar respect for Indian ways?

--How do Indians speak in the stories? What does a stylistic analysis of Indian speech patterns as reflected in fiction tell us about the popular conception of Indians as grunting, monosyllabic savages at one extreme, and as eloquent, dramatic orators at the other extreme?

--Which tribes are most often represented in short stories? For example, has the Sioux been more frequently treated than the Pueblo? If so, why and what has been the effect on the popular conception of the Indian?

--What are the most frequently perpetrated errors about Indian life?

--Can certain truths about Indians be portrayed more effectively in short stories than in other ways? For example, can the story convey what it feels like to be a Comanche more effectively than the historical or anthropological monograph can? If so, which stories have done so?

--What psychological explanation can be offered for the kinds of stories that have been written? Were the white writers attempting to defend the concept of "manifest destiny"? Do those writing sympathetically of Indians show signs of attempting to expiate feelings of guilt for the way Indians have been treated?

--Do stories written by Indian authors differ significantly or consistently from stories about Indians written by non-Indian authors?

We wish to express our thanks to the National Endowment for the Humanities, which provided the fellowship under which the project was begun; to Lehigh University's Office of Research and to Lehigh University's Humanities Perspectives on Technology program, for providing funds for technical and research assistance; to the staff of the libraries of the University of Arizona and Lehigh University, for their help in locating materials; to technician David Mastrobattista, of the Lehigh University Center for Information Sciences, for assistance in compiling information contained herein; to Martha Mills, Anne Beidler, and Gerald Joyce, for their assistance in locating and summarizing stories; to Lynne Gallagher, Jami Frank, Wendy Dudzinski, and Elaine Doyle, for helping to prepare the manuscript; and to Edward H. Spicer, of the Anthropology Department of the University of Arizona, for thinking the project was worth doing in the first place.

Scope and Use of Bibliography

In this bibliography we have included modern short stories about Indian characters. Although most of the writers of the stories are non-Indians, we are pleased to note that Indians themselves are coming increasingly to use the short story as a means of literary expression. We do not include here the traditional oral tales, myths, and legends recorded by anthropologists and folklorists (although, certainly, the work of some short story writers shows evidence of their having been influenced by these traditional stories); nor do we include, with only a few exceptions, stories written by European writers, stories about Mexican, Canadian, or Alaskan Indians, stories written for pre-teen juveniles, or stories written before 1890.

We have located most of the stories in one of two ways. The first involved tracing stories listed as being about Indians in the Short Story Index. The second was more difficult, since it involved our sitting down with whole runs of various journals and popular magazines and paging through one issue after another in search of stories with Indian characters. The bibliography makes no claims to completeness. It would have taken several more years and a great deal more money to search complete runs of every American magazine published since 1890. We feel confident, however, that we have located a sufficiently large number of stories to enable scholars to identify characteristic trends.

The stories are listed alphabetically by author. (Tribal affiliation of Indian authors, if known, is given in parentheses following the name.) The summaries are designed to give users of the bibliography a rough idea of who the Indian characters in the story are and what they do. Not intended to take the place of a reading of the full story, these summaries are meant only to guide scholars in determining which stories they will need to track down for their own purposes.

Important features of this bibliography are the two comprehensive indexes following the alphabetical listing of the stories. Scholars who wish to know what stories have been written about the Indians of a certain tribe should consult the Indian Tribes Index. By looking under, say, IROQUOIS, they will find the numbers of all of the stories which have Iroquois Indians as characters. We have had to make certain decisions along the way, however, and researchers should keep in mind: 1) Stories which mention only "Indians" without specifying a tribe are not listed in this index; 2) Some tribal names included are fictional; 3) Indian tribes merely mentioned in the stories--without having been directly involved in development of the plot--are not included; 4) Variant spellings of tribal names have been changed to the most common spelling for the sake of consistency (for example, "Paiute" has been changed to "Piute, " "Navaho" to "Navajo, " and so on).

The Subject Key Words Index may be used by those who wish

to locate stories in which there are HALF-BREED Indians, or stories about the REVENGE motive in fiction about Indians, or stories about EDUCATIONAL DISORIENTATION of Indians, or stories about RO-MANCE relationships between Indian men and white women, or SCI-ENCE FICTION/FANTASY stories about Indians. This index lists these and almost fifty other concepts or "key words" which identify recurring motifs in short fiction about Indians. Plot summaries have, of necessity, been kept brief; some key concepts in certain stories are indexed as such even though specific reference may not be apparent by reading the summary alone. (Additional information appears before each index.)

We believe that these two indexes will prove to be of partic-ular usefulness to scholars. A glance at the first index, for exam-ple, shows that the three tribes most frequently represented in Amer-ican short fiction are the Apache, the Navajo, and the Sioux--three of America's most militarily aggressive tribes. A glance at the second index, on the other hand, shows that the number of stories involving romance is about equal to the number involving killing. And if readers have assumed that the dominant stereotype in stories about romance would be that of the Indian male as captor or rapist of white women, they may be interested to note 1) that there are twice as many stories about love affairs between Indian women and white men as there are about love affairs between Indian men and white women, and 2) that there are far more stories about romances between Indian men and Indian women than there are about both kinds of interracial romances combined. We leave to others the fun of making--and exploring--similar discoveries.

P. G. B.
M. F. E.

ANNOTATED BIBLIOGRAPHY

1   Abbey, Edward. "Sunflowers. " <u>Western Review</u>, 4, No. 1
     (Summer 1967), 17-21.
          George Hayduke, an anthropology graduate student at the
     University of New Mexico, attempts to write his thesis: "A
     Study of the Sweatbath Ceremonials of the Havasupai Indians of
     Supai, Arizona. " He is distracted by a neighbor, the wife of
     his best friend, and seduces her.

2   Adams, Andy. "A Comanche Fight in the Tallow Cache Hills. "
     <u>Why the Chisholm Trail Forks and Other Tales of the Cattle</u>
     <u>Country.</u> Ed. Wilson M. Hudson. Austin: Univ. of Texas
     Press, 1956, pp. 232-36.
          Twenty Comanches, on their return to the reservation
     with a herd of stolen horses, are attacked by Texas Rangers.
     As a result most of the Comanches, including one woman, are
     killed. The Rangers find among the dead Indians' possessions
     the fresh scalps of white people, including women and children.

3   _____. "A Horse Herd Lost to Cheyennes. " <u>Why the Chis-</u>
     <u>holm Trail Forks and Other Tales of the Cattle Country.</u>
     Ed. Wilson M. Hudson. Austin: Univ. of Texas Press, 1956,
     pp. 36-39.
          Reservation Cheyennes are accustomed to asking for,
     and receiving, the gift of a horse or a cow as tribute from cow-
     boys taking their herds through a certain stretch of the Chisholm
     Trail. One tough Texas trail boss, however, will not give Chief
     Running Bull Sheep the tribute, but instead shoots the Indian.
     In the end the Cheyennes take the whole herd, the cowboys bare-
     ly escaping with their lives.

4   _____. "Indian-Style Fun. " <u>Why the Chisholm Trail Forks</u>
     <u>and Other Tales of the Cattle Country.</u> Ed. Wilson M. Hud-
     son. Austin: Univ. of Texas Press, 1956, pp. 111-15.
          A group of about twenty Cheyennes from the reservation,
     finding a lone cowboy in the camp, have some "fun" by taking
     his gun and shooting bullets into his campfire. Then they re-
     turn his empty rifle and disappear.

5   Adams, Jones. "In the Stronghold of the Piutes. " <u>Overland</u>
     <u>Monthly,</u> n. s. 22 (1893), 583-93.
          In early 1880 a large herd of horses is brought to
     southwestern Colorado under the protection of John Thurman,

Dick May, and Byron Smith. A notorious band of renegade
Piutes kills Smith and May and steals the horses. May's brother, William, organizes a party to seek revenge but is not successful.

6   Alcott, Louisa M. "Onawandah." Growing Up with America:
     An Anthology. Ed. May Lamberton Becker. Philadelphia:
     Lippincott, 1941, pp. 33-46.
         The good parson kindly takes in a lame and starving In-
     dian youth against the warning of his housekeeper, who fears
     that no Indian can be trusted in those colonial times. Later,
     savage Indians attack the community when the parson is away.
     The Indians carry off the parson's two children to their village
     many miles away. Onawandah, the Indian youth, is accused of
     being responsible for this evil act, but he proves his innocence
     and his loyalty to his friends by helping the two children escape
     from the village, and by saving their lives on the return trip.

7   Allen, Hervey. "A Boy Turns Turtle." In Other Days. Ed.
     Frances T. Humphreville. Chicago: Scott, Foresman, 1956,
     pp. 84-95. Originally published in The Forest and the Fort
     (New York: Rinehart, 1943).
         Salathiel Albine is taken prisoner by Shawnees at about
     six years of age. His mother and father had been killed by the
     Shawnees, but two childless members of the tribe (Big Turtle
     and his wife, Mawakis) accept Salathiel into their lodge as Little
     Turtle.

8   Allen, Merritt P. "The Second Race." Indians, Indians, In-
     dians. Ed. Phyllis R. Fenner. New York: Franklin Watts,
     1950, pp. 35-43. Originally published in Boy's Life (Feb.
     1949).
         David Elerson finishes last in a footrace in the army
     camp in 1779, but later he wins a second race, escaping from
     a dozen pursuing Indians.

9   Anderson, Dillon. "Forty Years of Firewood." Southwest Re-
     view, 36, No. 4 (Autumn 1951), 267-76. Reprinted in
     Claudie's Kinfolks (Boston: Little, Brown and Co., 1954)
     and in 21 Texas Short Stories, ed. William Perry (Austin:
     Univ. of Texas Press, 1954), pp. 176-89.
         Two drifting freeloaders (Claudie and Clint) get to the
     Waxahachie Reservation in time to see Chief Eaglebeak installed
     amid groundbreaking ceremonies for the new government-built
     gymnasium. (The Chief is portrayed as a slow-witted Indian--lazy,
     indolent, and easy to push around.) The Indians wear feathers
     and costumes for the occasion, borrowed from white people in
     town. Chief Eaglebeak lives in an old house, and gradually
     tears down a new one the government had built for him, using
     the wood for his fire. He decides to cooperate with the con-
     tractor of the new gymnasium--mainly because the much larger
     building will provide him with firewood for the next forty years.

10 Anderson, Edna. "Her Own People: The Story of a Managing
Mother. " Sunset, 40, No. 1 (Jan. 1918), 42-43, 58-61.
   Indian Mary, widow of a prosperous Irish rancher, had
raised four fair daughters. Celia and Sophy had married well,
and later Katie and Sheila made plans to marry. Indian Mary
gave them all generous wedding gifts. After the girls are all
gone, Mary leaves the ranch to implement a long-awaited plan;
she rides to another settlement to get a young Indian boy she
had seen a year earlier and had promised to raise, but she
learns that he has died. Upon her return to the ranch she finds
Katie with supper waiting for her. Indian Mary realizes that
her daughters are her own people after all, in spite of their
white blood.

11 Andrews, Mary Raymond Shipman. "A Messenger. " The Mili-
tants: Stories of Some Parsons, Soldiers and Other Fighters
in the World. New York: Scribner's, 1907, pp. 151-84.
   Miles Morgan, a young lieutenant, is sent out to warn
Captain Thornton that the "red devil" (Black Wolf) has gone on
the warpath. It is a most dangerous journey, but he soon
learns that God protects the good and the innocent. He discovers that he is followed by a small band of ponies, "each
with its load of filthy, cruel savagery"--that is, each bearing
an Indian. He is saved when an angel appears and takes him
to one side, and then causes the Indians to turn in fear from
a kind of vision of an enormous approaching army.

12 Annixter, Paul. "Circle Round the Mound. " Southwest Review,
29, No. 4 (Summer 1944), 588-93.
   On the Apache reservation in front of Heeny's Trading
Post, Carrick awaits Winstead's arrival. Winstead and an old
Indian, Joe Narrow Knees, take Carrick on a photography trip.
They notice the protective relationship between the rattlesnake
and the prairie dog, and Joe draws an analogy between the
greedy coyote/white man and the patiently wise rattlesnake/In-
dian.

13 Anthony, Wilder. "The Spotted Dog's Bride. " Overland
Monthly, n. s. 56 (1910), 290-91.
   A reservation agent teaches Spotted Dog how to cheat at
poker so he can win the girl he wants for his wife from her
stubborn and proud father.

14 Applegate, Frank. "The Apache Kid. " Native Tales of New
Mexico. Philadelphia: Lippincott, 1932, pp. 205-15.
   An Apache Indian's father is killed by another Apache.
Instead of waiting for due process under the white man's law,
the son avenges the misdeed by killing the murderer; then he
quickly escapes to the mountains, an outcast from both cultures.
He raids both whites and Indians--sometimes taking squaws
with him, but later releasing them. He kills a white lad (the
narrator's friend), and is finally killed by a rancher when he
attempts to steal the white man's horses.

15 _____ . "The Buried Treasure of Cochiti." Native Tales of New Mexico. Philadelphia: Lippincott, 1932, pp. 113-21.
The Indians bury a treasure when Spaniards threaten to take over their lands.

16 _____ . "The Founding of Hano." Native Tales of New Mexico. Philadelphia: Lippincott, 1932, pp. 15-23.
The Hopi residents of Walpi need help to fight off the Navajos; the willing assistants set up outside Walpi in a new area which they name Hano.

17 _____ . "A Hopi Affair." Indian Stories from the Pueblos. Glorieta, N.M.: Rio Grande Press, 1929, pp. 59-64.
Ta Ha, a Hopi boy, goes to a boarding school and learns that white men choose their own wives. His mother wants to follow the Hopi tradition of selecting a wife for him herself, so Ta Ha is much perturbed and divided in his loyalties. He loves Dawa, a Hopi girl from another mesa, and, deciding that love must come first, he writes to the girl, asking her to run off to have a white man's wedding. Dawa agrees, and they marry, but it turns out that she is the one picked by his mother anyway, so everyone is happy.

18 _____ . "The Hopi Famine." Indian Stories from the Pueblos. Glorieta, N.M.: Rio Grande Press, 1929, pp. 125-33.
In a terrible drought and famine, little Mungwu, his brother, and his widowed mother almost starve. Their fellow Hopis help for a while, but they become selfish when the food supply diminishes. The little family moves in with the Zunis, who give them temporary aid. The mother longs to return to Walpi, but can afford to do so only by selling Mungwu for a sack of seed corn. Many years later, after having lived in Mexico, he finally goes back to Walpi for a cheerful reunion with his mother.

19 _____ . "Hopi Susanna Corn Blossom." Native Tales of New Mexico. Philadelphia: Lippincott, 1932, pp. 169-78.
Susanna is sent to a California Indian school when she is a very young girl and returns at age nineteen, a stranger to her people and their ways. Too old to be a true Hopi bride, she accepts lovers, has three Indian sons, and then outwits both the Hopi tribal elders and the white agent when accused.

20 _____ . "An Indian Divorce." Native Tales of New Mexico. Philadelphia: Lippincott, 1932, pp. 257-63.
George Cloud-mountain wants a divorce from his fat wife so he can marry a California school graduate (Indian) who is too untrained and lazy to get a husband in the "usual" way--grinding Piki-flour. He wants a "regular" divorce, but is told he must first go through a legal marriage ceremony with the first woman, and then take two hundred dollars to a lawyer and file suit against her for divorce. He decides not to bother with the formalities, and remains with his first "wife" after all.

21 _____. "The Mystery of Manzano." Native Tales of New
       Mexico. Philadelphia: Lippincott, 1932, pp. 27-40.
          A fast-talking white man comes to town, bilks the Indians
       by getting them to unearth an old mission church, and then runs
       off with the treasure while they get drunk at his expense.

22 _____. "Sandia the Tragic." Native Tales of New Mexico.
       Philadelphia: Lippincott, 1932, pp. 79-89.
          When Sandia Pueblans suffer at the hands of the Spanish,
       they go to live among the Hopis. Later, when they are able to
       return to their own lands, they have lost their unique culture
       and tribal identity.

23 _____. "Tricks in All Trades." Native Tales of New Mex-
       ico. Philadelphia: Lippincott, 1932, pp. 43-48.
          A selfish priest tricks ignorant Indians into giving him
       some money.

24 Athanas, Verne. "Bridge Crossing." Hoof Trails and Wagon
       Tracks. Ed. Don Ward. New York: Dodd, Mead, 1957,
       pp. 1-15. Originally published in 1952, entitled "Crimson
       Crossing."
          When the wagonmaster is killed, a hired helper (Jonny
       Free) assumes leadership of the wagon train and wins his girl.
       There are several minor incidents involving Indians who come
       to beg food, steal livestock, etc.

25 Atherton, Gertrude. "The Bells of San Gabriel." The Splendid
       Idle Forties: Stories of Old California. New York: Fred-
       erick A. Stokes, 1902, pp. 371-78.
          California Indians attack the Spanish soldiers who are
       protecting the rising walls of the new mission at San Gabriel,
       when a "savage tribe" of "soulless fiends" attacks and kills them.
       Captain de la Toore fights bravely, but he too falls, leaving a
       fiancée in Mexico. Later she dies of a broken heart.

26 _____. "The Isle of Skulls." The Splendid Idle Forties:
       Stories of Old California. New York: Frederick A. Stokes,
       1902, pp. 255-80.
          A Santa Barbara priest learns that there is an island
       somewhere in the Pacific containing some unclaimed savage
       souls as well as the survivors of a shipwrecked European ship.
       He sets out to search for the island, taking with him a few con-
       verted mission Indians. He finds it, and convinces all except
       Dorthe to return with him to Santa Barbara. (Dorthe is the
       half-breed offspring of a native woman and a white sailor washed
       ashore, both now dead.) The priest's voyage home is unsuccess-
       ful; the ship is wrecked on some rocks, and only the priest sur-
       vives. He lives out his days with Dorthe on the Isle of Skulls.

27 _____. "Lukari's Story." The Splendid Idle Forties: Stor-
       ies of Old California. New York: Frederick A. Stokes,
       1902, pp. 327-37. Originally published in Cosmopolitan, 14,
       No. 1 (Nov. 1892), 29-34.

Lukari, a mission Indian, tells of an incident in 1837 when the "bad" Indians came down out of the San Diego mountains and carried off the two daughters of the Spanish rancher for whom she works.

28 _____. "The Vengeance of Padre Arroyo." The Splendid
Idle Forties: Stories of Old California. New York: Frederick A. Stokes, 1902, pp. 359-67.
Andreo and Pilar (two California mission Indians) love each other, but Padre Arroyo insists that they wait a year before marrying. Disobeying him, they run off together. When the soldiers return them to the Padre, he threatens them with punishment, then locks them in a dungeon for a week--in the same cell.

29 Atkey, Bertram. "Sitka." Outing, 54, No. 4 (Jul. 1909),
464-70.
Sitka is a strong young Eskimo male who resists some of his people's customs. When it is suggested by the "ankoot" (sorcerer) that Sitka's old mother should be placed out on the ice to die, thereby conserving food, Sitka kills him and his nephew. Their bodies, placed outside, are dragged away by two Arctic bears. The two bears thereafter return to the camp to ravage it. The superstitious Eskimos--except Sitka--believe that the bears are the spirits of the "ankoot" and his nephew. Sitka becomes quite unpopular--until Spring arrives and he masterfully kills the two bears.

30 Austin, Mary. "Agua Dulce." Lost Borders. New York and
London: Harper, 1909, pp. 82-93.
A stagecoach driver tells a story of an earlier period of his life: He had been camped at Agua Dulce, a water hole in the desert, working some mines. He fell in love with a local Indian girl, Catameneda; when the tribe left the area, Catameneda stayed behind with him. After a series of crises--robbery, illness, severe weather--the couple headed for the safety of Black Mountain, suffering hardships throughout the journey. Catameneda died and was taken by her lover back to Agua Dulce for burial.

31 _____. "Approaching Day." One-Smoke Stories. Boston:
Houghton Mifflin, 1934, pp. 237-42. Originally published in
American Mercury (Mar. 1926).
Two young Navajo men are interested in Approaching Day, a beautiful young woman of the tribe. One of them is afraid that because she is so beautiful, she would be an unfaithful wife. She marries the other man and dies in childbirth shortly thereafter. Many years later, the man who distrusted her because of her beauty asks to be buried next to Approaching Day when he dies: "He was like a man who at a feast has talked too much, and realizes suddenly that the feast is over and he has eaten nothing."

32 _____. "A'wa Tseighe Comes Home from the War." One-

Smoke Stories. Boston: Houghton Mifflin, 1934, pp. 39-52.

At an Indian soldier reunion in Oklahoma, the narrator (a San Juan Pueblo Indian) tells, in dialect, of his experiences during World War I.

33 _____. "The Basket Maker." Atlantic Monthly, 91, No. 544 (Feb. 1903), 235-38.

After many Piute braves die in battle at the border of Bitter Lake, their women carry on the way of life. Seyavi becomes the tribal philosopher, quickly learning that the way to understand life is to know the land on which it lives. The Piutes make use of the land and survive with only the barest of elements. Seyavi is a basket maker of special sorts--in every basket there is a definite, distinguishable quality which has a "touch beyond cleverness."

34 _____. "A Case of Conscience." Lost Borders. New York and London: Harper, 1909, pp. 26-41.

Sanders, an Englishman with a lung disease, goes to the American West for his health. Settling in the Sierra area he meets and starts living with Turwhase, a gray-eyed Shoshone woman. In one of his yearly visits to a Los Angeles doctor, Sanders learns that his illness has been cured. Immediately he longs to return to England, his mother, and the estate; he decides to leave Turwhase but to take their daughter along. Realizing the problems his half-breed child will cause in his homeland, Sanders returns the little girl to Turwhase and goes off to England alone.

35 _____. "The Coyote Song." One-Smoke Stories. Boston: Houghton Mifflin, 1934, pp. 34-38.

Cinoave, a Piute, is the only man in his tribe without his own special song. It is a sadness to him and thus, one day, he trades a bag of roots for a Coyote Song--one that will warm the hearts of his people and stir thoughts within them. He must, however, use it only for its intended purpose. The people praise it and the proud Cinoave sings it excessively, putting the people to sleep. So Old Man Coyote comes in the night and steals it away.

36 _____. "The Divorcing of Sina." Sunset, 40, No. 6 (Jun. 1918), 26-29, 74-75.

Black Rock Maggie "chases" Bill Brody (all characters Piute) for a long time, but he becomes enthralled with and buys young Sina for his wife. Sina, however, is quite unhappy with her sharp-tongued mother-in-law, with Black Rock Maggie's unrelenting visits, and with a husband who she believes does not love her. Sina goes home to her mother, Catameneda, and her father, Wind-in-the-face, yet she is not happy there either. Some time later, Sina overhears Bill rebuffing Black Rock Maggie's advances; Bill protests that he is uninterested--that he loves his wife. Sina returns to Bill.

37 _____. "The Governor's Eye." One-Smoke Stories. Boston: Houghton Mifflin, 1934, pp. 30-33.
     Governor Hernenegildo of the Presidio of Monterey, whose
eye had been put out by an Indian arrow, receives a new one.
Indians of the San Carlos Mission, who hate the Governor because of his harsh treatment of them, fear the miraculous ap-
pearance of the evil eye. Tonito sneaks into the Governor's
bedroom at night in order to destroy the eye and, in the confusion he creates, the Governor is punched in the eye. The
next day the eye is gone and the Governor is considerably hum-
bled by its loss.

38 _____. "Hosteen Hatsanai Recants." One-Smoke Stories.
Boston: Houghton Mifflin, 1934, pp. 226-36. Originally published in American Mercury (Mar. 1926).
     After thirty years of being a good Christian, a Navajo
man takes a second "wife" because his first one goes blind. She
becomes pregnant and they go to get married in the Christian
way, but the missionary is shocked and casts him out as a sin-
ner. He reverts to his tribal religion.

39 _____. "Instruction to the Young." One-Smoke Stories.
Boston: Houghton Mifflin, 1934, pp. 90-92.
     An Indian father teaches his son of the mysterious wis-
dom and power of animals and how to cooperate with these brothers of the wilderness so that both may prosper and be at peace
with one another.

40 _____. "The Little Coyote." Atlantic Monthly, 89, No. 532
(Feb. 1902), 249-54.
     Little Coyote is the illegitimate son of Moresco (a He-
brew storekeeper in Maverick) and a Piute woman named Choyita. Choyita raises Little Coyote. Eventually Choyita moves
away and Moresco marries a white woman. At seventeen, Little
Coyote learns the identity of his father. After some time, Moresco gives Little Coyote the job of tending a large sheep flock
he owns. The boy works with care and dedication because he
feels a fierce loyalty to his father. In a terrible snowstorm,
Little Coyote valiantly tries to get the sheep to shelter. The
rescue party arrives too late. Tears fall from Moresco's face
as he stoops over the young shepherd lying dead in the snow.

41 _____. "Mahala Joe." Atlantic Monthly, 94, No. 561 (Jul.
1904), 44-53.
     A white boy, Walter, and a Piute boy, Joe, grow up to-
gether in the Piute camp near Walter's father's ranch. When
they are fifteen, the two boys, who have sworn to be blood
brothers always, find themselves on opposite sides during a war
between the Piutes and the whites. Walter is secretly sent back
East to safety, but Joe is expected to fight the whites. He refuses to fight his brother and is called a coward by his people.
Joe's punishment is to wear a woman's dress as long as he lives.

42 _____. "The Man Who Lied About a Woman." One-Smoke
Stories. Boston: Houghton Mifflin, 1934, pp. 7-15.
Tall Flower, the adopted Navajo daughter of Tizessina,
a Jicarilla Apache, spurns all the Jicarilla youths, even the rich,
young Nataldin. However, when Tall Flower goes away for some
time, Nataldin, in order to preserve his ego, claims to have had
his way with her. When she returns, obviously pregnant, Nataldin lies, claiming to be the father, and marries, hoping to escape the punishment of a man who lies about a woman. His
hopes are crushed, however, when he looks on the newborn's
face--which is that of a white child.

43 _____. "The Man Who Made People Laugh." One-Smoke
Stories. Boston: Houghton Mifflin, 1934, pp. 83-86.
A Micmac (of the Algonquins) searches for seven years
for Glooscap, the Magic-Maker who will grant his wish to have
a noise that will make people laugh and be light-hearted. Glooscap gives him a wish in a bag which must not be opened until
he is among the people; however, the Indian opens it out of cur-
iosity on his way home and the noise rushes into him, making
him the container for it. Thus, whenever he speaks, whether
he be serious or humorous, the people are struck with uncon-
trollable laughter. The Micmac searches another seven years
for the Magic-Maker--who cannot take the wish back because,
after seven long years, the wish has become very much at home
in the Indian.

44 _____. "The Man Who Was Loved by Women." One-Smoke
Stories. Boston: Houghton Mifflin, 1934, pp. 217-25. Originally published in American Mercury (Mar. 1926).
Tsaysiki, a handsome young Navajo man, finds that many
women are attracted to him, and he is all too willing to accept
their favors. Among his women is a Christian convert who,
when she discovers herself pregnant by him, commits suicide.
Later Tsaysiki marries an older and more experienced woman
who, to get even with him for his philandering, gives him some
of his own medicine by cuckolding him.

45 _____. "The Medicine of Bow-Returning." One-Smoke Stories. Boston: Houghton Mifflin, 1934, pp. 131-35.
Taku-Wakin (Something Wonderful) is a Plains Indian who
goes to the mountains to keep the holy silence and to receive his
own special medicine. One-Who-Walks-in-the-Sky speaks to him
in his heart and gives him this medicine: Man can hurt nothing
without also hurting himself. Now called Bow-Returning, he is
revered for his great wisdom in never allowing himself to hurt
another creature. When he decides that he must leave his wife
and son in order to spread his teaching to the other tribes, his
strength of spirit begins to fade and his medicine is no longer
strong. Returning to his tribe, he finds that his wife has died
of grieving and that his son has been given to another. Bow-
Returning goes to the mountain to ask One-Who-Walks-in-the-Sky
why all this has happened, and his question is answered: "Did
I not also make woman?"

46   . "Mixed Blood." One-Smoke Stories. Boston: Hough-
      ton Mifflin, 1934, pp. 285-95.
            Venustiano de Vargas, an Indian with mixed blood (Taos
      Pueblo/Spanish), attends the Christian boarding school, where
      he becomes a Presbyterian, and begins to think he is better than
      the other Indians. He speaks English and wears pants rather
      than a blanket. Returning to his tribe to marry an Indian girl,
      he is rejected because he is not a true Pueblo. Venustiano is
      eventually brought back to the blanket by various pressures ap-
      plied by the tribe.

47   . "Papago Kid." One-Smoke Stories. Boston: Hough-
      ton Mifflin, 1934, pp. 63-83.
            Papago Kid, an Irishman from New Jersey, wanders
      around the West, seemingly unable to settle down. He becomes
      engaged to a Papago girl, but never gets around to marrying her.
      She marries an Indian, and Papago Kid dies of tuberculosis.

48   . "Papago Wedding." One-Smoke Stories. Boston:
      Houghton Mifflin, 1934, pp. 243-49.
            Shuler is a white cotton rancher in southern Arizona who
      lives for many years with "Susie," a Papago woman. They have
      many children together, even though they have not formally mar-
      ried. When Shuler becomes interested in a white woman with
      many hats, he tries to get rid of Susie--yet keep the children.
      His various ploys to buy Susie off and to get the court to give
      him custody of the children fail, however, and in the end the
      judge takes Shuler out to Susie's ranch and "makes the marriage
      paper" to legalize their union.

49   . "The Ploughed Lands." Lost Borders. New York
      and London: Harper, 1909, pp. 42-51.
            Curly Gavin, returning from a gold search, gets lost and
      becomes ill. He is rescued by a Shoshone Indian whose daugh-
      ter, Tiawa, nurses him back to health. She falls in love with
      Curly and offers to guide him back to white civilization. He
      notices her interest and becomes her lover, but the affair is
      short-lived. Tiawa returns to her people and marries a Piute.

50   . "The Spirit of the Bear Walking." One-Smoke Stor-
      ies. Boston: Houghton Mifflin, 1934, pp. 93-95.
            Hotandanai of the campody of Sagharawite tries not to
      think of Pahawitz-na'an, the Spirit of the Bear Walking, when
      he is hunting--for it is said that one who sees him without think-
      ing of him will become the mightiest hunter of his generation.
      However, Hotandanai tries too hard. Only when he is overcome
      with grief because of his son's death in battle does he finally see
      the Spirit of the Bear Walking.

51   . "Stewed Beans." One-Smoke Stories. Boston:
      Houghton Mifflin, 1934, pp. 170-74.
            An Apache named Two-Comes-Over-the-Hill has been
      fooling around with Spotted Horse's wife. To embarrass Two-

Comes-Over-the-Hill, Spotted Horse does not pour the water off
the stewed beans his wife is preparing for her lover, and as a
result Two-Comes-Over-the-Hill later emits gaseous eructations
in the Chiricahua Council meeting: "If water is not poured off,
then they make phutt-phutt!" Two-Comes-Over-the-Hill is humiliated and shamed by his friends, and as a result Spotted
Horse's wife refuses to see her shamed lover again.

52 _____. "The Way of a Woman." One-Smoke Stories. Boston: Houghton Mifflin, 1934, pp. 1-6.
An Indian forces his daughter to marry a man she does
not love. After their divorce, she realizes that she loves him
after all.

53 _____. "The White Hour." Munsey's Magazine, 29 (1903),
89-92.
The old medicine man, Mono John, names his daughter
"Evaly" after the local white school teacher, Eva Lee Matheson
of the Tres Pinos School. When the child grows older, Mono
John sends her to school, hoping that she will become a school
teacher like her namesake. Evaly, however, proves to be a
rather slow student. When she is sixteen years old a pneumonia
epidemic hits the settlements in the area. People blame the
medicine men and begin to plot their assassination. In despera-
tion, Evaly makes a two hundred-mile train journey to get John
Sides, a respected man (it is not clear whether he is Indian or
white), who talks the Indians out of murdering her father. The
exhausting trip leaves Evaly in a weakened condition and she
dies.

54 _____. "White Wisdom." One-Smoke Stories. Boston:
Houghton Mifflin, 1934, pp. 181-99.
Dan Kearny, son of a Ute woman and a white rancher,
is brought up in the white man's way. When both parents die,
Dan is raised by his Indian aunt but is a frequent visitor to
homes of whites. When he speaks out against traditional Indian
ways in favor of the new, white ways, the Indians dare Dan to
test his theories by taking a white wife. He tries to do so and
is rebuffed. In anger he marries an Indian woman and espouses
the old ways. Later, the narrator learns that Dan Kearny--now
Twice-Bitten, the Gray-Eyed Ute--is truly a white man, the son
of the white rancher and his deceased white wife!

55 _____. "The Woman Who Was Never Satisfied." One-Smoke
Stories. Boston: Houghton Mifflin, 1934, pp. 16-21.
A Navajo man has a wife who, though good to him in all
other things, is never satisfied to stay at one place for any
length of time. To please her, the man buys sheep so that they
might move from pasture to pasture for grazing. "'I think,'
said her husband good-naturedly, 'that even in the Underworld
you would not be satisfied!' But that was unlucky, to speak of
the death of a living person as a thing already accomplished."
She dies soon, but returns to her husband and with him seeks

the Trail to the Underworld. Together they find a white man suffering from the breathing sickness and she, presumably satisfied, disappears with him to the Underworld when he dies. "'I hope,' said the Navajo, 'that this time she will be satisfied.'"

56 Bahr, Jerome. "The Word Passer." Wisconsin Tales. Baltimore: Trempealeau, 1964, pp. 105-12.
      Volney is a college student, a descendant of Black Hawk, the great chief who had been captured and taken away to prison many years earlier. Volney chooses this particular Wisconsin town for college because it was here where Black Hawk had been captured by deceitful Winnebagos and turned over to the army. In the end, after graduation, Volney walks away from the town with his carved stick on which is recorded the history of his people. But unless Volney has children, he will be the last "word passer" of his people.

57 Ballard, Charles L. "Protection for Rosalie." Sun Tracks, 2, No. 2 (Spring 1976), 4-6.
      During an Indian dance in modern-day southern plains Indian country, the narrator talks with a friend about the time an old man named Jim Coldfire had used special "medicine" or magic to influence the actions of his granddaughter, Rosalie, in far-away Denver.

58 Ballard, Todhunter. "The Saga of Toby Riddle." With Guidons Flying: Tales of the U.S. Cavalry in the Old West. Garden City, N.Y.: Doubleday, 1970, pp. 1-16.
      Toby Riddle is the young Modoc wife of a white man. During the Modoc War she serves as an interpreter and messenger between the beseiged Captain Jack and General Canby's army. The arrogant Canby will not listen to Toby's warnings, nor to her advice about how to compromise with the Modocs. Finally the Modocs, convinced that there is no hope for a peaceful solution, shoot the peace commissioners, including Canby.

59 Baltimore, J. Mayne. "Sagebrush and Sand." Overland Monthly, n.s. 43 (1904), 343-47.
      Cossaga, a Klickatt reservation Indian, is a lazy, irresponsible drunkard who relies on his more industrious wife to gather food for their baby girl and themselves. Once when he is supposed to be watching the baby, he goes on a drinking spree and the little girl nearly perishes in a sand storm. A good white rancher rescues the child, but Cossaga believes (when he sobers up) that she has died, so he commits suicide. The rancher later brings the child back to her loving mother.

60 Barker, S. Omar. "Saddle or Nothing." Rawhide Men. Ed. Kenneth Fowler. Garden City, N.Y.: Doubleday, 1965, pp. 13-29. Originally published in The Saturday Evening Post (Apr. 9, 1949), entitled "My Gun Talks for Me."
      Blackie is a man and a half (half-Kiowa, half-Cherokee, and half-white) who has spent time in jail and now works for a

professional horse thief. There is honor among thieves, however, and Blackie is kind to the "kid" he trains until he (Blackie)
gets shot.

61 Barnes, Will C. "Just Regulars." Tales from the X-Bar Horse
      Camp: The Blue Roan "Outlaw" and Other Stories. Chicago:
      The Breeder's Gazette, 1920, pp. 45-57.
      Major Brown wipes out one of the last of the Apache
bands that refuses to stay on the reservation. Brown traps them
in a mountain cave, and then gradually (but methodically) kills
all of them.

62 _____. "The Navajo Turquoise Ring." Tales from the X-
      Bar Horse Camp: The Blue Roan "Outlaw" and Other Stories.
      Chicago: The Breeder's Gazette, 1920, pp. 74-85.
      A beautiful Eastern girl visits a Western ranch and im-
mediately gathers many admirers. She flirts a little with a Navajo man who gives her a very fine turquoise and silver ring.
Some whites tell her that if she wears it on her engagement
finger she is his. The next day, as the Indian rides toward her,
she panics and runs; he follows, swinging a lariat. Cameron
(a white man) shoots the Indian's horse and fires several "warning" shots that send the Indian crawling to escape. The dramatic
rescue makes the girl realize that she loves Cameron.

63 Bastow, E. "The Sobering of Joshua, the Shuswap." Wascana
      Review, 7, No. 1 (1972), 15-22.
      Joshua, a Shuswap Indian, awakens in his mother's house
after a long drinking bout. He thinks of the uselessness of his
life of endless drunkenness; he thinks of his three sons, the one
grown and the two who are home from mission school; and he
thinks of Seraphine, the wife who has left him. At dawn, Joshua
starts for home--everything suddenly oddly beautiful. Then, just
as suddenly, all his sorrows and problems seem to crowd back
into his mind. Joshua drowns himself in the nearby river.

64 Baylor, Byrd. "A Faint Glow Under the Ashes." Redbook,
      141, No. 3 (Jul. 1973), 73, 121-23.
      Maria goes to the Public Welfare office to get money and
is browbeaten by the woman working there: she must sign a
paper stating that her husband is guilty of non-support of their
children (thus sending him to jail); she must produce birth cer-
tificates for the half-dozen children and must promise not to
have any more; she must promise to find a house to buy or rent
(the one she was in was boarded up and condemned by the Board
of Health, and she is now living in an old car). At the end, after feeding her children beans and tortillas, she leaves them and
heads toward the B-29 Bar, which is as close as she will ever
get to the "electric lights."

65 _____. "The Winner." Redbook, 138, No. 5 (Mar. 1972),
      85, 163, 166, 168, 170.
      Mrs. Domingo, an old Papago grandmother whose hus-

band had died twenty-three years earlier, wins a swimming pool at the fair. Because her house is sub-standard, she uses the pool for living quarters.

66 _____. "Yes Is Better Than No." McCall's, Sep. 1972, 88-89, 118, 120, 122, 124.
　　　　Maria Vasquez (Papago), depressed because her house has been condemned and boarded up, goes to the B-29 Bar for beer. A brash young University of Arizona anthropology student comes in to survey Papago Indians about motivation and achievement levels; Maria and her friends, who have learned to provide answers the whites expect, do so. After the student leaves, they partake of a fly-in-the-beer ritual which is supposed to have some healing effects.

67 Beck, Ruth Everett. "Alone on the Trail." Overland Monthly, n. s. 57 (1911), 40-51.
　　　　Two Indian women (one old, one younger) talk as they walk around the Indian school. The young one wants to know whether she should marry for love or at her parents' bidding. The older one tells about how her own mother had married for love, rejecting the chief her parents had wanted her to have. She had been very happy.

68 Bedard, Brian. "The Celebrated Return of Simon Laughing Owl." South Dakota Review, 8, No. 3, (Autumn 1970), 50-57.
　　　　Old Simon Laughing Owl, his two sons, and his three cousins are sitting in and around an old battered auto with a flat tire. Hardly any other cars have passed throughout the day. One lady tourist stops to take their picture. Finally another tourist family stops, and the white man changes the flat tire for them. Spirits revive as the Indians from Power River Reservation head toward the Broken Arrow Inn for a wild Saturday night.

69 Beebe, William. "A Red Indian Day." Atlantic Monthly, 122, No. 1 (Jul. 1918), 23-31.
　　　　The narrator is an American soldier fighting in France during World War I. Much to his surprise he meets there a group of Iroquois Indians who are also American soldiers and who skillfully lead him on a dangerous but successful intelligence mission.

70 Bell, Ed. "Cherokee Blood." Story, 20, No. 93 (Jan. /Feb. 1942), 88-94.
　　　　Calfkiller is a small community in Tennessee where everyone claims Cherokee blood--especially Old Sooner (the football coach) and his sons, Will Buck and the narrator. Old Sooner's second wife, Widder, informs him that the new school principal is to be her sister, Dolly. Old Sooner is unhappy about this, especially when Dolly takes over his coaching job; however, Dolly helps the team to win the big game, and all are friends by the conclusion.

71 Benét, Stephen Vincent. "The Captives." The Last Circle:
    Stories and Poems by Stephen Vincent Benét. New York:
    Farrar, Straus, 1946, pp. 31-47.
        A Scottish army officer writes to a friend back home of
    an experience he had in America in 1764. It was his duty to
    oversee the release of some white captives from the Shawnee
    tribe. One, Mary Carmichael, especially fascinated him, for
    she seemed through her experience to have become transformed
    from a Britisher into something much different--a kind of new-
    primitive American woodswoman.

72 _____. "Jacob and the Indians." Tales of Our People:
    Great Stories of the Jew in America. Ed. Jerry D. Lewis.
    n. p. : Bernard Geis Associates, 1969, pp. 3-16. Originally
    published in 1938.
        Jacob Stein, a young Jewish immigrant in Philadelphia,
    wants to become established so that he can afford to get mar-
    ried. One proven, though dangerous, way to get rich is to trade
    with the Indians for beaver skins, so Jacob heads West. In the
    wilderness he learns a great deal about himself and the world.
    He is also captured by the Shawnees and narrowly escapes being
    burned at the stake. Eventually he runs away from the Shawnees
    and returns to Philadelphia, wiser and richer.

73 Berg, Alan M. "The Defeat of the Nez Percé." Voices of
    Brooklyn: An Anthology. Ed. Sol Yurick. Chicago: Amer-
    ican Library Association, 1973, pp. 188-204.
        A young English teacher is both intrigued and depressed
    by the white man's rape of the Indian throughout history. Inad-
    vertently, he participates in this rape by marrying an Indian
    (Nez Percé) student of his and then by not recognizing her loneli-
    ness and unhappiness. She commits suicide. Still disillusioned,
    the teacher becomes a truck driver. One night he and another
    unscrupulous fellow plan to rape a pretty young Indian girl.

74 Berlin, Lucia. "Angel's Laundromat." Atlantic Monthly, 237,
    No. 2 (Feb. 1976), 92-94.
        A Jicarilla Apache who claims to be chief of his tribe
    frequents a laundromat in Albuquerque, New Mexico. He forms
    a kind of friendship with a woman who also does her laundry
    there. The story begins and ends, however, with a failure of
    understanding and communication: "I don't know why Indians get
    so drunk.... I can't remember when it was that I realized I
    had never seen the old Indian again."

75 Berry, Erick. "The Ghost Village." Spooks, Spooks, Spooks.
    Ed. Helen Hoke. New York: Franklin Watts, 1966, pp.
    128-38. Originally published in Beckoning Landfall, by Erick
    Berry (John Day Co. , Inc.).
        Ellen is preparing a historical window display for the
    350th anniversary of the founding of Mount Desert Island, Maine.
    Having trouble reconstructing an accurate miniature model of an
    Abnaki village, she idly wishes that she might "see a real Indian

village." One day when Ellen is rowing her dinghy near the island, she sees smoke drifting up and goes ashore to investigate. Ellen finds an Indian village, mingles with the natives who willingly answer her questions, and sketches what she sees on small pieces of birchbark. She becomes increasingly aware that the historical scene of Mount Desert Island's discovery is actually taking place, and that she somehow has gone back through time to witness the scene. After trouble with the medicine man she senses the wisdom of leaving. Recalling the rest of the historical facts of the incident as she rows toward the mainland, Ellen reaches in her pocket and finds two small sheets of birchbark, each containing the charcoal sketch of an Indian. "It couldn't have happened. Yet it had."

76 Bixby, J. F. "Last Hunt of the Pawnees." Overland Monthly, n. s. 29 (1897), 52-61.
      In 1873 Major William Burgess and commissioners from Washington recommend that the Pawnees not go on their annual buffalo hunt, but Te-lah-hut-la-sharo (Sky Chief) fails to follow their advice. He leaves with a large party (including white men), reaches the buffalo range, and enjoys considerable hunting success. However, unknown to Te-lah-hut-la-sharo, the Sioux (old Pawnee enemies) prepare to attack them. A bloody slaughter follows.

77 Blackburn, Thomas W. "Arrows Fly Westward." With Guidons Flying: Tales of the U. S. Cavalry in the Old West. Garden City, N.Y.: Doubleday, 1970, pp. 17-36. Originally published in 15 Western Tales (1945).
      Longbow recognizes that his people are threatened by both the buffalo hunters and the settlers, but his father, the chief, trusts Washington and the recent treaty which insures his tribe the right to their land. Longbow discovers that the buffalo hunters have persuaded the settlers to join with them to exterminate the Indians. A kind white woman warns him, however, and Longbow leads his tribe to safety.

78 _____. "Welcome from Broken Jaw." Rawhide Men. Ed. Kenneth Fowler. Garden City, N.Y.: Doubleday, 1965, pp. 30-48. Originally entitled "Mountain Crossing," Collier's, (Apr. 8, 1950).
      Broken Jaw, chief of the Blackfeet, is at first angry when the new "factor" arrives to manage the fur post. White trappers have cheated the Indians, killed them, and ruined beaver runs. By the end, however, Broken Jaw makes a mutually profitable pact with the new factor.

79 Blackwood, Algernon. "The Valley of the Beasts." Alfred Hitchcock's Ghostly Gallery. New York: Random House, 1962, pp. 20-42. Originally published in The Wolves of God and Other Fey Stories (Dutton, 1921).
      Grimmond, an English hunter, is tracking an enormous wounded moose with Tooshalli, his Indian guide. The tracks

lead into the Valley of the Beasts, but Tooshalli refuses to go in, saying that it is the special valley of the god, Ishtot. He gives Grimmond a wooden talisman with which to appeal to Ishtot for help, and then leaves. When Grimmond enters the valley he seems gradually to turn into a beast, and is about to be killed by wild animals when he uses the talisman and, with the help of Tooshalli, escapes.

Bonin, Gertrude see Zitkala-Sa

80 Bonneau, Jean X. "The White Moose." Overland Monthly, n. s. 46 (1905), 71-75.
    Louis Paulin relates a story about the alleged ghost moose, the White Moose of Spirit Lake: Louis and his partner, Joe Pablo, were canoeing on the lake when they spotted the White Moose. Soon afterward, they found a small Indian girl and named her Echo Paulin Pablo. As Echo grew up, a love triangle developed: Echo loved Joe, Joe loved another local woman, and Louis loved Echo. When Echo learned that Joe had decided to marry the woman in town, she took the canoe out in the lake; the White Moose appeared, and the canoe floated ashore empty.

81 Borland, Hal. "Beaver." Story, 5, No. 25 (Aug. 1934), 60-66.
    Jim Bridger tells (in dialect) exaggerated tales of his beaver trapping days to a small group of mountain men. As soon as he had several pelts, he would usually steal Indian horses to carry them; however, the Indians invariably got back their horses, and Jim's pelts as well.

82 _____. "A Mule from Californy." Story, 6, No. 30 (Jan. 1935), 30-40.
    Old Black Harris, the only man ever to ride a famous red mule in California, tells (in dialect) an exaggerated tale of taming the mule, hunting and capturing "Californy horses and mules" for trade, and being chased by "Injuns" who want to steal the horses.

83 Bourke, Charles Francis. "The Vengeance." Outing, 52, No. 6 (Sep. 1908), 673-78.
    Captain Sharpe learns that the Comanches have obtained Mauser rifles and plan an uprising in retaliation for Chief Bull Bear's recent arrest. (The arrest had been based upon an accusation by Jim Cleaver, a well-digger on the reservation.) Military men go after the armed Comanches and find a dying white man, Jim Cleaver, whose last words have something to do with "vengeance." It is later learned that it was Jim who had smuggled the rifles to the Indians, and who had wanted Chief Bull Bear out of the way in order to take over his huge flock of sheep.

84 Bowman, James. "The First War Party." Indians, Indians, Indians. Ed. Phyllis R. Fenner. New York: Franklin

Watts, 1950, pp. 44-55. Originally published in Winabojo
(Albert Whitman, 1941).
Chief Fiery-Wind of the Oneida Indians is in charge of
training young warriors. He sends them out for a practice attack on a nest of hornets.

85 Boyce, George A. "Boy with Wind Sickness." Some People
Are Indians. New York: Vanguard, 1974, pp. 56-64.
Although only fourteen years old, Galthbahi has been away
from his Navajo family for two years. He quits his job as a
migrant farm worker, however, because he is tormented by a
patch of white hair he has on his head of otherwise black hair.
This is an evil mark, he feels, which sets him apart. Desperate, he goes to a white doctor for help; the doctor tells him only
that this white hair is nothing to worry about. There is only one
other source of help left to Galthbahi, so he seeks out a medicine man. After the medicine man's nine-day ceremony, Galthbahi's anxiety at last leaves him.

86 _____. "Changing Woman." Some People Are Indians. New
York: Vanguard, 1974, pp. 14-25.
No Luck, a young Navajo man, is very poor, yet he des-
perately wants to attend a Squaw Dance--to make a good impres-
sion on Bigeebah and her father, because he hopes to marry the
girl. On the way to the dance he is caught in an avalanche.
The earth pours down around him, and at his feet he sees a
yellow rock. This, he knows, is a gift from Changing Woman
(Mother Earth), so he takes it to the trader. The gold makes
him rich, and he marries Bigeebah.

87 _____. "Enough for Two." Some People Are Indians. New
York: Vanguard, 1974, pp. 137-49.
Nellie and Johnnie, two young Navajos, love each other.
Because they are very poor, they leave the reservation to look
for work in a city. They find jobs in a cannery, where Nellie
peels tomatoes all day and Johnnie operates huge machines.
They hate the work, they hate the prejudice against Indians, and
they miss the reservation. They do have each other, however,
and hope that they will be able to earn enough for two people to
live.

88 _____. "For Only Two Apples." Some People Are Indians.
New York: Vanguard, 1974, pp. 65-73.
While Jim Blackgoat's young son, Tsosie, is sick, a white
tourist couple appears at Jim's hogan. The intruders talk to
each other about these lazy Navajo Indians who lie around all
day, and the woman condescendingly gives each of Jim's two
children an apple. Tsosie wants to give her something, so offers her his beautiful silver and turquoise ring. The insensitive white woman is very pleased with the shrewd bargain she
has made with "only two apples." The next day Jim takes Tsosie
to the white hospital so that the boy can get well.

89 _____. "Girl with Seven Names." Some People Are Indians.
New York: Vanguard, 1974, pp. 97-113.
Smiley, a young Navajo girl, goes to school but does not
like it there. When she arrives, the white principal tells her
that Smiley is not a suitable name, and insists that she have an
Anglo name. Her mother picks the name Julia, and the principal adds Mitchell. The teachers mistakenly call her Virginia;
some of the students call her Owl Eyes (she wears glasses), and
sometimes Negrita (she is part black). Smiley also has a secret ceremonial name which, of course, she cannot use. Finally
she decides that she needs a new name--she picks, for herself,
Mary J. Laughter.

90 _____. "The Happiest Moment." Some People Are Indians.
New York: Vanguard, 1974, pp. 114-22.
A young Navajo couple have their first baby. Zonnie,
the mother, follows all the old Navajo customs before and during the child's birth. Her happiest moment comes when the baby
is a few weeks old and laughs for the first time. This means,
Zonnie knows, that the Sacred Spirit is entering into her child's
body.

91 _____. "Little No-Name's Grandson." Some People Are
Indians. New York: Vanguard, 1974, pp. 88-96.
An old Navajo grandfather, Little No-Name, is driving
his young grandson to his first day of white man's school. During the slow wagon ride, Little No-Name remembers how his
own father was killed when he tried to steal a calf in order to
feed his starving family. Little No-Name, who is very poor,
hopes that his grandson will be able to learn in school about a
new way of life so that he can escape the poverty that the older
Indians have always known. When they arrive at the school,
they are turned away. The principal tells them the school is
filled--there is no room there for even one more student.

92 _____. "Long Coat, Short Coat, and No Coat." Some People Are Indians. New York: Vanguard, 1974, pp. 74-87.
Peshlikai is a Navajo father whose third child is about
to be born. Long Coat, a missionary from the church with the
cross, comes to visit Peshlikai and to persuade him to send his
children to Long Coat's church. Soon another missionary, Short
Coat, comes from the church with the bell in order to convince
Peshlikai to send his children to Short Coat's church. Then No
Coat, who is still another kind of missionary, from still another
kind of Christian church, visits Peshlikai. Peshlikai, not wanting to offend any of them, decides to send one of his children
to each of the missionaries.

93 _____. "Navajos Have Heroes Too." Some People Are Indians. New York: Vanguard, 1974, pp. 1-13.
Yazzie, a young Navajo boy, wants to prove that he is a
man. He spends several days and nights on the rim of a canyon
where he hopes to capture an eagle. Although he sees no eagle,

he is bitten by a rattlesnake. Calmly and bravely he makes the
long journey to a doctor. His parents now realize that he is no
longer a little boy.

94 _____ . "The Patriot." Some People Are Indians. New
York: Vanguard, 1974, pp. 40-55.
Chee Bowman, who was a soldier in World War II, has
returned to a traditional Navajo life. He tries to instill in his
son, James, an appreciation for his Navajo heritage. Chee is
worried about this eighteen-year-old son who is failing in school,
who gets into trouble with the police, and who is generally un-
settled and without direction. After wrecking his family's new
pick-up truck, James joins the Marines. Soon he will be sent
to Vietnam. His father hopes that James will return to his Navajo home, but realizes that it will be up to the boy to decide.

95 _____ . "Salt Clan Girl." Some People Are Indians. New
York: Vanguard, 1974, pp. 123-36.
Elsie Salt Clan is a grown-up Navajo girl who has run
away from home because she does not want to marry Many
Goats, a wealthy but old Navajo man. She spends a year at an
elementary school learning English, where she falls in love with
the kind, white teacher. He is fond of Elsie, but he does not
love her. Because she is too old to remain at the elementary
school, and she still does not want to marry Many Goats, Elsie
agrees to enroll at a boarding school.

96 _____ . "Slow Talker Settles a Case." Some People Are Indians. New York: Vanguard, 1974, pp. 26-39.
A young Navajo man, Curly, very much wants a horse,
but his wife, who is older and more frugal, refuses to buy him
one. They go to a Squaw Dance, where Curly runs off with a
young woman who has a black horse. Months later there is a
trial. The young woman's husband wants Curly to pay him for
riding his horse and living with his wife; Slow Talker, the judge,
orders Curly to pay the husband twenty sheep. Curly's wife,
however, feels that the girl's husband is at fault; he should have
kept his young wife at home. So Slow Talker orders the husband
to pay Curly's wife twenty sheep. This settles the case happily.
Curly's wife then gives Curly a gift--a handsome horse.

97 Boyesen, Hjalmar Hjorth. "Zee-Wee." Overland Monthly, n. s.
24 (1894), 229-48.
At a young age Zee-Wee, daughter of Dakota Chief Don't
Know How and of Minona (his favorite wife), was sent away to
a mission school leaving her twin sister (Wauska) behind. After
being at the school for fourteen years, Zee-Wee becomes acculturated to white customs. She has a dear friend, Marion Gal-
laudet, with whom she shares the dream of returning to her people to uplift them from degradation. Zee-Wee does return--to
find a drunken father--and is disgusted with the "savage" way
of life. Aided by Wauska, Zee-Wee runs away after learning
that she has been sold to Crooked Gun to be his wife. She es-

capes to the U. S. Agency, grateful to be with her friend Marion once again.

98   Boynton, S. S. "Blackfeet and Bruin." Overland Monthly, n. s. 25 (1895), 258-61.

James P. Beckworth, who for several years had lived with the Crow Indians and had participated with them in battle against the Blackfeet, decides to journey to the California frontier. On the way he is found and pursued by three Blackfeet. Beckworth, unwittingly driven into a steep-walled canyon, climbs to seek protection, and discovers a cave which tunnels through the mountain. From his hiding spot he watches as one of the Indians is fatally attacked by a grizzly bear. He fights and kills a second Indian who discovers his hiding place, then hastens away with the three Indian horses, leaving the third Blackfeet behind.

99   _____. "A Close Call." Overland Monthly, n. s. 16 (1890), 644-48.

The narrator is a junior partner in a sheep's wool business. His job is to ride through the wilderness--often with thousands of dollars of gold coin in his saddle bags--to purchase wool. On one trip he stays at a public house where two men seem to be very curious about him. He is warned by a half-breed Indian named Bill (who had earlier that day been his guide to Rucker's sheep camp) that the men are robbers. The next day the two men ambush the narrator on the trail; he kills one thief and severely wounds the other.

100   Bradbury, Ray. "Perhaps We Are Going Away." The Machineries of Joy. New York: Simon and Schuster, 1964, pp. 89-93.

Ho-Awi awakens in fear "on a day that was evil for no reason." The shadow of his grandfather's hand gives the sign that the "Old Man" and Ho-Awi "must go on the Great Hunt." On their journey they encounter strange "creatures"; "summer goes," and "then the boy vanished in darkness, following the eagle and the hawk that lived in the stone body of his grandfather."

101   Brady, Cyrus Townsend. "In the Box Canon of the Gila." Harper's, 102 (Mar. 1901), 600-06.

After a church service, a major recalls a story about a sergeant who used to be in love with a certain girl. The girl, however, married another man. While on his rounds one day the sergeant found that the girl, her husband, and their child had been tortured and scalped by an Apache. Disobeying orders, the sergeant killed the Apache.

102   Brandon, William. "The Tomahawk." Atlantic Monthly, 200, No. 2 (Aug. 1957), 58-63.

Quince Keensy, an orphan, is the only full-blooded Indian attending Quincy Adams Junior High School. Mrs. Polling be-

friends Keensy and helps him to overcome various growing
pains. As the boy continues through school and takes a job
across town, he sees less and less of Mrs. Polling. When
she learns that he is leaving for college, she decides to give
him an old tomahawk. She hears that Keensy has promised to
visit her, but is very disappointed when he fails to show up.

103 Brereton, Charles V. "Casco Collects Damages." Sunset,
     58, No. 1 (Jan. 1927), 18-20, 66-67.
     Casco Billy (a Deep Valley Wylackie Indian), pushed by
Jenny, his energetic wife, reluctantly weeds the garden. There
he notices some water seepage and digs down to discover an
old water pipe leading to some not too distant agency buildings.
He turns on the valve slightly, covers the pipe, and builds a
pseudo-spring. Not only does the garden thrive, but Casco
profits with tips from thirsty passing motorists. When the
spring runs dry, the agency buildings are converted into a
creamery and the pipe is adapted to carry fuel oil. Hurst,
believing the new seepage to be indicative of an oil strike,
pays Casco Billy five hundred dollars for the small garden
plot. The Indians leave before the white man realizes he has
been outwitted.

104 _____. "Casco Omits a Detail." Sunset, 58, No. 3 (Mar.
     1927), 36-39, 60.
     Jenny grows impatient with her lazy husband, Casco Billy
(Wylackie Indian). She tells him that the white government, in
trying to rid Deep Valley of destructive digger squirrels, is
paying a bounty for each squirrel tail turned in. The ultima-
tum is "to work or else," so Casco goes out to catch squirrels;
however, he traps them, cuts off their tails, and lets them go
rather than killing them. He brings home the tails. Casco
holds out a bit of money to gamble every night, but a suspicious Jenny discovers the truth. Casco runs away, and a furious Jenny must reimburse the government man, Ross.

105 _____. "Casco Pans Out." Sunset, 54, No. 4 (Apr. 1925),
     30-32, 56, 60.
     On his way home, Wylackie Indian Casco Billy is nervous
about seeing his wife, Jenny. He has been gone for two months,
panning for gold with Jim Bluejay, and has only a small amount
of gold to show for his efforts. There is a fuss when he gets
home, during which the gold vial is broken on the floor. After
her anger subsides, Jenny sweeps out the "dirt" and fixes supper for Casco. The next day Gus Schmaltz, the Deep Valley
store keeper, comes to collect an old five dollar debt of Billy's;
Jenny agrees to trade him five chickens in full payment. The
next day, an excited Gus comes back and buys the property for
an outrageous price. Weeks later Jenny and Casco pass their
old place and see mining in progress. Gus had found gold in
the chickens that Jenny had traded him, and had assumed there
was a rich vein on the place. Actually, the chickens had eaten
the small amount of gold from Casco's spilled vial.

106 _____ . "Casco, the Goat Getter." Sunset, 48, No. 2
(Feb. 1922), 37-39, 50, 52.
   Indian Casco Billy, whose uncle has recently died, is
now Chief of the Wylackies. This new status does not impress
his wife, Jenny--but the fifteen dollars he earns does. In an
unusual moment of generosity, Casco gives ten of the dollars
to Jenny--which she promptly invests in four goats. Casco
manages to gamble the rest away playing poker at Bill Clive's.
While despairing about his poverty, Casco gets an idea: If
illegal deer jerky (dried meat) is a profitable item, why couldn't
he dry goat meat and sell it to Bill Clive as venison jerky?
He successfully does so, stealing Jenny's goats, one by one.
He gambles away his profit, and encounters "big trouble" when
an enraged Jenny and Bill Clive learn the truth.

107 _____ . "Casco Traps Trouble." Sunset, 55, No. 6 (Dec.
1925), 31-33, 56, 58.
   Jenny (Wylackie) grows angry with her husband, Casco
Billy, because he contributes no money for household expenses.
So Casco Billy decides to trap coyotes to collect the five dollar
bounty paid by the judge for each carcass. He catches two,
and also shoots a deer. Susie Bigfire, in a nearby cabin, ob-
serves the illegal deer kill. Casco takes one dead coyote into
the judge on two separate occasions--and collects twice. Angry
that Casco has not shared the deer meat with her, Susie Bigfire threatens to report his deer slaying. He bribes her not
to tell by giving her a red calico dress he had bought to surprise Jenny. When Casco goes to the judge with the same
coyote (for the third time) he hears the commotion of Jenny
and Susie fighting over the dress.

108 _____ . "A Christian Pro Tem." Sunset, 48, No. 5 (May
1922), 26-27, 52, 54, 56.
   Wylackie Indian Casco Billy is surprised when his wife,
Jenny, meets him in town after his return from jail. Jenny
cooks him a delicious meal, and announces that they should get
married "white style." Casco goes along with the plan and
signs a paper at the agency--which, he later learns, has given
Jenny access to his allotment. Jenny promptly exchanges this
for the local preacher's car. Casco, unhappy with his land
loss, gets an idea when Bluejay talks to him about bootlegging;
Casco tries to implicate the preacher in illicit liquor trade.
But the agent is too wise for Casco Billy. As the story ends,
it looks as if Casco will go to jail again.

109 _____ . "The End of the Rainbow." Sunset, 58, No. 4
(Apr. 1927), 24-25, 56, 58, 60.
   Coot Tashburn sells the Rainbow Mine to Casco Billy
(Wylackie) for twenty dollars--which Billy steals from Jenny,
his wife. Casco obtains all the proper legal papers and posts
them at Rainbow Mine. The mine, of course, is worthless,
but Casco bought it so that he would have some land outside of
town where he could fish. An irate Jenny and Judge Horons

soon arrive at the mine to arrest Casco for stealing Jenny's twenty dollars. Just then, Casco turns on the hydraulic monitor; this destructive watery force uncovers a sack of gold dust --which now legally belongs to Casco.

110 _____. "High Tide Come Quick." Sunset, 58, No. 6 (Jun. 1927), 9-11, 78-79.
Jimmy Crickett (a Siwash Indian policeman) and a white law officer are tracking the notorious Tah-an, who had recently wounded a young man (Jimmy's son-in-law) with a knife. They track him to an estuary's edge, but must wait for low tide in order to ford it. Once across the estuary, they make camp at an old cabin. The next morning, Jimmy and his sidekick catch White Eye, Tah-an's evil brother-in-law, and force him to tell the whereabouts of Tah-an. White Eye confesses that Tah-an had crossed the estuary the night before with the intention of killing the policemen, but has not returned. They find Tah-an in the river, near the bank, caught in a bear trap.

111 _____. "In the Mesh of the Law." Sunset, 59, No. 3 (Sep. 1927), 9-11, 77-78.
Jimmy Crickett (a Siwash Indian policeman) and a white law officer head up the river in a motorboat when they are shot at by Otter, an Indian salmon poacher and the object of their tracking expedition. The crafty Otter gets away, but returns later and approaches the motorboat silently in his canoe. The motorboat, however, strikes and destroys the canoe, leaving Otter to tread water in the dark night. Jimmy locates the poacher's huge net and drags it in a great arc, managing to capture the thief.

112 _____. "Jimmy Crickett, Hi-Jacker." Sunset, 60, No. 4 (Apr. 1928), 26-28, 64.
As Jimmy Crickett (a Siwash Indian policeman) and a white law officer patrol an estuary looking for poachers, their motorboat is struck and overturned by a speedboat. The two men swim ashore, warm themselves, and change clothing at Owl's cabin. In searching for the speedboat, they discover a liquor-smuggling operation. Jimmy and his companion, mistaken for "bums" in Owl's old clothing, are captured by the outlaws. Soon the crafty Jimmy uses the speedboat's machine gun to subdue the smugglers.

113 _____. "Man's Best Friend." Sunset, 48, No. 3 (Mar. 1922), 23-25, 64-67.
Wylackie Indian Casco Billy, who is in bad favor with his wife and several townspeople, decides to winter in a deserted cabin. Soon growing tired of the dull diet, he gets an idea when he notices a bear skin hanging on the wall. Knowing that hogs are frightened of bears, he decides to dress in the skin, lure some of the range hogs into a trap, butcher them, use some of the meat himself, and sell some of it in a distant town to get money for supplies. All goes well until he

realizes that the third hog he killed belongs to his wife, Jenny. Meanwhile, some suspicious people, including Jenny, start to track the "bear." All the dogs are confused by the tracks except Spot, Casco's own dog. After a chase, Casco is finally caught; he chooses jail rather than face Jenny's wrath.

114   . "Next Came Casco." <u>Sunset</u>, 47, No. 5 (Nov. 1921), 42-43, 64-65.

Casco Billy (Wylackie) returns to Ukiah from a six-months' jail stay for possession of illicit liquor; his wife, Jenny, kicks him out. A reluctant Casco gets drafted into a fire fight, but is well paid for his efforts. That night he gambles with some other Indians and wins everything, including Good Boy Joe's wife. When Casco again runs out of money, he decides to set a fire in order to earn fire-fighting wages again. Jenny realizes that Casco has started the fire, and reports him to the ranger for a twenty-five dollar reward. In the face of Jenny's anger and jealousy, Casco is happy to return to jail.

115   . "The Owl and the Pussycat." <u>Sunset</u>, 60, No. 5 (May 1928), 9-11, 66, 68.

Jimmy Crickett (a Siwash Indian policeman) and a white law officer are called into the agent's office, where they learn that old man Schell has been murdered and that Tom Brown Owl is being held as a suspect because he has been found drunk and carrying a large sum of money. Owl's attorney pleads insufficient evidence. Jimmy examines the money and then goes to investigate the crime site, where he finds a black kitten. Back at the jail, Jimmy tells a reconstructed version of the crime (which he claims the kitten has related to him), implicating Owl as the murderer. Owl confesses. The white officer later learns that a kitten's paw print on a five-dollar bill found in Owl's pocket had been Jimmy's primary clue.

116   . "The Rally Call." <u>Sunset</u>, 49, No. 6 (Dec. 1922), 12-14, 88-90.

Casco Billy, otherwise known as Little Wolf, hereditary Chief of the Wylackies, is in jail. He befriends the sheriff's son, whom he calls Little Chief. He has spent hours teaching the boy Indian calls and traditions. One day a condemned murderer escapes, taking Little Chief as hostage. Casco Billy is asked to help free the boy; he reluctantly agrees. Casco sneaks up to the deserted cabin hide-out. The plan is that Casco signal with a coyote wail when he wants the posse to close in; unfortunately, a real coyote wails before he is ready. A startled and desperate Casco throws his club at the murderer, knocking him unconscious. The boy is rescued and the criminal recaptured.

117   . "Red Magic." <u>Sunset</u>, 60 (Feb. 1928), 18-20, 54, 56.

Jimmy Crickett, a Siwash Indian, is a detective who brilliantly solves the mystery of the stolen gold dust and identifies the guilty man--a white mining foreman. (This is an interesting reversal of the typical "Tonto" story: the Indian is the smart one and the white lawman relies upon the Indian's judgment.)

118 _____. "Spirits of Medicine Mountain." Sunset, 59, No. 4 (Oct. 1927), 28-30, 58, 60.

Jimmy Crickett (a Siwash Indian policeman) and a white law officer are tracking Lo-et, the "no-good" son of White Eye. Singing Bird, Tom Joe's sister, has taken her own life because of Lo-et, and Tom Joe seeks revenge. Wanting to prevent a murder, Jimmy tries to force Lo-et into Medicine Mountain, the home of tribal spirits, hoping that Tom Joe will not follow-- thereby avoiding the onset of a tribal blood-feud. But both Lo-et and Tom Joe are already at Medicine Mountain. Tom Joe catches Lo-et, but is cornered by Jimmy. Lo-et escapes, but is killed by a bear. Jimmy believes this to be an act of the "Spirits of Medicine Mountain."

119 Brick, John. "The Captives." They Ran for Their Lives. Garden City, N. Y.: Doubleday, 1954, pp. 110-13.

Three whites (two men and a woman) are held captive by the Senecas. When the Indians are all drunk one night, the whites escape. One of the men stays behind to fight off the pursuers and is killed; the other two escape to the fort to be married.

120 Brimblecom, Charles E. "A Masque at an Old Mission." Overland Monthly, n. s. 17 (1891), 482-89.

Dick Fox, a young American who has sneaked off the ship "Betsy Tucker," comes into a small California town looking for his uncle. On the first day he sees Doña Isabel and immediately falls in love with her. Meanwhile, in the Santa Clara Mission, an Indian named Miguel shows Father Caraffa some gold he has found in the Sierra Nevada Mountains. The Father, who is quite an entrepreneur, cautions Miguel to secrecy. After being rejected by his uncle, Dick comes to the mission and becomes friendly with the Father. Eventually the Father sends Dick and Miguel to get the gold, and Dick wins Doña.

121 Brink, Carol Ryrie. "Massacre." Indians, Indians, Indians. Ed. Phyllis R. Fenner. New York: Franklin Watts, 1950, pp. 56-80. Originally published in Caddie Woodlawn (New York: Macmillan, 1935).

Acting on a rumor that Indians are gathering to attack the whites, many Wisconsin settlers band together to defend themselves. No Indians attack. Some of the whites talk of going to massacre Old John's camp of friendly Indians, but Caddie runs to warn John. He brings the young girl back, pledges his friendship to the white men, and promises never to attack.

122   Brooks, Florence E. "Tonitiah." Overland Monthly, n. s. 46
       (1905), 537-45.
       Tonitiah, a Pueblo Indian girl, confides in her girl friend,
Poyye, that she does not love Sopete, whom she is supposed to
marry the next day; she confesses that she loves Poyye's brother,
Tejos. Poyye wants to help her friend and her brother, so she
goes to Hannay for a potion to make Sopete refuse the marriage.
The potion kills Sopete, however, and Tonitiah is accused of
the murder. She is secretly tried by the Pueblo leaders and
secretly walled up and left to die. Tejos discovers Tonitiah's
tomb and frees her; but she soon dies and Tejos, clutching her
body, jumps off a cliff.

123   Brown, J. M. "Out on the Plains." Overland Monthly, n. s.
       16 (1890), 495-508.
       Some early ranchers have trouble with Apaches who want
to steal a herd of mules. The Apaches fail.

124   Brown, Will C. "Duel in Captive Valley." Bar 2 Roundup of
       Best Western Stories. Ed. Scott Meredith. New York:
       Dutton, 1953, pp. 117-33.
       Ilene had been captured by the Tonlawa Indians six years
ago. Now the half-breed Young-Knife wants to marry her, but
Lieutenant Blair, her old fiancé, comes to rescue her. He
must fight a deadly duel with Young-Knife, his former scout.
Lieutenant Blair wins.

125   Buchan, John. "In the Dark Land." Path of the King. Bos-
       ton: Houghton, 1921, pp. 227-42.
       Daniel Boone and some friends try to locate their lost
companion, Jim Lovelle, but find him too late, burned at the
stake of some Mingo Indians.

126   Bullock, Alice. "Star for Teco." Arizona Quarterly, 10,
       No. 1 (Spring 1954), 17-24.
       Morning Star and Eagle Feather (of Acoma Pueblo) have
a son after many years of waiting. They name him Telcolote
(Owl)--Teco, for short. Teco is a mute, but learns in his
early years to love the stars and to play the flute--his only
voice. Teco's parents are killed by a car while returning
from Grants where they have taken Teco to a white doctor.
One night much later, Teco climbs to Acoma to find Morning
Star and Eagle Feather. He falls into some water (and presumably drowns) as he reaches for a star.

127   Burchardt, Bill. "Wine Without Price." Spurs West. Ed.
       S. Omar Barker. Garden City, N. Y.: Doubleday, 1960,
       pp. 55-67.
       A young couple and their baby homestead near the Co-
manche reservation. When the man goes back to Kansas for
some supplies, his wife is befriended by the half-breed son
and daughter of a neighboring cattleman.

128 Burson, Fred. (Ute). "Why Not? It's New Years!" Arrows
Four: Prose and Poetry by Young American Indians. Ed.
T. D. Allen. New York: Pocket Books, 1974, pp. 115-20.
A young Indian named Drew wanders around Salt Lake
City early in the morning of January 1. He befriends a wino
named Turkey who is part-Cherokee. They have a cup of coffee and a cigarette together. Then Drew goes to his sister's
house where, treating him like a grown-up for a change, she
offers him a beer.

129 Burton, Frederick R. "The Courting of Mahngequay: A Story
of Life Among the Ojibways Before the Days of the Reservation." Craftsman, 13, No. 1 (Oct. 1907), 1-13.
Maskenozha and Mahngequay (Loon-girl) are the son and
daughter of old Megissun and his wife, Sibequay, of the Ojibway tribe. One day Iggadom, a very strong but boastful brave,
announces his intention to marry Mahngequay. The old men
of the tribe tease him, saying that he should first court the
girl before making such statements. A slender brave named
Tebikoosa seems upset by the incident. When Iggadom courts
Mahngequay in the traditional Ojibway manner, he is turned
down; later, Tebikoosa wins Mahngequay and has a grand wedding feast.

130 _____. "Ibenese, the Provider." Craftsman, 15, No. 4
(Jan. 1900), 447-553.
The Ojibway brave, Ibenese, son of Megissun and Sibequay, has fallen in love with Segwunequay, daughter of the
widow Wabigan. He gives her a courting gift of bears; however, Wabigan bitterly chastises him for not bringing skins or
meat, and forbids the relationship. A shamed Ibenese leaves
the village and attempts to forget the lovely Segwunequay, but
he cannot. He returns home, resolved to provide for the widow
and her daughter, and to win Segwunequay for his wife. On a
hunting trip he kills three deer--one for the widow, and the
other two for the hungry village. Wabigan finally consents to
the marriage.

131 _____. "Rebellion of Maskenozha: A Sequel to the Visit."
Craftsman, 13, No. 6 (Mar. 1908), 631-42.
Maskenozha (an Ojibway brave) and Eliza Robinson (his
new half-breed wife) travel to his home, where they discover
that Sibequay (Maskenozha's mother) has left on a visit. Despite the fact that his mother disapproves of Eliza, Maskenozha
sets up house in his mother's wigwam; Megissun (his father)
is rapidly won over by Eliza's kindness. When Sibequay returns and banishes Eliza from her house, the couple live with
Tebikoosa and Mahngequay, Maskenozha's brother-in-law and
sister. Eliza and Maskenozha survive the long winter months,
but then Eliza, heavy with child, has a bad fall. Sibequay ultimately offers to help Eliza, but it is too late; both the girl
and her baby die. Maskenozha soon leaves his home, never
to return.

132 _____. "Visit: An Ojibway Romance." <u>Craftsman</u>, 13,
      No. 5 (Feb. 1908), 493-504.
      Sibequay, Megissun's squaw, notices her husband's dis-
content as autumn approaches, and he remembers that Shingebis had incurred a debt to him (fifty summers earlier) of
four buffalo skins which had never been paid. Megissun announces that he will visit his cousin, who lives in the same
village as Shingebis. The debt is easily settled after Megissun arrives. During the course of the visit, Sibequay's son,
(Maskenozha) falls in love with Eliza Robinson, the adopted
half-breed daughter of Waboos, son of Shingebis. Sibequay,
however, is violently opposed to a union between her son and
a half-breed and refuses to consider a marriage. As they
part, Maskenozha promises to return one day for Eliza.

133 Cable, George Washington. "Belles Demoiselles Plantation."
      <u>The American Tradition in Literature</u>, Vol. 2. Ed. Sculley
      Bradley et al. 3rd ed. New York: Norton, 1967, pp.
      512-26. Originally published in <u>Scribner's Monthly</u> (Apr.
      1874); later collected in <u>Old Creole Days</u> (1879).
      The De Charleu family property in New Orleans had been
unfairly divided between the white Colonel--who got Belles Demoiselles Plantation on the banks of the Mississippi River--and
his blood relative, half-Choctaw Injun Charlie--who got a row
of dilapidated houses in town. When Colonel De Charleu realizes that the river bank is eroding and his beautiful mansion
is doomed, he tries to arrange a swap of properties with Injun
Charlie. The old Indian puts De Charleu off repeatedly but
finally agrees. As the two approach the plantation to make the
deal, they watch with horror as the mansion suddenly collapses
"with one short, wild wail of terror--sunk, sunk, down, down,
down, into the merciless, unfathomable flood of the Mississippi,"
and De Charleu's seven daughters are carried along with it to
their deaths. Injun Charlie cares for the Colonel until the
grieving father joins his seven <u>belles</u> <u>demoiselles</u> "in paradise."

134 Cady, Jack. "Ride the Thunder." <u>The Burning and Other</u>
      Stories. Iowa City: Univ. of Iowa Press, 1972, pp. 107-18.
      Originally published in <u>Overdrive</u> (1967).
      Joe Indian, a half-Creek Indian, is a truck driver who is
hated and feared by other drivers. They are shocked by Joe's
cruelty to the turkeys he transports. Joe is torn between his
Indian belief that all animals deserve respect and the white
man's insensitivity to all nature. Finally the animal spirits
take their revenge and force Joe's truck to crash. Thereafter,
all trucks avoid that stretch of highway because it is haunted
by the animal spirits.

135 Calkins, Frank Welles. "Big Gun: A Santee Brave." <u>Outing</u>,
      40, No. 2 (May 1902), 142-46.
      Two white men are having a peaceful morning camped on
the Wattering when they sight a group of Indians chasing another
Indian. Recognizing the lone Indian as Big Gun, one of the

white men, Jules, shoots at the pursuers, scaring them away.
Big Gun, a Santee Sioux, tells how he had gotten separated
from his hunting party and had been attacked by a band of Chip-
pewas. Later Jules tells how he came to know Big Gun. Jules
and his family had once lived at Dead Horse Lake with the Santees. Their enemies, the Assiniboins, had burned their camp,
forcing the Santees onto an island in the lake. The Assiniboins
captured Jack, Jules's son, and threatened to burn him alive.
Big Gun, a young man then, offered to fight five Assiniboins
in return for Jack. The Assiniboins agreed, so Big Gun swam
across the lake and fought bravely, saving the boy's life.

136   Calkins, Harriet Bates. "What Happened on Half Way Grade."
        Sunset, 16 (Feb. 1906), 386-88.
            A greenhorn proves his worth to the local old-timers by
        standing up to a group of Indians who have attacked the stage-
        coach. He shoots the lovely young girl "to save her" from the
        Indians who are dragging her off, and is then nearly killed
        himself.

137   Calvin, M. Stowe. "Dry Husks." New Mexico Quarterly,
        6, No. 4 (Nov. 1936), 299-303.
            A young Navajo silversmith, Juan, brings Maria to his
        hogan. Soon they have a child, Little Blue-Bird. Juan be-
        comes sick and can no longer work at his craft; however, one
        day a Hollywood agent approaches him and offers a job on the
        movie set at Vas Quez Rocks. Against Maria's wishes, he
        goes. In the dangerous role as Grey Eagle's "double," the
        horse and rider slip and fall down a cliffside. Juan is killed.

138   Cameron, William Bleasdell. "A Mule-Skinner's Coincidence."
        Overland Monthly, n.s. 28 (1896), 463-69.
            One night on the Dakota reservation, after headman Ta-
        tonka Nompa finishes relating a story, the narrator asks a
        humpback Indian how he received the conspicuous scar over
        his right eye. The Indian explains in very bad English, "O,
        damn 'Melican man shoot un fol noting." A year later the nar-
        rator meets an old friend, mule-skinner Jim Vue, and learns
        of the encounter Jim had had with this Indian. It was Jim who
        had shot "Humpy," thinking he had killed the Indian.

        Campbell, W. S. see Stanley Vestal

139   Carleton, S. "The Tall Man." Atlantic Monthly, 99, No. 1
        (Jan. 1907), 36-44.
            The narrator, a white woodsman, is blinded by a curable
        eye disease. If he can reach a doctor in the nearest town, he
        will be cured. He can only reach the town, however, if his
        Indian companion, Louis, guides him there through the woods.
        Louis is afraid because the woods are haunted by an Indian god
        who forbids trespassing there. Lost in the woods, they meet
        the god, who leads them safely to the town.

140 Carlyle, Jean Claude. "Mas-col-lo, the Mighty Medicine Man."
     Overland Monthly, n. s. 16 (1890), 533-35.
        Mas-col-lo rushes from the sweat house to Medicine Hill,
     thinking he has been called by the great Savior, Un-koi-to.
     His lover, Shu-na, follows him, is rebuffed, and leaves. Mas-
     col-lo is attacked by a puma. He kills it, but is caught under
     its weight. As he nears death, he calls for Shu-na, who re-
     turns, believes Mas-col-lo to be dead, and stabs herself to
     death. Mas-col-lo is found, barely alive, and miraculously re-
     covers to become a famed and powerful medicine man.

141 Carousso, Georges. "The Sting of the Lance." Bar 5 Roundup
     of Best Western Stories. Ed. Scott Meredith. New York:
     Dutton, 1956, pp. 56-72.
        Black Cloud, a Cheyenne "hot head," has become the ar-
     rogant chief of a combined Indian force of thousands about to
     attack an undermanned fort staffed by fever-ridden soldiers.
     The smart Captain Brandon, however, outwits the proud Chey-
     enne chief by drawing him into an attack on thirty-five soldiers
     in a perfect defensive position. Black Cloud is defeated and
     loses his following.

142 Carpenter, Helen M. "The Mitchells." Overland Monthly,
     n. s. 26 (1895), 292-96.
        Jim Mitchell (black) and his Indian wife, Ellen, live in
     a cabin with their dog near Jim's old master. Jim is old and
     quite sick. Through the years Ellen had kept close contact
     with her people and they, in turn, had continually sought goods
     from her. When Jim dies Ellen sells the land, and the money
     is quickly dissipated by her fellow tribesmen. One day, when
     she is not at home, a male slave who had unsuccessfully tried
     to take Jim's place, destroys the contents of her cabin. Ellen
     returns to her people.

143 Carr, Mary Jane. "Traps of Quicksand." This Land Around
     Us. Ed. Ellis Lucia. Garden City, N. Y.: Doubleday,
     1969, pp. 350-59.
        Wagon train leaders, having just led their train across a
     dangerous river, camp on the other side near some Crow In-
     dians. The leaders, Stephen and Henri Devine, are wary of
     the Crows, who are reputed to be skillful thieves. They agree
     to give the Crows a meal, but won't let them near the wagons.
     After the Indians depart, Stephen and Henri are very pleased
     with the clever way they thwarted the thieves. Then they re-
     alize that the Indians have walked away with all the white
     men's plates and cups.

144 Carter, Russell Gordon. "The Crimson Arrow." Young
     Readers' Indian Stories. New York: Lantern Press, 1951,
     pp. 108-25.
        Waquoit, a young Penacook Indian from what is now New
     Hampshire, is torn between loyalty to his tribe and his friend-

ship with a white man (John Stanwood) at the outbreak of King Phillip's War in 1675. Waquoit helps his friend to escape when the Indians are on his trail.

145   Carver, Mary Alden. "The Indian Who Was a White Man."
      Overland Monthly, n. s. 52 (1908), 462-65.
          Silent Pete, a half-breed Indian, and Adolph St. Claire, a Frenchman, are both lumberjacks at Cedar Lake Camp. This is to be Adolph's last winter working there because in the spring he is supposed to wed Nora; unfortunately, Silent Pete also loves Nora. One day Adolph is severely injured and Silent Pete brings Nora to Adolph's bedside so that she can see him before he dies. To Pete's dismay, however, Nora's appearance inspires Adolph to recover. The night before Adolph is scheduled to leave, Pete weakens a bridge over which Adolph is to travel. Upon his return to camp he sees Nora, who pours out her thankfulness to him. Pete, guilt-stricken, returns to the bridge and repairs it.

146   Case, Victoria. "When the Indians Came." This Land Around
      Us. Ed. Ellis Lucia. Garden City, N.Y.: Doubleday,
      1969, pp. 350-59.
          A rowdy group of young Molalla (Cayuse) Indians plan to prove their manhood by attacking some vulnerable settlers. When the Indians see that teen-aged Walter and his elderly aunt are alone and without horses, they head for their cabin to begin their rampage. The two whites expect to die, but Walter, without a weapon, bravely confronts the Indians on a log bridge, demanding that they pay the toll before they cross. The Indians, who are young and inexperienced also, are startled. The Indian leader's pony, frightened by Walter's loud voice, slips off the bridge--carrying the leader with him into the river. The other Indians laugh and go home. Walter has proved his manhood.

147   Catherwood, Mary Hartwell. "The Chase of Saint-Castin."
      Atlantic Monthly, 72, No. 429 (Jul. 1893), 60-72.
          Saint-Castin, a French nobleman, lives among the Abnaki Indians. He loves the nun-like daughter of the Abnaki chief, but she tells him she will never marry. He is persistent, however, and finally she relents.

148   _____. "The Cobbler in the Devil's Kitchen." Harper's,
      95 (Aug. 1897), 414-21.
          Owen Cunning is an Irish cobbler who lives near a beach (called the Devil's Kitchen) on Mackinac Island. One day a squaw named Blackbird pays an unexpected visit to Owen. She leaves a gold coin with a bird's outline carved on one side. Through a fur trapper he learns that his cousin (John McGillis) is married both to Blackbird and to another woman. Owen confronts John and they fight. Owen claims he has a token to prove John isn't the widower he claims to be, and as John is leaving on his boat Owen shows him the gold coin the Indian

squaw gave him. John admits that he is married to Blackbird. When Owen returns to his kitchen, he finds a beaver-skin coat that Blackbird had left him.

149 _____. "The Kidnapped Bride." Atlantic Monthly, 74, No. 443 (Sep. 1894), 326-34.
A beautiful young French woman, Celeste Barbeau, loves Gabriel Chartrant, a young Frenchman who also lives in Cahokia, a frontier Illinois town. They want to marry, but Celeste's father pledges her to an older, richer man whom Celeste hates. Gabriel and his friends, disguised as Potawatomi Indians, plan to kidnap Celeste on her wedding day. The abduction takes place, but the kidnappers are real Potawatomies. Gabriel follows them, however, and retrieves Celeste.

150 _____. "Marianson." Harper's, 96 (Dec. 1897), 92-98.
A young Canadian attached to the British Army during an attack upon Mackinac Island attempts to desert, but an officer spots the youth and sends a Sioux Indian to scalp him. The deserter discovers a cave, enters, and finds a woman (Marianson) asleep. She awakens and feeds the young man, then leaves to arrange his escape. When she returns she realizes that the Sioux has accomplished his assignment.

151 Chamberlain, William. "Proud Guidon." Rawhide Men. Ed. Kenneth Fowler. Garden City, N.Y.: Doubleday, 1965, pp. 65-108. Originally published in The Saturday Evening Post (Feb. 4, 1956).
The greenhorn Lieutenant Landseer grows to manhood in charge of a company of soldiers outnumbered five to one by off-reservation hostile Sioux.

Chapman, Leslie see Leslie Silko

152 Chase, Clyde Scott. "Liolah." Overland Monthly, n.s. 38 (1901), 138-42.
Liolah, a Puget Sound Indian, falls in love with a white man who finds her unattractive. She does not realize this, however, so when he perishes in a spring flood she lives as a Christian virgin--devoted and faithful to him until her death at age seventy.

153 Chesnutt, Charles W. "A Midnight Adventure." The Short Fiction of Charles W. Chesnutt. Ed. Sylvia Lyons Render. Washington, D.C.: Howard Univ. Press, 1974, pp. 85-88.
Jones feels superior to the poor, uncivilized Indians he sees in a Wild West Show. That night in a park he sits down near a bronze statue of an Ojibway Indian. The Indian seems to speak to him, to capture him, and then to be about to strike him with a sledge hammer. The Indians are punishing him because his people have taken their land. Just as Jones is about to die, he wakes up. It was only a dream.

154   Chidestar, Ann. "The Beach Boy." <u>Atlantic Monthly</u>, 178,
      No. 5 (Nov. 1946), 80-84.
           Charles Bixby, a successful businessman, is married to
      a young woman, Flora, who had grown up in the wooded area
      of Bird Island. He hires Skidmore Fenner, a Chippewa, to
      work in the boathouse. Flora and Skid become good friends,
      but when local gossipers suggest a closer relationship between
      the two, Charles confronts the Indian about it.

155   Churchill, Claire Warner. "Kal-a-ka-lah'-la, the Wild Goose."
      <u>Slave Wives of Nehalem</u>. Portland, Ore.: Metropolitan
      Press, 1933, pp. 79-90.
           Kal-a-ka-lah'-la, once princess of the Yakimas, is now
      the slave wife of Shilth-lo, chief of the Nehalem. When she
      and All-chee, Shilth-lo's other wife, both bear him sons on
      the same day, Kal-a-ka-lah'-la arises and trades sons with
      All-chee, knowing that this way her son will eventually become
      chief. Unfortunately her son dies during the night and Kal-a-
      ka-lah'-la, growing weaker, realizes she will die too. Seeking
      revenge against the tribe's women, who belittle her because of
      her slave status, she requests that upon her death the baby in
      her arms (really All-chee's baby) be sold to another tribe as
      a slave.

156   _____. "Le-mo-lo, the Untamed One." <u>Slave Wives of</u>
      <u>Nehalem</u>. Portland, Ore.: Metropolitan Press, 1933, pp.
      49-75.
           A prophecy of an ancient slave girl, Tsealth, states that
      one day Tal-a-pus, the tribal diety, will marry a maiden of
      the Oregon coast Nehalem tribe. Le-mo-lo believes herself
      to be that maiden, so when she learns that arrangements have
      been made for her to marry Tish-ko-lo (the old medicine man
      whom she despises) Le-mo-lo tells her people that they will
      bring evil upon themselves. The marriage takes place, how-
      ever, and that night Le-mo-lo kills Tish-ko-lo with magic.
      The chief and several tribesmen take Le-mo-lo to the beach
      for punishment. She calls for a sign of favor from Tal-a-pus.
      Just then, a shipwrecked white man--the first white man the
      Indians have ever seen--washes ashore. Le-mo-lo and the
      rest of the Indians think the man is Tal-a-pus and that the
      prophecy has come true.

157   _____. "My-ee-na, the Singer." <u>Slave Wives of Nehalem</u>.
      Portland, Ore.: Metropolitan Press, 1933, pp. 31-46.
           My-ee-na, a Coos slave, lives among the Nehalem peo-
      ple. She is the widow of Ul-ken whom she had never loved;
      instead, she loves Ul-ken's brother, Yak-a-la. My-ee-na lives
      with her mother-in-law, who alone has the power to release
      My-ee-na from the mourning period, leaving her free to re-
      marry. While Yak-a-la is away on a trading trip, Kah-loken
      tries to make My-ee-na marry the slow-witted Klo-nass, but
      the clever My-ee-na feigns a dream about her dead husband.
      This bad omen cancels the marriage plans. When Kah-loken
      dies soon afterward, My-ee-na and Yak-a-la are married.

158 _____. "Ock-li-put-li, the Lily." Slave Wives of Nehalem.
Portland, Ore.: Metropolitan Press, 1933, pp. 3-28.
Ty-yel-a-ho, an Oregon coast Nehalem Indian, makes
gaming sticks for the native gambling game. He loves a young
slave maiden, Ock-li-put-li, who is owned by Oo-lux. Oo-lux
gambles and loses the girl to Tish-ko-ko who, in turn, loses
her to Ty-yel-a-ho. A bitter Tish-ko-ko tries to poison Ty-
yel-a-ho, but the intended victim discovers the poison in his
food. The next day Ty-yel-a-ho cleverly retaliates, causing
Tish-ko-ko to lose his position as tribal medicine man. Ty-
yel-a-ho and Ock-li-put-li are married.

159 Clark, James W. "Broken Spirits." Two Saps and Fourteen
Other Stories. Los Angeles: DeVorss and Co., 1942,
pp. 111-18.
Two traveling salesmen arrive at a Pueblo village hoping
to sell farm machinery to the Indians. While there they get
to know the old missionary, who after twenty-two years is dis-
couraged and wants to leave, and a young Indian, Thunder-
Cloud, who had been away at one of the government schools.
While the salesmen are visiting the Pueblo, the members of
the tribe go into the kiva to hold a trial for an Indian who had
gotten drunk and had beaten his wife. At the end, the two
salesmen and the priest leave and everyone seems sad.

160 Clark, Walter van Tilburg. "The Anonymous." The Watchful
Gods and Other Stories. New York: Random House, 1950,
pp. 67-92. Originally published in Virginia Quarterly Review.
Gates is a sensitive white teacher at an Indian boarding
school. He is coerced into tutoring Peter Carr (a rich young
Navajo man) in literacy and "culture." Peter has no interest
in his Indian heritage, nor in Jenny, the Shoshone girl who
offers herself to him. It turns out that he is being kept by
the wealthy owner of a New Mexico dude ranch who intends to
marry him once he is "educated," and then to keep him around
the ranch for display.

161 _____. "The Pretender." Atlantic Monthly, 169, No. 4
(Apr. 1942), 482-91.
Joe-Jack (Indian) transports Jed Southwick to and from
Smoky Lake, where the white man resolves some personal anx-
ieties.

162 Coatsworth, Elizabeth. "The Attack." Indians, Indians, Indians. Ed. Phyllis R. Fenner. New York: Franklin Watts,
1950, pp. 188-201. Originally published in St. Nicholas
Magazine (Aug. 1935).
Five hungry Indians, carrying French rifles, attack a
frontier home when the menfolk are gone. The women trick
the Indians and sneak off to the garrison.

163 Cohoe, Grey. (Navajo). "Great Spirit Protect Us." South
Dakota Review, 9, No. 2 (Summer 1971), 163-67.

A young Navajo boy and his crippled sister bring the
sheep home to their hogan, only to find that their parents have
gone to a squaw dance. During the night, thinking of all the
stories they have heard concerning evil spirits, the children
are terrified when they hear a disturbance outside. What they
believe to be a monster jumps upon the hogan roof, but then
leaves. The boy decides that he must leave his sister to get
his parents. She agrees. When the family returns they find
only the little girl's head. Later hunters go to a sacred butte
to kill the evil monsters, but the boy remains forever sad at
the loss of his dearly beloved sister.

164 _____. (Navajo). "The Promised Visit." South Dakota
Review, 7, No. 2 (Summer 1969), 45-56. Reprinted in De-
sign for Good Reading, ed. Schumacher (New York: Harcourt Brace Jovanovich, 1969); also reprinted in American
Indian Authors, ed. Natachee Scott Momaday (Boston: Houghton Mifflin, 1972), pp. 106-16, and in The American Indian
Speaks, ed. John R. Milton (Vermillion, S.D.: Dakota
Press, 1969), pp. 45-56.
A young Navajo man is driving his brother-in-law's truck
back to Shiprock after having been to Window Rock for an in-
terview concerning a tribal scholarship. A bad storm overtakes him. When suddenly he sees a figure on the highway,
he considers--but quickly brushes aside--the old Navajo superstitions concerning ghosts. He stops for the hitchhiker, a
young and beautiful Navajo girl, and the young man instantly
falls in love. He offers his maroon sweater to the chilled girl,
Susan Billy. When he leaves her at the path to her hogan, she
promises to visit him some night. Several days later, under
the pretense of getting his sweater back, he goes to visit her.
He learns from an old man that Susan has been buried in a
nearby crumbling hogan for ten years. The young man wonders if and when Susan's ghost will visit him again.

165 Comfort, Will Levington. "Red Brennan of the Seventh."
Trooper Tales: A Series of Sketches of the Private Soldier.
New York: Street and Smith, 1899, pp. 97-104.
Red Brennan, a white deserter, dies at Custer's last
stand. The Indians do not mutilate his body, however, because
of the love of an Indian, Kate Poison-Water, who keeps them
away. Kate is "a serpent in cunning, a tigress in strength
and agility--a Sioux squaw in general deviltry."

166 Condie, LeRoy. "My Name Is Hope Martine." New Mexico
Quarterly, 36, No. 2 (Summer 1964), 179-84.
Hope Martine, a Navajo girl (more or less "orphaned"
by a dead mother and a drunken father), is raised by her
grandmother (Shinali) and sent to Phoenix for nurse's training
at a white man's school when she is about eleven years old.
She returns after five years and is given a Navajo puberty
ceremony but, seeing her father and others drunk, she leaves
and returns to the school to stay with the white teacher: "I
do not think I shall go back to Navajoland."

167 Conley, Robert J. (Cherokee). "A Lone Oak in Kansas."
     Indian Voice, 2, No. 2 (Mar./Apr. 1972), 30-31.
        An old Indian decides not to fight the whites anymore,
     and tries to be friendly. Finally he is moved to Kansas to a
     horrid reservation. When he returns home for a visit he finds
     that his land and family burial ground have been plowed under.
     Back in Kansas, he and his son go for a horse ride and four
     Sac Indians shoot arrows at them, pinning his son to a tree.

168 _____. (Cherokee). "The Night George Wolfe Died."
     Indian Voice, 2, No. 3 (May/Jun. 1972), 9.
        George Wolfe, a Cherokee, is doing rather well in the
     white man's world--he has been educated, runs a general store,
     is mildly prosperous, has been elected to the Cherokee Na-
     tional Legislature, etc. On his way home from a meeting one
     night, Wolfe is beaten up by a drunk white. He fights back,
     knocks the drunk out, but is thrown into jail by the white law-
     man. He decides to give up being white: George Wolfe "dies,"
     and he "never spoke another word of English."

169 Connor, James F. "Shadow on the Desert." Southwestern
     Mosaics. Ed. Jo Gwyn Baldwin. El Paso: Boots and
     Saddle Press, 1969, pp. 84-87.
        Little Wolf, a Mimbres Pueblo Indian, notices a large
     troop of men and animals approaching Mimbres. It turns out
     that they are Spaniards seeking the city of Cibola with its
     streets paved with gold. Little Wolf lies, sending them to
     Apache country, and then returns to Mimbres. The Indians
     decide that they must leave before the strange white men re-
     turn; they abandon their pueblo.

170 Cook, William Wallace. "Aquastor." Overland Monthly, n.s.
     33 (1899), 14-19.
        At Albuquerque Bob Graham meets an old friend, Grantly,
     on a westbound train. Grantly, racked with consumption, is
     traveling to Laguna in hopes of regaining his health. He seeks
     Aquastor, an ancient Eastern charm owned by Quacal, a Na-
     vajo medicine man. Grantly carries a blue topaz, given to
     him by an old Navajo chief, which is to help him obtain an
     audience with Quacal. Grantly fails to steal Aquastor from
     the crafty Indian and dies.

171 Cooke, Grace MacGowan. "The Sacred Meal." Sunset, 29
     (Oct. 1912), 371-82.
        Virchow Raines, a young Philadelphia artist painting at
     Oraibi in Hopiland, is tricked into thinking he is engaged to a
     Hopi maiden when his mother unknowingly accepts some sacred
     corn meal left by the girl (it was meant to indicate her interest
     in Honve, a Hopi orphan painter staying in the house with his
     white "mother"). The comedy of errors works out fine, though:
     The maiden, Keewanee, marries Honve; Raines's girlfriend
     (Gertrude) is brought in from Philadelphia and they, too, are
     married.

172   Coolidge, Dane. "Sparrow Hawk." Sunset, 29, No. 2 (Aug.
        1912), 127-34, and 29, No. 3 (Sep. 1912), 283-88.
             Sparrow Hawk and her husband, Pistola (both Cheme-
        huevis), live in Ehrenberg. Pistola is so jealous that he forces
        Sparrow Hawk to go with him to his gold claim in the moun-
        tains. She escapes from Pistola, and is saved from death in
        the desert by Jim Orcutt (white), the only inhabitant of Flow-
        ing Wells. Sparrow Hawk falls in love with him, but Jim does
        not want to take her as his wife because he suffers from a
        lung disease. She returns to Ehrenberg, but finally runs away
        and returns to Jim.

173   Coolidge, Grace. "The Indian of the Reservation." Short
        Stories of the New America. Ed. Mary A. Laselle. New
        York: Henry Holt, 1919, pp. 109-19.
             The Indian Bureau official calls a meeting of reservation
        Indians to explain why the Indians should sell half of their res-
        ervation to white people: so that they will have money to buy
        water rights to the river that runs through the reservation.
        After considerable debate a majority of the Indians decide that,
        since they are like children, they must do what the White
        Father tells them to do.

174   _____. "Place of Thanksgiving." Collier's, 52 (Sep. 27,
        1913), 17.
             The narrator, a rancher, and a half-breed, driving down
        a valley, see a man up on the rocks who (according to the
        half-breed) is Old Plenty Elk, praying and fasting for his sick
        wife. The half-breed then says that Indians always give thanks-
        giving, and tells of an incident in his childhood when his mother
        made him give thanks at a spring in the desert. After hearing
        a description of the spring, the rancher realizes that it is lo-
        cated on his property.

175   Corle, Edwin. "Bank Holiday." Mojave. New York: Live-
        right, 1934, pp. 43-53.
             Several Indians want to go into the bank in Coachella, but
        (apparently because of the 1929 stock market "crash") the bank
        is closed. Failing to understand the complex circumstances,
        they decide to sit and wait.

176   _____. "Big Min." Mojave. New York: Liveright, 1934,
        pp. 147-62.
             Big Min (Piute) initiates young Piute boys into sex, but
        her husband shows little concern. One day some white men
        convince him to be jealous, to beat up his wife, and to kill
        her lover. Later, when he comes home and finds her with a
        Shoshone man, he beats the Shoshone to death and kicks his
        wife. Then the two bury the dead man. Big Min confesses
        and the two go to jail, but no case is proved and they are re-
        leased.

177   _____. "A Burnt Offering." Mojave. New York: Live-
        right, 1934, pp. 54-73.

The Piute Black Horse changes his name to Tony Black, moves into a white man's house, works on the highway, has lots of money, and so on. His mother refuses to change, and she dies. Then arises the conflict: should he burn the house, as in the old way, or not burn the house, as in the white way? A white man talks him out of burning it, and he leaves the house to a white family. Then a terrible wind blows down his new house, and he loses his trees and his job, so he decides he has to appease the gods. He goes back and sets the old house afire, with the family in it (they get out). Tony is prosecuted and sent back to live on a reservation in a hogan, and he is finally happy and contented.

178 _____. "One More Hero." Mojave. New York: Liveright, 1934, pp. 94-100.
Bluebird, a minor hero in the first World War, now just sits in a little desert town in the Mojave Desert and refuses to answer questions of tourists--that is, unless they ask about his Distinguished Service Cross.

179 Courtright, Eugenie. "Death Song." Atlantic Monthly, 145, No. 5 (May 1930), 637-49.
A wide-eyed, idealistic young white woman, Sarah Boggs, gladly accepts her new job as clerk in a Sioux agency. With her very romanticized view of Indians, she does more harm than good. Helpless to reform the Indian Service, which she believes is corrupt, Sarah loses her mind and her life in a vain attempt to murder an insensitive bureaucrat.

180 _____. "Kinda Lonesome." Atlantic Monthly, 146, No. 5 (Nov. 1930), 610-21.
Titus Big Hawk, a young Sioux boy, attends a government Indian school. Because he is artistic and sickly, the school nurse, the principal, and the local priest befriend him. In their desire to "help" him, they coddle him and inadvertently estrange him from his family and his culture.

181 _____. "Two Insurgents." Atlantic Monthly, 148, No. 5 (Nov. 1931), 631-43.
Betsy Lane, an idealistic young clerk at a Sioux agency, defies her superior, a corrupt, racist Indian agent, and tries to help Bear Ghost, an aging Sioux chief. Bear Ghost is so oppressed by the agent that he resorts to armed resistance. Out of pity, Betsy encourages him, even though she knows he will die in the struggle.

182 _____. "Yours Lovingly." Atlantic Monthly, 144, No. 6 (Dec. 1929), 806-17.
A young Potawatomi boy, Julius Pokagan, is dying of tuberculosis. Throughout his final stay in the hospital, he is befriended by a kindly clerk in the superintendent's office of the Indian school where Julius has been a student. The insensitive school superintendent, however, callously refuses to care about lonely, dying Julius.

183 Coxey, Willard Douglas. "An Aboriginal Coquette." Tales by
     the Way: Little Book of Odd Stories. Chicago: n.p.,
     1898, pp. 38-47.
         Singing Bird, daughter of Chief Patonka-I-Yotanka, flirts
     with many of the young men of the tribe, even the poor and
     lazy brave named Yellow Crow. The chief's adopted son,
     Waubluijo-Ta-Ke (Sitting Eagle), a prosperous hunter, wants
     Singing Bird for his wife; Black Bear, an Indian educated in
     a white school, also wants to marry her. Sitting Eagle and
     Black Bear fight with knives to determine who will be Singing
     Bird's husband, but she stops the fight, informing them that
     she has decided to be Yellow Crow's squaw.

184 _____. "The First Trail." Romances of Old Berkshire.
     Great Barrington, Mass.: The Berkshire Courier, 1931,
     pp. 31-64.
         One of the first (early seventeenth-century) Dutch settlers
     in the Berkshires is Diedrik who, along with his wife, makes
     his home in the wilderness. Soon a baby girl is born to them,
     and within a few years they become friendly with a small band
     of Pequot Indians. Ultimately the daughter, Gertie, falls in
     love with Little Fox, the chief's son; much to her parents' dis-
     may, she marries him and moves to the village. Gertie is not
     happy as a hard-working squaw, however, and after three years
     drowns herself. Soon her mother dies of grief for her lost
     daughter, but Diedrik takes an Indian wife and becomes one
     of the tribe. He even joins King Phillip in his war against
     the whites. Diedrik is killed and scalped by white soldiers
     and their Mohican allies in 1676, and the white men are amazed
     to discover that one of the "Indians" is really white.

185 _____. "The Indian Dreamer." Romances of Old Berk-
     shire. Great Barrington, Mass.: The Berkshire Courier,
     1931, pp. 7-30.
         An old Algonquin chief named Sho-no-wee-naw hopes that
     his son, Os-so-waun, will be a great warrior and accomplish
     revenge against the tribe's many enemies. Os-so-waun, how-
     ever, is a dreamer and a coward who not only refuses to fight,
     but also becomes friendly with a girl from an enemy tribe.
     When the lovers are discovered by the girl's father, the girl
     throws herself off a cliff to her death. Her people then attack
     the Algonquin village, killing all the men except Chief Sho-no-
     wee-naw, who lives out his sad life to a great old age alone--
     "the last of his tribe."

186 Craddock, Charles Egbert. "A Victor at Chungke." Harper's,
     100 (Mar. 1900), 509-26.
         Two braves play an old Indian game--chungke. Wyejah,
     the undefeated champion, and Otastite (man-killer), an English
     captive since his childhood, engage in a contest which ends in
     a draw. Otastite asks Abram Varney (an English trader re-
     cently returned from Charlestown) for news of his family in
     Charlestown and confides to Varney that he would like to leave

the Cherokees. Learning of Otastite's desire, the old chief
is very sad, but he agrees to grant the young brave his freedom if Otastite can beat Wyejah at chungke. If he loses the
game he must stay. Otastite wins, but Wyejah accidentally
kills him with the chungke stone. Both Abram and Wyejah
flee for fear of their lives.

187   Crane, Stephen. "The Battle of Forty Fort." Cassell's Maga-
       zine, n. s. 23 (May 1901), 591-94.
       Young Bennet, at age sixteen, joins a regiment to fight
the British and the Indians in a battle in Pennsylvania's Wyoming Valley. When the left flank of the Americans is routed,
Bennet drops his rifle and runs home to where his father,
"Ol' Bennet," is reading his Bible.

188   _____. "'Ol' Bennet' and the Indians." Cassell's Magazine,
       n. s. 22 (Dec. 1900), 108-11.
       The Indians around Wilkes Barre, Pennsylvania, hate one
of the white settlers, "Ol' Bennet," because he kicks them when
they get drunk. One day Indians capture him and his son while
they are plowing their fields. A few days later, after a furious
and bloody fight, "Ol' Bennet" and his son defeat their Indian
captors and head back toward the settlements.

189   _____. "The Surrender of Forty Fort." Last Words.
       London: Digby, Long, 1902, pp. 81-88.
       John Bennet, after the Americans have lost the battle of
Forty Fort in Pennsylvania's Wyoming Valley, sends his wife
and female children to the fort (which is to be surrendered)
and heads off himself, with his two sons, over the mountains
to Stroudsburg.

190   Currier, Susan Lord. "The Ending of the Watson Case."
       Overland Monthly, n. s. 33 (1899), 437-41.
       Martha Watson waits for a court ruling on the legality
of her marriage to John, her late husband. In his youth John
had married an Indian, fathered a half-breed son, Henry, and
later married Martha. Henry contests the legality of his
father's second marriage and, therefore, Martha's right to
inheritance. Martha learns that the marriage is legal, but she
bequeaths the land to Henry in a letter. She is murdered that
night. Henry is accused of the murder and is about to be
lynched when his real Indian mother comes forward and confesses to the crime.

191   Curtis, Anna L. "The Ghosts of the Mohawk." Spooks,
       Spooks, Spooks. Ed. Helen Hoke. Franklin Watts, 1966,
       pp. 167-74. Originally published in Ghosts of the Mohawk
       and Other Stories, by Anna L. Curtis.
       John Ferris, a pioneer settler in the Mohawk Valley,
lies ill with fever. His older daughter, Annie, comes in from
milking with the news that she has seen an Indian. Fearing
attack that very night, Annie and her sister, Lukey, put on

white sheets, mount stilts (which their father had gotten in Belgium years earlier), and walk around the cabin, thus frightening the Mohawks away.

192   Curtis, Wilmetta. "A Double Stroke." Overland Monthly, n. s. 38 (1901), 332-37.
      Jim Long, a white miner, lives with Mollie, an Indian woman. Later he takes a second "wife," Majella, and has a son, Pete, by her. Mollie, possessive of Pete and jealous of Majella, forces Jim to send Majella away, keeping the child. Majella returns later in the night, murders Jim and Mollie, and takes her baby.

193   Daixel, Sheen. "My Indian Mother." The New Country: Stories from the Yiddish About Life in America. Ed. Henry Goodman. New York: YKUF Publishers, 1961, pp. 481-98.
      A young writer from New York hitchhikes around the West to find out about Indians for a series of stories he wants to write. He spends a few weeks at the Hopi reservation where he strikes up a friendship with O-ta-ka, a young Hopi painter. Then he spends a couple more weeks with the Yosemite Indians. There he massages the sore back of an old Indian woman, who becomes his "Indian mother."

194   Daugahnogae, and Oledoska. "The Warclub That Killed the White Captain." Indian Voice, 1, No. 3 (May/Jun. 1972), 16-17, 47.
      Hubert Logan (Seneca), having tried the white man's way but having found it unsatisfying, returns to the tribe of his youth. When the white agent, Hamilton, breaks up the Gahnah-o-uh Dance at Harvest Festival Time, Logan grabs his old ancestral war-club and murders him. Logan's only defense at his trial is that he did not kill the white man--his Medicine Club did.

195   Davis, Julia. "Two for One." Atlantic Monthly, 163, No. 6 (Jun. 1939), 773-78.
      Two drunk Shoshone boys, Ibbepah and Johnny, kill a drunken hobo who refuses to buy them whiskey. The two boys are sentenced to death.

196   _____. "White Justice." Atlantic Monthly, 151, No. 6 (Jun. 1933), 689-95.
      A young Piute boy, Imyo Weismiller, kills a white cowboy who has cheated him out of some money. A white judge sentences him to death, but Imyo's parents plead with the judge to save the boy. The judge convinces the governor to send Imyo to school instead.

197   Day, Bess Eileen. "A Tree on the Prairie." Southwest Review, 41, No. 4 (Autumn 1956), 366-69.
      During a November snowstorm, Hester Moore awaits the return of her husband, Vierck. Her baby is cold and sick,

and Hester is running out of fuel. She sees Indian riders and
is afraid because she remembers earlier visits when Red
Feather, a Crow, had tried to bargain with Vierck for her.
Hester watches the Indians hoist and secure a long bundle into
her cottonwood tree. At last Vierck comes back and informs
Hester that the Indians are there to fulfill Red Feather's last
request--to have his body placed in the tree near "Pale Squaw."

198 de Angulo, Jaime. "Wife of Cheating Frog." Independent,
     117 (Aug. 21, 1926), 206-07.
     The narrator (white) tells of a personal observance of
     Achomawi death. He had been living with Cheating Frog in
     order to learn of Indian lore. Cheating Frog's wife was quite
     ill and steadily grew worse; neither her father's powers, nor
     their daughter's ministrations, nor an old Modoc's singing
     could make her well. When death finally came, the narrator
     found her death rattle and the wails chilling.

199 Defender, Adelina. (Pueblo). "No Time for Tears." An
     American Indian Anthology. Ed. Benet Tvedten. Marvin,
     S.D.: Blue Cloud Abbey, 1971, pp. 23-31.
     Moon Rainbow, Allen, and Stephen, three children from
     Jemez Pueblo, go to the family cornfield to hoe corn. Moon
     Rainbow thinks about some of the unpleasant experiences she
     has had: the time the sisters at the Catholic mission forced
     her to write over and over, "I will not go to the protestant
     church"; the time the teacher at the public school made her
     write over and over, "I will not talk Indian." She thinks about
     the good things also: her grandfather, her artist father, the
     beauty of the village.

200 DeHuff, Elizabeth Willis. "The Grinding Stones." New Mexico
     Quarterly, 2, No. 4 (Nov. 1932), 299-311.
     Pah-ah-pi and Tam-pohva do nothing except quarrel dur-
     ing their four years of marriage, so Pah-ah-pi approaches
     O-coo-wha (his lazy brother-in-law, married to Tam-pohva's
     sister, Poh-lah-mee-mee) and suggests that they exchange
     wives. They agree and the trade is planned. Pah-ah-pi is
     readily accepted, but O-coo-wha must go twice to Tam-pohva
     before she agrees to the arrangement. A year later, both
     have additions to their "new" families.

201 _____. "Pink Skin Strangers." New Mexico Quarterly, 8,
     No. 4 (Nov. 1938), 229-39.
     Miss Howper, a New England woman, attends a Pueblo
     religious ceremony to obtain material for her doctoral disser-
     tation. She is crude and impolite. She sees in the dance only
     what she already believes, listens to the nonsense of a man
     who makes up stories for a quarter, and leaves before the
     ceremony ends.

202 _____. "Witch-Bears: A Tale of Tomas Pueblo." South-
     west Review, 23, No. 1 (Oct. 1937), 84-103.

Tom Bradley lives with his Indian wife, Tah-la-si, and their seven children in Tomas Pueblo. Though white, Tom had tried very hard through the years to adopt Indian ways and fit into the community. As a surveyor, however, he is richer than most, thereby incurring jealousy--especially that of Mahsah-yah-ni-mah, the ex-suitor of Tah-la-si, and of old See-kahkoo-kee, the poorest man in the village. One day Tom comes home to find his baby quite ill; when a brass ring found around the baby's wrist is removed, the baby becomes well. The illness is blamed on the "shy-gay-e-kaye"--the witch-bears. Tom finds this hard to believe, but other misfortunes to his family and animals follow. One day when Tah-la-si fails to return from the trading post, Tom finds her half-scalped. Tah-la-si says that two witch-bears did it, but that she was able to stab them with a butcher's knife. Tom and his brother-in-law track the "bears," and the bloody trail leads to a cave where two bear skins and two wounded men, See-kah-koo-kee and Mahsah-yah-ni-mah, are found. The two fugitives jump from a precipice to their deaths.

203 de la Cuadra, José. "Hungry Dog." Southwest Review, 29, No. 3 (Spring 1944), 406-09.

  José Tupinamba, a Quechua-speaking Indian, leaves his baby, Michi, and five-year-old son, Santos, alone in his hut. His wife, Chasca, is at the master's house--where she is both maid and lover. José finds a lost lamb and returns it to the sheepfold. Conqueror, the guard dog, should be there but is missing. José waits with the sheep and soon Conqueror returns, his tail between his legs, carrying the purple diaper of Michi and a baby's bloody arm.

204 de Paola, Daniel. "The Returning." Best American Short Stories, 1965. Ed. Martha Foley. Boston: Houghton Mifflin, 1965, pp. 45-56. Originally published in Prairie Schooner.

  Willis Darkcat, fed up with the kind of life that the Blackfeet are forced to live on the reservation in Oklahoma, decides to run away. To accomplish this, he must kill a member of the posse. Near the Mexican border he comes to a house, enters, and finds a woman and her baby very sick from diphtheria. He nurses them back to health. After several days have passed, the woman's husband (a deputy who had been part of the posse hunting him down) returns home. He thanks Darkcat for saving his family, then gives him a horse and a day's head start, promising to come to gun him down the next day. They part in mutual respect, knowing that one must die at the hands of the other.

205 de Quille, Dan. "An Indian Story of the Sierra Madre." Cosmopolitan, 19, No. 2 (Jun. 1895), 180-95.

  Three prospectors, Captain Ben Denton, Burt Colrick, and Dick Nordine, realize that they are being followed by five Apache braves. They kill the Apaches and, fearing for their

safety, decide to disguise themselves in the Apache dress of
the dead Indians. While undressing the bodies, they discover
twenty-nine thousand dollars. The newly-rich men ride on,
but are apprehended by Mexican soldiers. The prospectors
reveal their disguise and are forced to show the Mexicans the
Apache bodies. Once back at the site of the killings, the prospectors attack the Mexicans, then Apaches attack the prospectors. The prospectors manage to slip away and are able to
keep the money.

206 Derleth, August. "That Heathen Alonzo." Country Growth.
     New York: Scribner's, 1940, pp. 113-19.
         Aunt Mary is angry when she fails to convert Alonzo,
     the Indian gardener, to Catholicism. To save face and get
     rid of him at the same time, she accuses him of stealing her
     wedding ring from her dresser. Alonzo, however, gets even
     by walking in (clothed in his underwear) when she is about to
     tell a group of her lady friends about the thievery, and an-
     nouncing that she had left her ring in the sand where they had
     been swimming together.

207 Deutsch, Alfred H. "Agenda for Tomorrow." Bruised Reeds
     and Other Stories. Collegeville, Minn. : St. John's Univ.
     Press, 1971, pp. 121-30.
         Eighty-year-old Father Reuben, for many years a mis-
     sion priest to a group of Indians, visits with David Leanbuck,
     an Indian who quietly listens to the priest's problems. Father
     Reuben talks about his years with his Indians and about how
     little he has accomplished among them. It has been difficult
     for him, he realizes, because the Indians are lazy and often
     drunk. The worst Indian characteristic, Father Reuben says,
     is that they always put things off until tomorrow. As the priest
     rambles on about Indians, it becomes clear that Father Reuben
     himself has also become a chronic procrastinator.

208 DeVries, Marvin. "Stage to Yuma." The Saturday Evening
     Post Reader of Western Stories. Ed. E. N. Brandt. Garden
     City, N.Y. : Doubleday, 1960, pp. 52-68.
         The stage to Yuma is attacked by ten Apaches, but the
     cool Ibsen takes charge. Although several of the stagecoach
     occupants die in the battle, Ibsen succeeds in killing all but
     one of the Apaches, saving the lives of a woman and child.

209 Dew, Natalie Manson. "Tisare." Out West, 29, No. 3 (Aug.
     1908), 153-58.
         Tisare, an Indian boy at an Indian school, catches a
     mouse and gives it to Miss Muffet, a cat belonging to the red-
     haired clerk's wife. She has been kind to Tisare and he, in
     turn, is fascinated with her, though he understands little of
     what she says to him. One day he sees Black Coyote's wife
     (Arapaho) steal Miss Muffet. Tisare courageously runs away
     from school, follows Black Coyote and his wife, sneaks into
     their camp at night, and rescues Miss Muffet. He returns the

cat to her worried mistress, and is given a green ribbon for
his heroic efforts.

210   Dickinson, Cyntitha Caldwell. "Nina, An Indian Maiden's Eas-
       ter." Out West, n. s. 7, No. 4 (Apr. 1914), 218-25.
       William Yates, an Indian Commissioner in Utah, lives in
a comfortable cabin with his wife, Sarah; they are good people,
well-liked by the Indians. One day an old Indian woman asks
Mr. Yates to take into his care an eight-year-old Indian girl
named Nina. After her initial fears are overcome, Nina grows
to love the Yates family. When Sarah dies, Mr. Yates returns
to England, leaving the farm to Nina's care. Three years
later, Yates returns with a second wife and gives the farm to
Nina, who marries "Gentleman Jim" Juanea.

211   Downing, Linda. (Cherokee). "Day of Confusion." Arrows
       Four: Prose and Poetry by Young American Indians. Ed.
       T. D. Allen. New York: Pocket Books, 1974, pp. 57-59.
       The narrator recalls the day her father sent her and
her sister to an orphanage. "Every time I think about it now,
a big lump forms in my throat and sometimes a tear or two
comes out, but it does no good to cry so I'll try to do what
Dad told us, 'Finish school and make the best.'"

212   Drum, Charles S. "The Digger Indians." Southwest Review,
       55, No. 3 (Summer 1970), 268-74.
       In 1866 the narrator's father, Amos Bell, took the family
to California. Although he was only eight years old at the
time, the narrator remembers and tells of the trip. Toward
the end of the journey, as they traveled across the desert,
they noticed that they were being followed by Digger Indians
who were apparently surviving on the wagon train's leavings.
The Indians closed in as the family neared its destination, but
after a few days disappeared. One man rode back to find them
all dead.

213   Eastlake, William. "A Bird on the Mesa." Harper's, 223
       (Oct. 1961), 57-63.
       Rabbit Stockings, a Navajo cowboy, tracks a stray heifer
toward a high mesa. On the mesa a white man named Peter
Wingo has just unloaded ten Mexicans he has illegally flown in
from Mexico, abandoning them to almost certain death (since
there is no known way down from the mesa). The cow, however, finds a way to the top through a cave inside the mesa.
She emerges just as the airplane begins to take off; Wingo
swerves to avoid hitting the cow and crashes to his death below the mesa. The Mexicans are led down to safety by Rabbit
Stockings, who has followed the cow.

214   _____. "Dancers in the Scalp House." Penthouse, 5, No.
       4 (Dec. 1973), 102-03, 202, 204-05, 208-10.
       Mary-Forge, a young redhaired Anglo "teacher" in a
"school" of her own, leads some Navajo Indians into a revo-

lutionary protest against a giant billboard advertising the construction site of a new Penthouse Club. The Indians win over
an FBI agent and tear down the billboard, thus restoring the
view of Painted Bird Mesa.

215 _____. "The Death of Sun." Prize Stories 1974: The O.
Henry Awards. Ed. William Abrahams. Garden City,
N. Y. : Doubleday, 1974, pp. 242-60.
    A white woman, Mary-Forge, lives among the Navajo In-
dians and leads them in a campaign to save the eagles from
the rifles of white men. Mary-Forge and the Indians especially
want to protect Sun, a beloved golden eagle that lives near them.
A white rancher, who recently shot Sun's mate, is now pursuing Sun in a helicopter. While the rancher shoots from the
helicopter at both the eagle and the Indians, Mary-Forge and
her Navajo friends try to shoot down the helicopter. Sun understands that he is doomed and dives into the helicopter,
causing its destruction--as well as his own.

216 _____. "The Medicine Men." Harper's, 210 (Mar. 1955),
54-62.
    Kurt Heinitz arranges and promotes a foreign-car rally
in New Mexico. When Coyotes-Love-Me tries to stop them
from crossing lands newly planted with winter rye, Heinitz hits
the Navajo on the skull with a wrench and the cars tear up the
fields. The white trader tends to Coyotes-Love-Me's wounds
and promises the Indians that he will also deal with Heinitz.
The Navajos, however, plan to use their own "medicine" against
the offender; they bind Heinitz with ropes, drench his clothes
with gasoline, and come to the trading post for matches. When
the trader stops them, the Indians say that their "cure" was
"just a scare."

217 _____. "The Quiet Chimneys." Harper's, 210 (May 1955),
45-50. Reprinted in The Best American Short Stories, 1956,
ed. Martha Foley (Boston: Houghton Mifflin, 1956), pp.
123-33.
    Plagued by famine, George Bowman (a white trading post
operator) and two Navajos (Rabbit Stockings and "Quicker-Than-
You") decide to kill a deer out of season. Although they get
a good line on one, all three miss (deliberately?) or refuse to
shoot, so the deer escapes. Bowman returns to his post taking the Indians along, and shares with them the last of his few
groceries.

218 _____. "What Nice Hands Held." Gallery of Modern Fiction: Stories from the Kenyon Review. Ed. Robie Macauley.
New York: Salem Press, 1966, pp. 383-93. Copyright
1963; reprinted by permission of Simon and Schuster.
    Tom Tobeck, a Zia Pueblo Indian, "marries" a Navajo
girl, Nice Hands, but he soon tires of her and runs off to a
motel with a white girl. Nice Hands, taking a rope with her,
goes to the motel and hangs him.

219 Eastman, Charles A. (Santee Sioux). "The Chief Soldier."
    Old Indian Days. Boston: Little, Brown, 1907, pp. 114-33.
    [Charles A. Eastman also writes under his mature Sioux
    name, "Ohiyesa" (meaning "Winner").]
        A brave Sioux (in 1862) is ordered by his corrupt chief
    to attack the whites. In fulfilling the assignment he forfeits
    the aura of "heroism" he had previously enjoyed, so both his
    wife and children shun him. One child becomes a missionary
    after the outcast departs.

220 _____. (Santee Sioux). "The Gray Chieftain." Harper's,
    108 (May 1904), 882-87.
        Two Indians on a hunting trip in the mountains see the
    Gray Chieftain, who is the head of the mountain goats. They
    choose not to kill him, but rather to observe him and the goats.
    They are fascinated by the degree of organization in the moun-
    tain goats' lives. After the goats flee, the hunters find that
    the Gray Chieftain is still asleep in a special place.

221 _____. (Santee Sioux). "She-Who-Has-A-Soul." Old Indian
    Days. Boston: Little, Brown, 1907, pp. 208-18.
        This is a missionary story about Black Robe, who came
    to the Sioux in Montana. The chief's youngest daughter, She-
    Who-Has-A-Soul, is the only one who is friendly to the priest,
    and he gives her a cross.

222 _____. (Santee Sioux). "The Singing Spirit." Sunset,
    20 (Dec. 1907), 112-21.
        Antoine is a Canadian mixed-blood who works at gathering
    buffalo hides for the Hudson Bay Company. One day he is car-
    ried off by a huge buffalo herd until he escapes, without a horse
    and miles from his friends. He sets up a camp with a new-
    found friend, a bear, Ami. That spring some hungry Yankton
    Sioux, out looking for buffalo herds, come to his camp. He
    befriends them, and all ends well.

223 _____. (Santee Sioux). "The Song of the Birch Canoe."
    Craftsman, 23, No. 1 (Oct. 1912), 3-11.
        Ayashe, a young Algonquin maiden, tells her mother that
    she wants to make her first canoe. The girl's father, Chief
    Medweasunk, lectures Ayashe on the seriousness of the under-
    taking; and Ayashe's grandmother, Kezhikone, takes her to the
    Manito Rock to make an offering. Ayashe's mother helps to
    gather the birch bark, slender cedar poles, roots, and pine
    pitch. Then all help Ayashe build her first canoe, which is
    dedicated to Ogama, the medicine man.

224 _____. (Santee Sioux). "War Maiden of the Sioux." Ladies'
    Home Journal, 23, No. 9 (Aug. 1906), 14.
        Smoky Day, an old Sioux story-teller, recounts the tale
    of the war maiden: Tamakoche, chief of the Hunkpapa Sioux,
    had a beautiful daughter, Makatah, and had three sons who had
    died bravely as warriors in battle. The lovely Makatah, though

she had many suitors, refused to take a husband until she had visited the land of the Crow, the killers of her brothers. When a war party made ready to go to Crow land, Makatah requested to go along. She spurred the men in battle to bravery, but just as defeat seemed certain, many of her suitors fled to save their lives; however, Little Eagle not only saved Makatah's life, but the battle as well. Unfortunately, Little Eagle was killed. Upon her return to camp, Makatah declared herself Little Eagle's widow and never married.

225 Edgar, W. M. "One Wagon-Train Boss of Texas." Outing, 39, No. 4 (Jan. 1902), 381-83.
In 1866, a wagon train of twenty-six men, women, and children is attacked in Limpio Canyon by two hundred fifty-one Mescalero and Lipan Apaches under Chief Gordo. The wagon master relates the story of a four-day fight which ends in agreement that the Indians will leave when they are given all the corn in the wagons.

226 Eggleston, Sister M. Florian, O. S. F. "The Earth Colors." Arizona Quarterly, 17, No. 4 (Winter 1961), 352-60.
Tonio Begay, a young Navajo boy, has been inspired at school by Sister Angelica to paint. He wants to enter some pictures in the forthcoming ceremonial at Gallup, but he has no paints. He cannot earn money to buy them because his father disapproves and wants Tonio only to be a sheep herder. One day as he is tending the flock, Tonio meets some people from the State University who are looking for "earth colors" with which to paint. Now realizing how he, too, can make a paint from a mixture of colored earth and water, Tonio paints and enters three beautiful pictures in the competition. When one of the earth color paintings wins a blue ribbon, Tonio's father brags--but the boy quietly turns away "to look for his mother."

227 Emerson, Larry. "A Tale of Two Worlds." Sun Tracks, 1, No. 3 (Spring 1972), 11-15, 18-21.
In this fantasy, seven hundred thousand Indians in the Fifth World go into the Canyon de Chelley to live. Eventually they argue and come out again, only to find (to their joy) that the whites have all disappeared--leaving the earth polluted with cans and waste paper. The Indians start setting up their own nations and governments again.

228 Eubanks, L. E. "The Treasure of the Tomb." Out West, n. s. 2 (Aug. 1911), 144-48.
A half-breed, Ben, asks the Seattle shopkeeper, Tom Lane (white), if he would be interested in earning forty thousand dollars. Tom is interested, so Ben tells him about a secret eighty-thousand-dollar gold cache in an Oregon grave. Ben's great-grandfather, Chief Bear-Killer, had asked to be buried with his wealth because he had no son to leave it to-- only two daughters. The two daughters passed this secret to

their daughters at the time of their deaths, and Ben's mother then told him the secret on her deathbed. Tom and Ben find the gravesite, but the next morning Tom awakens to find Ben stabbed to death. Tom hears someone, pauses, then recognizes Inez, a half-breed he had met and loved years earlier in Alaska. The girl identifies her mother as the "other" granddaughter of Chief Bear-Killer--and as Ben's murderess. Tom and Inez decide to marry and forget the "secret" treasure.

229   Evarts, Hal G. "One Night in the Red Dog Saloon." Spurs West. Ed. S. Omar Barker. Garden City, N. Y. : Doubleday, 1960, pp. 81-97. Originally published in The Saturday Evening Post (1953).
        Lew Zane pulls a cactus from the hoof of a lame camel, one of the remnants from the cavalry camels used thirty years earlier. Later that same camel helps him to scare some of Black Eagle's renegade Apaches back to the reservation.

230   Farrar, Addie. "An Indian Girl's Revenge." Overland Monthly, n. s. 47 (1906), 89-91.
        Harold Semple, a handsome Easterner, works as a cowboy in order to regain his health so that he can marry Alice; however, Harold is rather flirtatious, and pays considerable attention to an Indian girl named Mary. When Harold is well he tells Mary that he is returning East to marry. Mary protests, but then wishes him happiness. A few days later Harold runs into Mary on a deserted trail. She overpowers him, ties him to a tree, and leaves him to die in the desert. When a storm comes up, however, lightning frees his bonds, and he returns to Alice to become a faithful husband.

231   Farrell, Cliff. "Fiddle-Footed." The Saturday Evening Post Reader of Western Stories. Ed. E. N. Brandt. Garden City, N. Y. : Doubleday, 1960, pp. 69-83.
        Eb is a confirmed bachelor until some homesteaders move in next to his shack. They have a pretty and efficient daughter, Josie Belle. Eb and Josie Belle are alone together when the Comanches attack, wounding Eb. Josie Belle's "generalship" against the attackers convinces him that he should marry her, so Josie Belle gains a double victory.

232   Fast, Howard. "The Mohawk." The General Zapped an Angel: New Stories of Fantasy and Science Fiction. New York: William Morrow, 1970, pp. 55-64.
        A young Mohawk man, Clyde Lightfeather, in traditional Mohawk costume, sits in the lotus position on the steps of St. Patrick's Cathedral in New York City. He wants to meditate about "God's time." The police and the news media are astonished, but Father O'Connor permits him to stay for a while. Despite his training, the sympathetic priest admires the Indian's bold and direct approach. After meditating all night, Lightfeather leaves, satisfied that he has at last been granted a moment of God's time. Father O'Connor doesn't know what God's time is, but wishes he could find out.

233   . "Neighbor Sam." Patrick Henry and the Frigate's Keel and Other Stories of a Young Nation. New York: Duell, Sloan, and Pearce, 1945, pp. 71-93.

Sam "Squire" Burton, for twelve years the judge in a frontier district at the time of the Revolution, has a series of troubles: his well goes dry, the weather is bad, a wolf comes into his farm, and, to top it off, a Harvard lawyer comes to town, courts his daughter, and wins the local judicial election. Sam has a chance to regain his self-respect, however, when he organizes the neighbors against renegade Shawnees after they burn down his house and barn.

234   . "Spoil the Child." Out West. Ed. Jack Schaefer. Boston: Houghton Mifflin, 1955, pp. 107-18. Originally published in The Saturday Evening Post (Aug. 6, 1938).

A white family is traveling west by wagon. Two attacking Indians kill the father, leaving the twelve-year-old son in charge. Later, as his mother gives birth to a baby in the wagon, he kills one of the Indians, hitches up the mules, and heads west again.

235 Faulkner, William. "The Bear." Go Down, Moses. New York: Random House, 1942, pp. 191-331. Originally published in The Saturday Evening Post (May 1942).

With the help and advice of old Sam Fathers, half-black and half-Chickasaw, Ike McCaslin and his friends track down Old Ben, the bear.

236   . "A Courtship." Collected Stories of William Faulkner. New York: Random House, 1950, pp. 361-80. Originally published in Sewanee Review (1948).

Boon Hogganbeck, a white man, and Ikkemotubbe, a Chickasaw, are both in love with the indolent sister of Herman Basket. They have an eating contest and then run a long race to determine who shall be her husband. When the two runners return from the race, they discover that Herman Basket's sister has married Log-in-the-Creek, a harmonica-blowing Indian who has not participated in the contests.

237   . "A Justice." Collected Stories of William Faulkner. New York: Random House, 1950, pp. 343-60. Originally published in Faulkner's These Thirteen (1931).

Sam Fathers tells about his mother and father: His mother was a black woman brought by Ikkemotubbe (Doom) to the village. An Indian named Craw-ford became enamored of the woman, even though she had a black husband. After a time the woman gave birth to a son who was clearly Crawford's son, not the black man's. When the black husband complained to Doom, Doom named the child "Had-Two-Fathers" (later shortened to "Fathers"). Then Doom decreed that Crawford must build a fence around the black man's cabin, a fence so high that Craw-ford could no longer get in to bother the black woman.

238 _____. "Lo!" Collected Stories of William Faulkner.
New York: Random House, 1950, pp. 381-403.
   The President of the United States receives a delegation
of Indians who seek a determination about whether a certain
Indian is guilty of murder. The leader of the delegation, Francis Weddel, is half-French and half-Chickasaw. The President
proclaims the Indian innocent. After a time the President is
again asked by the Indians to hand down a judgment, this time
concerning the ownership of a ford across a certain river in
Mississippi.

239 _____. "Mountain Victory." Collected Stories of William
Faulkner. New York: Random House, 1950, pp. 745-77.
Originally published in The Saturday Evening Post (Dec.
1932).
   Part-Choctaw Saucier Weddel, a major in the Confederate
army, returns to Mississippi in 1865, after the Union victory.
He stops for the night with a Union sympathizer in Tennessee,
and is shot by the fanatical son of the Tennessee mountaineer.

240 _____. "The Old People." Go Down, Moses. New York:
Random House, 1942, pp. 163-87. Originally published in
Harper's (Sep. 1940).
   Sam Fathers, part-Chickasaw, initiates Ike McCaslin into
manhood after Ike kills his first buck. Sam's early history is
recorded, as is that of Ikkemotubbe, who uses poison to make
himself chief of the tribe.

241 _____. "Red Leaves." Collected Stories of William Faulkner. New York: Random House, 1950, pp. 313-41. Originally published in The Saturday Evening Post (Oct. 25,
1930).
   The Indians of Yoknapatawpha County have a problem.
Their chief, Issetibbeha, has just died, and they must delay
his burial until they can locate the black man (his personal
slave) who must be buried with him. Two Indians, Three
Basket and Louis Berry, talk about Issetibbeha's predecessor,
the shrewd and calculating Ikkemotubbe (Doom), and his suc-
cessor, the fat and moronic Mokketubbe. They discuss how
easy life was before they had black slaves to worry about. In
the end the terrified black man is brought in, and the burial
can proceed.

242 _____. "The Waifs." The Saturday Evening Post Stories,
1957. New York: Random House, 1957, pp. 18-28.
   Byron Snopes sends his four half-breed children (the
mother is a Jicarilla Apache) by railway express to Flem
Snopes. They terrorize the town--stealing things, killing and
eating a five-hundred-dollar dog, slicing a man who tries to
peek in on them at night, and trying to burn at the stake another who tries to make hunting dogs out of them. Finally,
Flem sends them back to Byron.

243   Fetler, James. "The Indians Don't Need Me Any More." The
      Literary Review, 16, No. 4 (Summer 1973), 434-46.
      A spiritually dry English professor concludes that he is
      unhappy, so he obtains a divorce and (altruistically) helps the
      Indians at Alcatraz by sailing there with canned goods, blan-
      kets, etc. He finally realizes that this is merely an excuse
      for action or confrontation and, at the end, is left with nothing.

244   Fiedler, Leslie. "Bad Scene at Buffalo Jump." Nude Croquet.
      New York: Stein and Day, 1969, pp. 251-65.
      Professor Baro Finkelstein, a Jewish friend of the Indian,
      idealizes the Indian way of life as closer to nature, and hap-
      pier and more peaceful than his own. He talks one of his
      graduate students, George, into taking him back to the reser-
      vation to participate in a peyote ceremony of the New American
      Church. George, who has lost all contact with the reserva-
      tion, is reluctant, but does as he is asked. They both try the
      peyote; George has some success, but Baro gets sick. As a
      result of this experience, and their contacts with "real" Indians,
      they seem to agree that the white way of life is better for
      them after all.

245   Fisher, Clay. "The Chugwater Run." The Oldest Maiden
      Lady in New Mexico and Other Stories. New York: Mac-
      millan, 1962, pp. 133-62.
      He Dog is a Wind River Cheyenne who had years earlier
      murdered Johnny's parents. Now Johnny, a young man, gets
      his revenge. He Dog has captured the pretty daughter of the
      commander of the fort, and is holding her as hostage for a
      ransom of fifteen cans of gunpowder. Johnny delivers fifteen
      pounds of fake gunpowder, and then manages (after securing
      the girl's freedom) to blow that up, thus ruining the prestige
      and power of He Dog and assuring that he will never again be
      able to stir the Cheyennes into making war.

246   _____. "The Hunting of Tom Horn." The Oldest Maiden
      Lady in New Mexico and Other Stories. New York: Mac-
      millan, 1962, pp. 194-215.
      Charlie Shonto, of the Arizona Cattleman's Association,
      rescues Tom Horn (Indian) from some cowboys about to hang
      him for stealing cattle. Charlie takes Tom into custody; but
      Tom escapes. Later Tom returns to help Charlie escape from
      Broken Mouth, chief of a band of Mescalero and Chiricahua
      Apaches.

247   _____. "Pretty Face." The Oldest Maiden Lady in New
      Mexico and Other Stories. New York: Macmillan, 1962,
      pp. 105-32.
      Hurd Clinton, a white man with a blood brother among
      the Hunkpapa Sioux, goes fur trapping with the half-breed,
      Piute Montera. He learns that the half-breed is cheating him
      by having made a deal with six Piutes under Mad Bull. A
      beautiful Piute girl, Wastewin ("Pretty Face"), is supposed to

seduce Clinton as part of a plot to rob and murder him. Instead, she falls in love with him, finds out that her brother
is Hurd's blood brother, and saves his life; later he saves her
life and they ride off into the sunset with all the furs.

248 _____. "The Skinning of Black Coyote." Western Bonanza.
       Ed. Todhunter Ballard. Garden City, N. Y.: Doubleday,
       1969, pp. 247-69. Originally published in Esquire (1951).
       A band of Arapaho Indians is hired by a white wagon-
master to steal a wagon load of guns. Tracy, raised by Oglala Sioux and now a wagon train scout, has learned enough
from the Indians to outwit the thieves.

249 Flower, Elliott. "The Law and the Indian." Atlantic Monthly,
       106, No. 4 (Oct. 1910), 483-90.
       John Red Deer persists in hunting and fishing on his
tribe's land which now belongs to the United States Government.
John knows that his tribe long ago sold the land but retained
the hunting and fishing rights. A game warden feels sorry for
John, but he repeatedly arrests the Indian. Finally John kills
the warden and is brought to trial. The lawyers and the judge
and the jury all feel very sorry for the Indian, but still they
sentence him to death.

250 Floyd, M. "A Phantom of the High Sierra." Overland
       Monthly, n. s. 21 (1893), 378-88.
       An Indian guide tells this story about the Ghost of Susie
Lake to two white fishermen: Two Indian groups came to Susie
Lake each summer to fish. The leader of one group was
Hahma, whose son was Mantua; the leader of the other was
Ahmona, whose daughter was Taon-Tish. Mantua and Taon-
Tish planned to marry. One day, however, a group of Span-
iards--the first white men the Indians had ever seen--came
into the camp. They stayed on for some time and their leader,
Don Casa de Marlo, became enamored of Taon-Tish. She,
however, rejected him. One stormy evening, de Marlo saw
Taon-Tish come across the lake in a canoe, captured her, and
gave her a choice between him and death. When she called for
Mantua, de Marlo stabbed her and threw her body into the lake.
Mantua believed she had drowned, until five years later. When
he saw her ghost at Susie Lake, he discovered her murder and
vowed vengeance. Eventually he stabbed the Spaniard to death.

251 Fontaine, Robert. "My Only Indian." Atlantic Monthly, 189,
       No. 1 (Jan. 1952), 42-44.
       The narrator's Uncle Louis meets an Indian man in a
bar and brings him home. He is very proud of his pet Indian,
who is "childlike and primitive." Uncle Louis tries to find a
job for the Indian, who doesn't want to work, but does want a
squaw. Finally Uncle Louis hires the Indian to an ugly widow.
The Indian is to be her gardner; fortunately, she has no garden.

252 Fontana, Bernard L. "The Green Dog." Arizona Quarterly,
17, No. 1 (Spring 1961), 56-62.
   Carlos, a reservation Indian boy, is caught between the
old ways--Indian customs and Indian superstitions--and the new
ways--white civilization encroaching upon the Indian reservation in the form of new building construction, modern medical
care, and education. An old medicine man places a "green
dog" curse on Carlos' father (a policeman) for having arrested
him for drunkenness.

253 Foote, Mary Hallock. "The Trumpeter." Atlantic Monthly,
74, No. 445 (Nov. 1894), 577-97, and 74, No. 446 (Dec.
1894), 721-29.
   A beautiful young girl, Meta, is half-Bannock. She falls
in love with the handsome cavalry trumpeter at the fort, marries him secretly, and bears his son. Faithless, he moves to
another fort and refuses to take her along. Meta and Ross,
the baby, are left homeless and penniless. Meta soon dies,
but Ross is raised by the same white family that raised Meta.
The trumpeter suffers a series of misfortunes until he is a
lame, broken man--a dirty bum who has nothing and nobody.
At age thirty-four, he throws himself into the river to die.

254 Footner, Hulbert. "Nanesis Macgregor: A Story of Atha-
basca." Sunset, 26 (Jan. 1911), 17-25.
   Nanesis (a half-breed Cree Indian at Caribou Lake) is
betrothed by her father to Hooliam, a proud, imperious, in-
considerate fellow who turns out to be a coward. She makes
her own match with a better man.

255 Forbes, Mrs. A. S. C. "El Molino Viejo." ("The Old Mill.")
Mission Tales in the Days of the Dons. Chicago: A. C.
McClurg, 1909, pp. 307-44.
   Salvador (whose father was an Indian and whose mother
was a mulatto) is the head shepherd at Simi Ranch, responsible for a large caravan of Indians traveling with stock and
grain to "El Molino Viejo," the Old Mill that had been built
by the San Gabriel Mission. Fearing rumors of robbers in the
area, Salvador buries his master's gold and silver on a hill
near the mill. Waylaid by thieves, Salvador is fatally wounded.
Before dying, however, he dictates the location of the gold to
Padre Lopez, who writes the account in Greek for the sake of
secrecy. Years later the document is acquired by two young
scholars who know Greek. They search for the treasure but,
haunted by Salvador's ghost, they finally give up the hunt.

256 _____. "Matilija." Mission Tales in the Days of the Dons.
Chicago: A. C. McClurg, 1909, pp. 83-103. [See "Amatil
and Olna," by Mrs. Fremont Older, which uses the same
or similar characters, setting, and plot.]
   Chief Matilija and his people live in the Ojai Valley, the
"Nest." Soldiers from Mission Buenaventura come to Ojai for
recruits at the mission; the beautiful daughter of Matilija is

taken. She is there for four years, but finally escapes and returns to her beloved homeland. During the marriage feast for Matilija's daughter, the soldiers come and kill almost everyone except Matilija's daughter and her new husband. Although the girl tenderly cares for him, the boy soon dies of serious wounds sustained in the battle.

257 _____. "The Story of Little Rossiya." Mission Tales in the Days of the Dons. Chicago: A. C. McClurg, 1909, pp. 137-55. [See "California's First Princess" (by Mrs. Fremont Older) which uses the same or similar characters, setting, and plot.]

Russian Prince Alexander Rotcheff and his wife, Princess Hélène de Gagarin, come to live in the California colony of Fort Ross, which had been established in 1811 by Ivan Alexandrovich Kuskof. The beautiful princess is a social asset to the fort; many fiestas are exchanged between Fort Ross and Mexican General Vallejo and his people of Sonoma. An Indian chief, Chief Solano, falls in love with Hélène and plots her capture; however, Vallejo learns of the plan and talks Solano out of it. The Rotcheffs return to Russia.

258 _____. "The Story of San Juan Capistrano." Mission Tales in the Days of the Dons. Chicago: A. C. McClurg, 1909, pp. 47-66.

In 1865 word is sent out to the Indians that the San Juan Capistrano Mission (which had been destroyed by a terrible earthquake in 1812) is to be restored. Carina, a beautiful half-Indian, half-Spanish girl, is ecstatic at the prospect of the rededication fiesta. At the fiesta her happiness is complete when she marries her lover, Benito.

259 _____. "Terésa, the Popeloutechom Neophyte." Mission Tales in the Days of the Dons. Chicago: A. C. McClurg, 1909, pp. 277-303.

About 1797 the San Juan Beutista Mission is founded by Father Francisco Fermin de Lasuen in the San Benito Valley among the Popeloutechom Indians. The Indians love the music of the mission's small pipe organ best of all. One of the mission's dedicated young Indian neophytes, Terésa, goes berrypicking and does not come back to the mission. A year later she shows up at the Father's quarters with a baby. She tells how she had been captured by Felipe Guzman, how she had borne his child, and how he had refused to marry her. The sick baby soon dies and Terésa is ill for weeks. As she regains her strength, Terésa learns that the Indians are revolting. Seeing them outside the Father's door, she runs to the organ and plays. The music quiets the rebellion, but Father Francisco later finds her dead beneath the cross.

260 _____. "Wana and Ahzi-Papoose." Mission Tales in the Days of the Dons. Chicago: A. C. McClurg, 1909, pp. 183-95.

Wana (Indian), wife of the handsome half-breed, José Ramon, is out of supplies and starving at the mission. One day, when José is away from the mission, Wana decides she will walk to meet him. Against the Padre's orders she searches for José, but they fail to see each other when their paths nearly cross. Wana lies down to sleep, never returning to the mission. Francesca, Wana's sister, goes to look for her, but she never returns either.

261 Foreman, L. L. "Wagon-Tongue North." Hoof Trails and Wagon Tracks. Ed. Don Ward. New York: Dodd, Mead, 1957, pp. 195-231.
    Dice Gould, a trail boss, loses cattle he is supposed to be taking to the Oglala Sioux reservation when the herd is stampeded by a dishonest range king. Dice takes up with a second herd (owned by a young lady), and saves the day by getting his own herd back--but only with the help of a party of Sioux from the reservation.

262 Forrest, Elizabeth Chabot. "Seveck Builds a Cabin." Story, 15, No. 78 (Jul./Aug. 1939), 20-28.
    Seveck is an Alaskan Eskimo who tries desperately to follow the white man's law because he thinks it is the best path for his people. He is betrothed to Kiana, the daughter of his mother's sister--as is customary--but wishes first to build a cabin, and then to marry Kiana according to white man's law. One day, when mink are out of season, Seveck finds a mink drowned in his fish trap. Peterson, the game warden, later examines Seveck's catch and sends him to jail, accusing the Eskimo of deliberately killing the mink. Seveck spends some time in jail and is repulsed by the conditions; however, when he gets out, he still endeavors to follow white ways. After the cabin is built, he and Kiana try to get married, only to discover that it is against white man's law for first cousins to marry. Seveck at last turns his back on white man's law.

263 Forrest, Williams. "Message." The Saturday Evening Post, 230, No. 35 (Mar. 1, 1958), 34-35, 90, 92, 94.
    Andy Andrews (white) is camping on his move from Arizona to New Mexico. He had quit his job as scout on the San Carlos Apache reservation because he felt that the Indians were unjustly treated, and he is on his way to see his friend, Ten Hellman. After a few days, Apaches boldly confront Andy, telling him that they want him to carry a message to the reservation. The message is that Red Arm is on the war path. Red Arm then hands Andy a cask; in it he finds the head of Ten Hellman.

264 _____. "Test by Torture." The Saturday Evening Post Reader of Western Stories. Ed. E. N. Brandt. Garden City, N.Y.: Doubleday, 1960, pp. 96-108. Originally published in The Saturday Evening Post, 230, No. 13 (Sep. 28, 1957), 43, 88, 92, 97-98.

A brave white trapper releases the Apache Tuzimo from slavery to a Mexican sheep rancher. Tuzimo returns to his tribe, but he leads them back to capture several Mexicans as well as the mountain trapper. As the Apaches are about to begin the torture-killing of their captives, the trapper requests that Tuzimo torture only him, and, if he dies bravely, let the others go free. Having learned from this trapper that bravery and compassion can honorably exist in the same man, Tuzimo releases all of them.

265 Forrester, Izola. "Shoot-'em-on-a-rock." St. Nicholas Magazine, 40 (Jul. 1913), 805-07.
   Charlie Boy Brooks tells Mildred, the Colonel's young daughter, that a box of cartridges is missing from the newly-arrived supply wagon, and that the Indians are suspected of theft. It is later learned that the missing cartridge box had fallen off the wagon and was later found and hidden by Little Cloud, a six-year-old Indian boy, who thought they were fire-crackers. Little Cloud had wanted Charlie Boy to show him how to explode the cartridges on the rocks. Charlie Boy dutifully arrests Little Cloud, much to the Colonel's amusement.

266 Foster, O'Kane. "The Thousand Dollar Cloud." Story, 26, No. 112 (Mar./Apr. 1945), 75-86.
   Movie director Barclay, on location in the West shooting a "Cowboys and Indians" film, uses Indians from a local tribe. There are several problems--a rapidly depleting budget, poor lighting conditions (a cloudy day), a very temperamental actress, and an Indian chase scene which must be reshot several times. Santiago, the Indian who plays the leader, is cast as a crafty red man who derives pleasure from acting stupid for the whites. The story closes with what seems to be a perfect "take"--until someone notices an automobile climbing the mountain in the distant background of the scene.

267 Foust, Juana. "Burial at Muleshoe." Story, 4, No. 1 (Feb. 1934), 20-26.
   Jim Strickland, recently deceased, is being buried.
Among others present at the grave are his wife (Prairie), son (Young Jim), and a Cherokee (Redbird Sixkiller), who provided the coffin.

268 Fowler, Kenneth. "Army Wife." Spurs West. Ed. S. Omar Barker. Garden City, N.Y.: Doubleday, 1960, pp. 98-117. Originally published in 1952.
   A tough cavalry officer, Captain Tooner, gets to show his bravery when renegade Cheyennes attack the wagon train he and his men are escorting.

269 _____. "Brothers of the Bugle." With Guidons Flying: Tales of the U.S. Cavalry in the Old West. Garden City, N.Y.: Doubleday, 1970, pp. 37-54. Originally published in Dime Western (1948).
   Captain Wayne Starrell is concerned about the rivalry

between two of his lieutenants: Vance Rhinelander, a very
proper West Point graduate; and Terry Boylan, a sloppy soldier, but a rugged and wise outdoorsman. Starrell believes
that discipline is essential, so when he leads a troop after the
Nez Percé, he trusts Rhinelander to scout for him. Rhinelander advises Starrell to follow the trail through a canyon.
Boylan disagrees, but is overruled. The Nez Percé ambush
the cavalry in the canyon and almost annihilate them. Starrell realizes his mistake and now admires Boylan.

270 Fox, Norman A. "The Fitness of Sean O'Fallon." Rawhide
     Men. Ed. Kenneth Fowler. Garden City, N.Y.: Double-
     day, 1965, pp. 141-56. Originally published in New Western
     Writing (Jun. 1947), entitled "Too Dumb to Die."
       Sean O'Fallon, newly arrived from Ireland, is too big to
     be a Pony Express rider, but he lands a job as a station hand.
     He gets a chance to prove his courage and win the hand of his
     lady when some marauding Piutes kill one regular rider and
     wound a second. Sean carries the mail through after killing
     four armed Piutes with a club.

     Foxe, Andrew see Bernard Wolfe

271 Fraser, W. A. "The Way of a Half-Breed." Outing, 36,
     No. 1 (Apr. 1900), 3-6.
       Maxepeto, a half-breed Blackfeet, settles near Trapper's
     Landing because the area is reputedly lax about law enforce-
     ment. "Those who knew him best said he was exclusively
     bad." The Trapper's Landing Trading Company's factor, the
     undisputed boss of the area, one day asks Maxepeto to find
     and bring in Nonokasi as his wife. Though Maxepeto does not
     particularly want a wife, he complies. Later, when Maxepeto
     returns from a trip, he tells the townspeople that his wife has
     become ill and has died. When Nonokasi's coffin is acciden-
     tally dropped, it is discovered that she has been beheaded.
     Maxepeto serves seven years in jail for his atrocity.

272 Frazee, Steve. "Great Medicine." Bar 3 Roundup of Best
     Western Stories. Ed. Scott Meredith. Freeport, N.Y.:
     Books for Libraries Press, 1954, pp. 45-83.
       Little Belly, a young Blackfeet leader, is determined to
     learn what the special medicine of the white fur trappers is.
     He allows himself to be captured by the trappers so that he
     can observe them. He finally decides that the special medi-
     cine is in the round silver watch that the white man consults
     frequently, so he steals it and rides off to his people. Little
     Belly brings back a strong force to attack (now that he has
     their invincible power through the watch), but when the watch
     stops running he angrily throws it away. In the ensuing battle
     the Blackfeet are defeated. Little Belly discovers that part of
     the white man's strong medicine is mercy, a quality which the
     Blackfeet people had previously misinterpreted as weakness.

273 Frederick, Judge White Bear. (Hopi). "How BIA and Indian
     Joe Got to Heaven." <u>Wassaja</u>, 4, No. 9 (Sep. 1976), 6, 20.
         "This is the life story of Indian Joe, who lived on this
     planet a long, long time, born on this earth many years before
     the white man came." Indian Joe sees his people exploited,
     his land confiscated, and his traditions undermined by the "peo-
     ple ... from the East." Several of the "invaders" die, go to
     heaven and are placed by St. Peter in small, unfinished houses
     in direct proportion to their earthly value and contribution.
     When Indian Joe dies and enters heaven, St. Peter assigns
     him to a mansion on a hill with "beautiful flowers and birds,
     and animals, on that place."

274 Frink, Maurice M. "Policeman Four-Eagle." <u>Out West</u>, n. s.
     1 (May 1911), 403-05.
         Major Reed, an Indian agent also known as "Little
     Father," tells this story to Hawkshield, an old Indian warrior:
     Four-Eagle, an Indian policeman for the Deer River Agency
     in '88, suddenly quit his job to marry Calls-the-Dawn, and to
     live in Stony Creek near some troublesome Indians. One day
     Major Reed received a message that Medicine Owl and others
     were headed toward the Bear Shoulder Hills settlement, but
     the signaler indicated he would try to detain them at Porcupine
     Pass. The whites intercepted Medicine Owl in time to save
     the settlement, but found the signaler, Four-Eagle, fatally
     wounded. Four-Eagle requested reinstatement as a policeman
     before he died.

275 Galpin, Cromwell. "The Corn People: A Story of Zuni."
     <u>Overland Monthly</u>, n. s. 38 (1901), 218-25.
         When there is a famine in Zuni, the Indians grow corn
     in order to survive.

276 Garfield, Brian. "The Glory Riders." <u>With Guidons Flying:
     Tales of the U. S. Cavalry in the Old West</u>. Garden City,
     N. Y. : Doubleday, 1970, pp. 55-72.
         Iron Feather, a prominent Sioux, is a captive of the U. S.
     Army. Lieutenant Joe Diamond, who hates Indians because
     some Sioux had once killed his wife, is in charge of transport-
     ing Iron Feather to General Custer. During this dangerous
     journey, Diamond resists an attack by would-be Sioux rescuers.
     He also grows to like Iron Feather.

277 Garland, Hamlin. "Big Moggasen." <u>The Book of the Amer-
     ican Indian</u>. New York: Harper, 1923, pp. 89-92.
         Big Moggasen is an old Navajo chief who refuses to co-
     operate with the Indian agency. His people complain that they
     want wagons, clothes, food, sweets, etc. --all of which other
     Navajos get. Big Moggasen finally talks with the agent, who
     agrees to give the Indians these things if Big Mogassen will
     send twenty Navajo children to the agency schools. The chief
     refuses and returns to the hills.

278   _____. "The Blood Lust." The Book of the American Indian. New York: Harper, 1923, pp. 105-09.
Little Robe, an aging Cheyenne guide, tells John Seger
about the time he raided a Mexican village for horses. In the
pursuit afterward his five-year-old daughter had been shot. So
great was his need for revenge that Little Robe went back later
with some men and killed all the Mexicans in the village.

279   _____. "A Decree of Council." The Book of the American
Indian. New York: Harper, 1923, pp. 121-24.
The Cheyenne Big Nose foolishly gambles away all of his
possessions, including his clothes and his two wives; he then
goes around the camp begging for handouts. The council meets
and agrees to give Big Nose clothing and a tepee, and return
to him only his sharp-tongued wife (but not the young, attractive one) as a punishment.

280   _____. "Drifting Crane." The Book of the American Indian. New York: Harper, 1923, pp. 127-32.
Drifting Crane (chief of the Sisseton Indians) is naturally
resentful when Henry Wilson brings cattle into his lush valley
and settles down permanently, because he knows that many
more whites will soon come also. Drifting Crane tries to make
Wilson leave, but the white man convinces him that the whites
will come anyway: "It's got to be. You an' I can't help n'r
hinder it."

281   _____. "Hotan the Red Pioneer." Prairie Song and Western Story. Freeport, N.Y.: Books for Libraries Press,
1971, pp. 247-59. Originally published in 1928.
When John Seger sets up a mail route across Indian
country in Oklahoma, he decides to let each of five tribes relay the mail across its own territory, a runner from each tribe
passing the bundle to the next runner. The Indians agree to
take "the white man's road" in this fashion, and Seger is delighted when the first mail arrives on time, brought by Hotan,
a Cheyenne.

282   _____. "The Iron Khiva." The Book of the American Indian. New York: Harper, 1923, pp. 25-35.
The Hopi Indians long resist attempts of the white man
to force them to attend white schools and white churches, but
they usually make token concessions to avoid military confrontation. They resist most strongly when told they must send
two boys to a school in the East, but two boys are finally se-
lected when the cavalry is summoned. After these two commit
suicide rather than go, however, the white officials back off
on their demands.

283   _____. "Lone Wolf's Old Guard." The Book of the American Indian. New York: Harper, 1923, pp. 77-84.
Lone Wolf, an old Kiowa chief, refuses to let the cattle
company run a fence through his camp. The two sides come

very close to fighting over the issue. Finally Lone Wolf agrees that if the soldiers come to build the line, then he will know that it is a legal move. The soldiers arrive, and the Indian chief backs down.

284 _____. "The New Medicine House." The Book of the American Indian. New York: Harper, 1923, pp. 39-48.
Indians at the Rosebud Reservation bitterly distrust a white nurse and refuse to go to her little hospital, preferring their own medicines and medicine men. When a Cheyenne (Robert) gets pneumonia he spends some time in the hospital but seems only to become sicker. Finally he is permitted to return to his family. At home, perhaps because of the friendly atmosphere, perhaps because of the doings of Tah-You (the medicine man), perhaps because it would have happened anyway, Robert recovers.

285 _____. "Nistina." The Book of the American Indian. New York: Harper, 1923, pp. 15-22.
When Hawk is punished for his part in an uprising by being sent to Florida, he leaves the lovesick Nistina behind. Intensely loyal to each other throughout their long separation, both Hawk and Nistina learn to read and write so that they can communicate by letter.

286 _____. "Pogosa, or The Lost Mine of Shushonnie." Prairie Song and Western Story. Freeport, N.Y.: Books for Libraries Press, 1971, pp. 276-93. Originally published in 1928.
Pagosa is an old Sioux woman who remembers the good old days. Some white miners get her to tell them where to find the lost gold mine of the Shushonnie. On the trip to show them, Pagosa returns to the grave of her husband and dies there. The miners, following her directions, find the mine.

287 _____. "Red Plowman." Craftsman, 13, No. 2 (Nov. 1907), 181-82.
Osca, an old Indian chief, steadily plows his field as a party of Arapahos rides by. The young men taunt the old chief for doing "squaw's work," but Osca puts them in their place by showing them his numerous scars and explaining that he had never begged anything from the white man. The force of his proud speech shames the young men.

288 _____. "The Remorse of Waumdisapa." The Book of the American Indian. New York: Harper, 1923, pp. 113-17.
Old Chief Waumdisapa is angered by another Sioux who wants to be the tribe's chief. Waumdisapa kills the challenger during a council meeting. Because he has murdered a "brother" he considers himself unfit, so Waumdisapa sets aside his chief's robes.

289 _____. "Rising Wolf--Ghost Dancer." The Book of the American Indian. New York: Harper, 1923, pp. 51-63.

Rising Wolf (apparently a Sioux) tells of how he became a medicine man, how white doctors gradually took away his business, and how he participated in the great Ghost Dance that was to destroy the white man and bring back the buffalo and the dead people.

290   . "The River's Warning." The Book of the American Indian. New York: Harper, 1923, pp. 67-74.
The Cheyenne Big Elk recalls the time when he was a young man eager to become a recognized warrior: he lead a dozen braves to the agency where they were to steal the agency horses. Going in alone to check things out, Big Elk was so impressed with the kindness of the Quaker agent that he backed down from making the raid. After returning to camp the other braves taunted Big Elk so much that, to save face, he decided to go ahead with the raid after all. When the river rose three days in succession so that they could not cross to carry out their plans, the Cheyennes all agreed that this was a sign from the Great Spirit to make peace, not war. The raid was cancelled.

291   . "Sitting Bull's Defiance." Prairie Song and Western Story. Freeport, N.Y.: Books for Libraries Press, 1971, pp. 210-22. Originally published in 1928.
An agent is sent from Washington to make a treaty with the "Blackfoot Sioux" in Montana, but when he gets to Montana he discovers that there is no such tribe. As a substitute he tries to make a treaty with Sitting Bull, but the proud chief refuses.

292   . "The Storm Child." The Book of the American Indian. New York: Harper, 1923, pp. 95-101.
A small Teton Sioux child wanders off alone just before a terrible blizzard, and none of Chief Waumdisapa's men can find any trace of him. They are delighted and grateful when "Blazing Hand," a young white outlaw, brings the child back to the camp. Ona (the youngster's mother) wants to marry the white man, but he moves on.

293   . "The Story of Howling Wolf." The Book of the American Indian. New York: Harper, 1923, pp. 135-55.
Howling Wolf is one of the last Cheyennes to visit the Indian agent; he has long hated whites because one of them had, for no apparent reason, shot his brother. The friendly agent wins him over, and the Indian agrees to cooperate with white authorities. But when Howling Wolf delivers some hides to town for the agent, he is set upon by some drunken whites. Then, unjustly accused of starting a fight, he is thrown into jail. The agent fails to obtain his release, and when Howling Wolf tries to escape, a mob attacks and mutilates him.

294   . "Wahiah--A Spartan Mother." The Book of the American Indian. New York: Harper, 1923, pp. 1-12.
Seger, a white teacher at the Cheyenne reservation, has

a discipline problem with Atokan, a rebellious fourteen-year-old boy who plays hooky. Deciding to whip the boy even though he knows the Cheyenne parents may kill him for doing so, Seger wears out two willow switches breaking Atokan's spirit to obtain the desired cooperation and obedience. The parents, realizing a necessity for the teacher's action, do not interfere.

295 Garrard, Christopher. "The Inheritance of Emmy One Horse."
South Dakota Review, 6, No. 1 (Spring 1968), 3-12.
Samuel Talks-in-Circles, a "crazy" old Indian who had once been a respected shaman of the Yanktonais, is now a hermit living under a bridge, and making spells which he believes causes automobile accidents. One day some men came to repair the bridge; they tear down Sam's shack and force him to leave. Emmy One Horse, a half-breed who has colored images constantly buzzing around her, is being teased by young boys who call her "crazy." She escapes and is later asked to go fishing with Les, Bill, and the Riley boys. She refuses because she vaguely understands that their motive is to take sexual advantage of her. Samuel Talks-in-Circles and Emmy One Horse talk as they are sitting on the river bank. Sam accidentally falls into the river, leaving Emmy his "magical sticks."

296 Garthwaite, Marion. "Jamie's Ghost Horse." Spooks, Spooks, Spooks. Ed. Helen Hoke. New York: Franklin Watts, 1966, pp. 51-58. Originally published in Story Parade (1952).
Twelve-year-old Jamie is crossing California when Chief Five Hats sees the boy's mother and tries to buy her for his wife. He first offers five horses, then ten, and then fifteen. To get rid of the Indian and his small band of tribesmen, Jamie sneaks away from the wagon at night and (dressed up as his mother's ghost) frightens the superstitious Indians away.

297 Gerard, Mary Ann. (Blackfeet). "It's My Rock." Arrows Four: Prose and Poetry by Young American Indians. Ed. T. D. Allen. New York: Pocket Books, 1974, pp. 31-39.
Meg has a favorite rock down by the ocean, one which she shares for a time with Richard, a handsome young man. When she discovers that Richard has had a homosexual relationship with Aaron, she takes some LSD which Richard had given her earlier. She winds up in a mental institution, from which she writes the story. She longs to get out and "return to my rock forever."

298 Gerrard, Ernest A. "A Gruesome War Dance." Outing, 39, No. 4 (Jan. 1902), 404-07.
Two white men, hunting by the Loup River, have killed two deer. Able to carry only one, they hire a Pawnee to take the other one into their camp. The deer never arrives, so the two white men go to the Pawnee camp that night. A feast of venison is being celebrated in Doctor Big Bear's tepee. When the white men demand return of the deer, the Indians become

belligerent, dancing a war dance around the white men.
Spotted Horse, a friend of the whites, stops the dancing, allows the two men to leave, and returns the meat to them the
next morning.

299 Gihon, Thomas. "An Incident of the Gold Bluff Excitement."
     Overland Monthly, n. s. 18 (1891), 646-61.
        In 1850 a group of whites makes an exciting expedition
     up the Klamath River to search for gold. The Indians rob and
     attack the miners, but the narrator, having been wounded and
     nearly killed, "bore them no ill will,--the first aggression
     came from our side."

300 Gillmor, Frances. "Matriarch." Southwest Review, 34 (Win-
     ter 1949), 50-54.
        A Navajo "first wife" struggles reluctantly to accept the
     fact that her husband is about to take a second wife. Finally
     she is able to accept her fate.

301 _____. "Spread His Sheepskins Smooth." Mademoiselle,
     Jan. 1945, pp. 119, 170-72.
        A Navajo girl returns to the reservation after being away
     at a white-run boarding school, but finds that she must forget
     some of the white ways if she is to live among her people
     again. She is very much attracted to a young man who has
     also recently returned from boarding school. She wants to
     marry him, but discovers that he is a member of her own
     clan. Because Navajos do not permit marriage between mem-
     bers of the same clan, she is faced with the decision of whether
     to disregard her tribal traditions or to marry another man her
     parents pick out for her. Finally she agrees to marry the man
     from another clan whom her parents have selected.

302 Godden, Rumer. "No More Indians." Gone: A Thread of
     Stories. New York: Viking, 1968, pp. 6-30.
        A "modern" Indian who is supposed to dress like white
     men and stay peacefully on the reservation goes berserk, be-
     lieving he is an old-style Indian. He murders and scalps a
     white man. One young boy claims to have seen both the In-
     dian and the corpse, but no one believes him. Later, when
     the boy himself is murdered by the Indian, they realize that
     his story was true.

303 Gordon, Caroline. "The Captive." Old Red and Other Stor-
     ies. New York: Scribner's, 1963, pp. 213-56.
        Indians attack the house of a white woman (Jinny Wiley)
     thinking it belongs to a white man who had killed one of their
     tribe. Her four children are murdered and she is dragged
     back to the Indian camp. The old chief, Crowmocker, treats
     her kindly--apparently adopting her to take the place of his
     own dead daughter. Crowmocker eventually sells Jinny to
     Mad Dog (who wants her, apparently as his wife), but before
     Mad Dog can claim his prize she escapes. After a breath-
     taking pursuit Jinny reaches the fort safely.

304 Gorman, R. C. (Navajo). "Nowhere to Go." The Man to
   Send Rain Clouds: Contemporary Stories by American Indians. Ed. Kenneth Rosen. New York: Viking, 1974, pp.
   61-65.
      A white sailor on leave picks up a Navajo hitchhiker re-
   turning from the Indian activities at Alcatraz. The Navajo
   shares his bottle of wine with the driver, and explains to his
   new friend about how Navajos and Apaches used to fight for
   "fun" until they realized that too many of the young men were
   being killed off. At the end the Navajo youth agrees to stay
   a little longer with the sailor--because "I have nowhere to go."

305 Grady, Gwynn, and Ray Hogan. "Bitter Sunset." With Guidons
   Flying: Tales of the U.S. Cavalry in the Old West. Garden City, N.Y.: Doubleday, 1970, pp. 73-81. Originally
   published in True Western Magazine (1955).
      Geronimo holes up in the mountains with his small band
   of starving Apaches. With no water and very little food, they
   are weary from their long flight. Charles Gatewood, a U.S.
   Army officer, bravely visits Geronimo in his last stronghold.
   Geronimo surrenders.

306 Graham, Robert Bontine Cunningham. "A Hegira." Thirteen
   Stories. Freeport, N.Y.: Books for Libraries Press,
   1969, pp. 110-32. Thirteen Stories of 1969 is the reprint
   of a 1900 edition.
      Eight Mescalero Apaches are captured by Mexicans and
   detained far from their homeland. They escape, however,
   and the six men, the woman, and a boy begin their long journey
   north. One by one they are killed by Mexicans and Americans,
   until all are dead. Only their pet white dog survives to mourn
   at the grave of the last Apache, his wife, and the child.

307 Graves, John. "The Last Running." Atlantic Monthly, 203,
   No. 6 (Jun. 1959), 39-45. Reprinted in The Best American
   Short Stories, 1960 (Boston: Houghton Mifflin, 1960), pp.
   112-25.
      Starlight, an old Comanche, comes to Texas from Okla-
   homa to visit his one-time enemy, and later friend, Tom Bird,
   a white rancher. Tom has a small herd of buffalo, including
   one fine bull named Shakespeare. Starlight and eight other
   Comanches convince Tom to give them Shakespeare so that they
   can have one last buffalo kill. The Indians don their old clothes,
   get out their spears and arrows, and attack the released bull.
   All of this takes place in 1923--after the range has been fenced
   off.

308 Green, Richard G. (Oneida). "Bronze My Skin, Dark My
   Eyes." Indian Voice, May 1973, 18-20, 30-31.
      Morning Star, a Mohawk Indian girl, lost her "Indianness"
   when she attended the white high school and became a Christian.
   Thus estranged, she feels out of place back on the reservation,
   and soon becomes bored. She decides to marry Titus Henhawk

(Tie), a young reservation lacrosse player who represents the old Indian ways. When she becomes pregnant, they discuss wedding plans, but disagree about whether to have an Indian ceremony or white ceremony. She wants the white; he and his grandfather want the Indian. They cannot resolve the conflict, so they break up. Her parents take Morning Star to a white hospital for the baby's birth. The baby is sick at first, but everything works out when she decides to reject the white ways.

309 _____. (Oneida). "The Coming." Indian Voice, Apr. 1973, 26-29.
Nineteen-year-old Rolland Longboat (Indian) leaves New York and travels northward to carry out his grandfather's dying wish--to take some ceremonial tobacco to a Longhouse meeting. There is a war going on in which the Soul Brothers (black) are trying to kill the whites, while the peaceful Indians try to remain close to the earth. Rolland seems eventually to fulfill his grandfather's prophecy that "... people of all origins would gather in peace at a great council hosted by the Iroquois...."

310 _____. (Oneida). "Private Strangers." Indian Voice, Apr. 1973, 34-35, 46-47.
Joyce, a two-time divorcée, and Simon, an unhappily married Mohawk businessman, are having an affair. On one of their monthly rendezvous they both have news: hers is that she is pregnant, that Simon is not the father, and that she plans to marry the other (white) man the next day; Simon's news was to have been that he was getting a divorce to marry Joyce.

311 _____. (Oneida). "Sometimes a Lonely Business." Indian Voice, 1, No. 10 (Dec./Jan. 1971/72), 16, 26-27.
Larry Little Cloud goes out "to do the work of a man," in this case to buy a bike at an auction. His friend José cannot go along so Larry goes alone. His father says ominously, "Perhaps then it is willed that you should do this thing alone. Being a man is sometimes a lonely business." The lad learns that the bikes he wants are bought by others for forty-five dollars (he has only five dollars to spend) or by young kids for fifteen cents (as a "gift" from the auctioneer). He finally goes home bikeless, lies to his mother--saying that the bikes were old and broken and not worth five dollars--and agrees that he needs new sneakers more than a bike.

312 Greenberg, Joanne. "L'Olam and White Shell Woman." Summering: A Book of Short Stories. New York: Holt, Rinehart, and Winston, 1966, pp. 163-74.
A Jewish girl works as a waitress for a few weeks during the annual Gallup Tribal Fair. Her associates, Bessie and Alice, are Navajo girls. They gradually come to discover that there are many cultural and religious similarities between Navajos and Jews. At the end of the fair the Navajo girls invite their white friend to come with them to the squaw dance.

313 Grey, Zane. "The Breaker of Wild Mustangs." Yaqui and
     Other Great Indian Stories. Ed. Loren Grey. New York:
     Belmont Tower Books, 1976, pp. 97-101. Originally pub-
     lished by Harper (1920).
        An unnamed Navajo demonstrates skill and perseverance
     in roping and breaking a wild mustang, Silvermane, for a white
     rancher, August Naab.

314 _____. "Daughter of the Moon." Zane Grey's Greatest
     Indian Stories. Ed. Loren Grey. New York: Belmont
     Tower Books, 1975, pp. 63-142. Originally copyrighted in
     1954.
        To avoid fulfillment of a prophecy of doom for the She-
     boyah people, Nashta, Daughter of the Moon--the secret love-
     child of Taneen, a Rock clan chieftain, and the queen of the
     outcast Antelope clan--is banished from the tribe. Taneen
     overrules the medicine men's decision, and Nashta stays. Blue
     Feather, a spy for the rival Nopah tribe, comes to the She-
     boyah lands and gains the confidence of the people, all the
     while intending to return to his own tribe and lead an attack
     against the Sheboyas; when he falls in love with Nashta, how-
     ever, Blue Feather lies to the Nopahs, saying that the She-
     boyahs have nothing worth taking. When they attack anyway,
     and it seems that either side could win, Nashta betrays her
     own people for the love of Blue Feather--and the last of the
     Rock clan, except for Nashta, dies at the hands of the Nopahs.

315 _____. "The Haunted Spring." Zane Grey's Greatest In-
     dian Stories. Ed. Loren Grey. New York: Belmont Tower
     Books, 1975, pp. 33-62.
        Wingenund, Chief of the Delaware tribe, rescues a young
     woman, Nell, and two surviving missionaries, Jim and Mr.
     Wells, when their Moravian Mission, the Village of Peace, is
     massacred by "a brutal liquor-crazed band of Huron Indians."
     Lew Wetzel, an Indian hunter who had earlier vowed vengeance
     against Wingenund, tracks down the group but allows the Indian
     to leave because of his kindness to the whites. Later, again
     pursuing Wingenund, Wetzel spares his life again when he over-
     takes the Indian performing a "Christian" burial for his dead
     daughter.

316 _____. "The Hogan of Nas Ta Bega." Yaqui and Other
     Great Indian Stories. Ed. Loren Grey. New York: Bel-
     mont Tower Books, 1976, pp. 141-200. Originally published
     in Argosy (1915).
        This is the story of John Shefford: "As a boy he had
     yearned to make himself an artist. His family had made him
     a clergyman; fate had made him a failure." After being ousted
     by the church, Shefford goes to Utah in search of Fay Larkin
     and a lost village of Cottonwoods. He is befriended by a former
     Navajo Chief, Nas Ta Bega, who had been educated by whites
     but who had renounced white ways and returned to his tribe.
     Shefford eventually finds inner peace in his new environment

but, when the story ends, is still seeking the whereabouts of Fay Larkin.

317 _____. "The Land of the Wild Musk-ox." Yaqui and Other Great Indian Stories. Ed. Loren Grey. New York: Belmont Tower Books, 1976, pp. 103-39.
  Jones, a white trapper, and Rea, a white free-trader, defy an Indian council order not to hunt the sacred musk-ox in the North country. (Jones wants to bring back live musk-ox calves.) Jones and Rea survive temperatures as low as seventy degrees below zero and attacks by white wolves; the men use their last bullet to kill a caribou for food when they are near starvation. The night before reaching home with their prize, all the little musk-oxen are killed. "Moccasin tracks told the story of the tragedy."

318 _____. "Nophaie's Redemption." Zane Grey's Greatest Indian Stories. Ed. Loren Grey. New York: Belmont Tower Books, 1975, pp. 143-85. Originally published by Curtis Publishing Co. (1922-23). [After Zane Grey's The Vanishing American was serialized by Ladies' Home Journal in 1922-23, some individuals and religious groups pressured the Curtis Publishing Co. into refusing to publish the story in book form unless substantial portions were cut. Grey's original final chapters appear as the short story, "Nophaie's Redemption."]
  Nophaie is nursed through an influenza epidemic by whites. He rides off to Nothsis Ahn (the sacred mountain of the Great Spirit) to examine his life, and to resolve the inner conflict between his Indian heritage and his white education--eventually rejecting his Indian ways and accepting Christianity. After quelling a Nopah and Noki uprising against whites, Nophaie returns to Mariam, his white love.

319 _____. "Siena Waits." Zane Grey's Greatest Indian Stories. Ed. Loren Grey. New York: Belmont Tower Books, 1975, pp. 9-32.
  According to ancient Indian prophecy, a great chief would one day be born to save his people from starvation and slavery, and to found a new tribe on the shores of a lake. Siena hears a call "to the last of the Crows." He kills eight moose to keep his people from starving, and later leads his people from slavery (by the hated Crees) far northward--"and there, on the lonely shores of an inland sea, he fathered the Great Slave Tribe."

320 Grinnell, George Bird. "Bluejay Visits the Ghosts." Harper's, 101 (Nov. 1900), 840-45.
  Bluejay seeks his sister, Ioi, in the Land of the Ghosts. He finds her surrounded by bones, but she insists that the bones are actually his brother-in-law. That night a crowd of people appears and Bluejay finds that they are turned into bones if he raises his voice. These people try to convince Bluejay

that the twigs and the leaves are actually salmon and trout.
He leaves, but his boat burns and Bluejay dies. Now dead,
he returns to the Land of the Ghosts and remarks about the
beauty of the place. He asks about the handsome brave with
Ioi, and learns that it is his brother-in-law--the very same
thing Bluejay saw as "bones" when he was alive.

321 _____. "The Girl Who Was the Ring." Harper's, 102
(Feb. 1901), 425-30.
Four brothers and their sister live together. In order
to get food, the boys put their sister on a swing to attract
buffalo, then kill some with their spears. One day a coyote
convinces her to call the buffalo, but the buffalo capture the
girl and transform her into a "ring" used for the Indian stick
game. The coyote then gathers a badger, a kit fox, a rabbit,
a hawk, and a blackbird, to trick the buffalo while they play
the stick game. Taking the ring, the animals relay the girl
("ring") back home where, at the lodge, the brothers kill most
of the buffalo and restore their sister.

322 _____. "Little Friend Coyote." Harper's, 102 (Jan. 1901),
288-93.
Suyesaipi is a Piegan girl who marries a Blackfeet named
Front Wolf. One day she begs Front Wolf to let her accompany
him on a trip. He warns her that it is dangerous but allows
her to go along. While on the trip the Blackfeet are deceived
by the chief of the Kutenais, and all are killed except Suyesaipi.
She escapes but is soon lost; however, a coyote guides her
back to her home village. In return she leaves some food for
the animal.

323 _____. "The Medicine Grizzly Bear." Harper's, 102
(Apr. 1901), 736-44.
A poor Pawnee boy is trapped in a grizzly bear's cave.
The bear has pity on the boy, teaching him special powers and
making him safe from harm. The Pawnee, now renowned for
his powers, allows his best friend (the chief's son) to be captured by the grizzly--and this young Indian is taught to be a
great healer. The Pawnees prosper under the guidance of the
two braves. When the grizzly bear dies, the two Indians soon
follow him in death--but not before they pass their special
knowledge on to their sons.

324 Grove, Fred. "Hostage Trail." Spurs West. Ed. S. Omar
Barker. Garden City, N.Y.: Doubleday, 1960, pp. 146-60.
Originally published in Texas Rangers (1957).
Captain Carnett is assigned to take some supplies and
Comanche hostages through rough territory where angry settlers
want to hang all the Indians. The hostages, led by old Eagle
Heart, dress up in army uniforms and help to scare off the
irate mob.

325 _____. "War Path." With Guidons Flying: Tales of the

U. S. Cavalry in the Old West. Garden City, N. Y. : Doubleday, 1970, pp. 83-96.
To-hauson, a Kiowa army scout, leads Captain Howard and his troop on the trail of Big Bow and his fleeing band of Kiowas. Howard is not sure of To-hauson's loyalties, but must depend on him. The clever To-hauson, not wanting to mislead Howard deliberately, takes him not to Big Bow, but to a band of white horse thieves instead.

326 Gulick, Bill. "The Marriage of Moon Wind." The Saturday Evening Post Reader of Western Stories. Ed. E. N. Brandt. Garden City, N. Y. : Doubleday, 1960, pp. 96-108.
Two fur trappers become partners, but their rivalry in practical joking gets serious when it involves their marriage to two Shoshone sisters.

327 _____. "Squaw Fever." Bar 2 Roundup of Best Western Stories. Ed. Scott Meredith. New York: Dutton, 1953, pp. 203-30.
Charlie Smith and Bear Claw agree to guide a wagon train to Oregon. Charlie is naively infatuated with a beautiful but manipulative and inconstant white girl, but soon learns his lesson about white squaws, and decides to settle for Bear Claw's sister-in-law instead--at a bargain price of ten horses.

328 _____. "Thief in Camp." Spurs West. Ed. S. Omar Barker. Garden City, N. Y. : Doubleday, 1960, pp. 161-79. Originally published in The Saturday Evening Post (1958).
Some friendly Crows come to a wagon train for a free meal. One, Wolf Runner, stays for a few days, and is accused of stealing a rifle that a couple of the white boys had lost in the river. In the end Wolf Runner is exonerated.

329 _____. "Two-Faced Promise." Bar 1 Roundup of Best Western Stories. Ed. Scott Meredith. New York: Dutton, 1952, pp. 53-64.
The surveyor for a new railroad to the West takes a chance by believing Chief Qualchee's word that there is a good pass through the mountains to the north of Indian land.

330 Guthrie, A. B. "Mountain Medicine." The Literature of the American West. Ed. J. Golden Taylor. Boston: Houghton Mifflin, 1971, pp. 299-307
Clell, a trapper who had once been with Lewis and Clark, finds himself the captive of a group of Blackfeet, a tribe he thinks of as "the meanest Indians living" and against whom he had once fought as an ally of the friendlier Crows. Because of his calm bravery, the Blackfeet give him a chance to run for his life, naked and unarmed, as they pursue him. After killing his closest pursuer, Clell dives into a beaver pond and hides inside a beaver lodge, thereby successfully eluding the Blackfeet.

331 Hall, James. "The Indian Hater." Legends of the West.
     Philadelphia: Harrison Hall, 1832, pp. 247-62.
         An unnamed narrator, on his way West through Illinois,
     stops at a small village for supplies. A farmer there tells
     him about Samuel Monson, who hates Indians and is suspected
     of occasionally killing some. On his return trip East, the nar-
     rator hires a Potawatomi Indian guide, who is suddenly shot.
     Monson steps from the brush and explains his hatred of Indians.
     Much earlier, Indians had horribly murdered Monson's wife,
     children, and mother; he had sworn to revenge their deaths
     for the rest of his life.

332 Hall, J. C. "A Narrow Escape All Around." Overland
     Monthly, n. s. 17 (1891), 73-76.
         In 1861 Henry Goodrich, Henry Martin, Jared T. Kim-
     berly, and the narrator start on foot from San Francisco to
     cover the more than 150 miles of desolate wilderness to Cres-
     cent City (home of the Eel River Indians). After spending the
     night at a mail service station, they continue their journey but
     soon lose the trail. Goodrich and Martin leave the other two
     to rest and protect their goods while they start back to the
     station for advice. The two are gone so long that Kimberly
     sets out after them, leaving the narrator alone. Later, an
     exhausted Kimberly returns to the narrator to tell of an Indian
     attack on the station. All survived, and everyone except Kim-
     berly had fled to Wood's Ranch. Kimberly, alone, faces the
     danger of returning for the narrator, and they soon catch up
     with the other men.

333 Hansen, Joseph. "Mourner." South Dakota Review, 5, No. 1
     (Spring 1967), 25-34.
         His finances having taken a bad turn during the Depres-
     sion (in Stander, S. D.), Henry Nelson takes a job as traveling
     salesman, and (because his wife has recently died) leaves his
     eleven-year-old son, Briggs, with Sheriff Meiser's family.
     The boy learns from the sheriff's son that there is an Indian
     in jail, so they visit him. (Briggs had been earlier fascinated
     with Indians after having seen some in a rodeo.) Later that
     night, Briggs sneaks into the jail, frees Charlie Two Horses,
     and demands that he be locked up in Charlie's place. Charlie,
     a sleepy harmless drunk, goes along with the plan. When
     Henry returns, the sheriff relates the story, but is willing to
     forget it, blaming Briggs' actions on the boy's being upset
     about his mother's death.

334 Harris, R. A. "A Friend of the Sioux: A True Story of
     Western Adventure." Overland Monthly, n. s. 34 (1899),
     53-58.
         In 1846 (in western Texas) Shorty Wilson of the U. S.
     Infantry saves a drunken Sioux brave from drowning. The
     scene then shifts to western Wyoming (in 1858) where a sol-
     itary rider, "Stub," travels through Blackfeet country with his
     pack horses. After a skirmish with three Blackfeet braves, he

reaches Sioux country--where he is surprisingly well-treated
by a camp chief. It is revealed that "Stub" is actually Shorty
Wilson, and the Sioux chief is none other than the Indian whose
life he once had saved.

335   Hart, Hazel. (Chippewa). "Ge Chi Maung Won." Arrows
      Four: Prose and Poetry by Young American Indians. Ed.
      T. D. Allen. New York: Pocket Books, 1974, pp. 165-71.
      An old Chippewa woman tells her grandchildren the story
      of her birth, her mother's death in childbirth, and her father's
      death from smallpox eight years later. "And soon the Great
      Spirit will come for me, and someone else will learn the
      meaning of life and death."

336   Hart, William S. and Mary E. "Sidewalk Pennies." --And
      All Points West! Binghamton, N.Y.: Lacotah Press,
      1940, pp. 153-61.
      An old man sits on Olive View Hill talking with Sadie and
      Lucy, two little half-Sioux, half-Cheyenne girls. He tells them
      how he had once fought their ancestors at Fort Phil Kearny.
      After buying them ice cream and letting them play with his dog,
      Horatio, he seems to fall asleep. Officer Red Brady comes
      along and determines that the old man is dead. He rushes the
      little girls off to their mother, Minnie One Feather, calls the
      wagon to come for the man's body, and gives Horatio to the
      two Indian girls.

337   Harte, Bret. "Dick Boyle's Business Card." [Bret Harte's]
      Complete Works, Vol. 10. Boston: Houghton Mifflin, 1896,
      pp. 234-64.
      Dick Boyle jokingly gives his business card to a harm-
      less-looking Indian at the stagecoach station. A few hours
      later he finds it along the road miles away, and correctly sus-
      pects that the Indians will ambush the stage. When they do,
      only he and the lovely Miss Cantire survive. Because of his
      bravery and good judgment the girl decides she likes him after
      all.

338   _____. "A Drift from Redwood Camp." [Bret Harte's]
      Complete Works, Vol. 2. Boston: Houghton Mifflin, 1878,
      pp. 342-64.
      Elijah Martin, named "Skeesicks" by the other men at
      Redwood Camp, is called "cowardly, untruthful, selfish, and
      lazy." When Redwood Camp is flooded, Martin survives by
      floating away on a plank. He drifts into a Digger Minyo In-
      dian camp, steals food, dons Indian clothes that he finds near
      the smoke house, and lies down to sleep. When he awakens,
      Martin is surrounded by Indians who acclaim him their new
      "great chief." He plays the charade for some time, having a
      profound positive effect on the tribe; but when he has a love
      relationship with the Indian agent's wife, complications multiply
      and the tribe is wiped out or sent to the reservation. "Skeesicks,"
      born survivor, returns to Redwood Camp--with secrets intact.

339 _____. "The Mermaid of Lighthouse Point." [Bret Harte's]
         Complete Works, Vol. 10. Boston: Houghton Mifflin, 1896,
         pp. 164-85.
              Pomfrey is a lighthouse keeper off the coast of California;
         his assistant (Jim) is a Digger Indian from a nearby village.
         One day Pomfrey notices a blonde girl swimming in the waves.
         It turns out that she is Olooya, a half-breed descendant of a
         sailor who had deserted from Admiral Drake's ship many years
         earlier. When Pomfrey indignantly refuses to buy the lovely
         Olooya from her brother for forty dollars, the brother sells
         her to a visiting treasure-seeking sailor.

340 _____. "Muck-a-Muck: A Modern Indian Novel after
         Cooper." [Bret Harte's] Complete Works, Vol. 1. Boston:
         Houghton Mifflin, 1878, pp. 78-85.
              Muck-a-Muck, "an untrammeled son of the forest," is
         a parodic image of one of Cooper's noble Indians. At the end
         Natty Bumppo sees Muck-a-Muck with what he thinks is the
         scalp of Geneva Tomkins, the judge's daughter, and shoots the
         Indian. It turns out that the scalp was only a wig.

341 _____. "The Princess Bob and Her Friends." [Bret
         Harte's] Complete Works, Vol. 3. Boston: Houghton Mif-
         flin, 1878, pp. 51-65.
              Princess Bob, the daughter of a Klamath chief, is res-
         cued and raised by a sympathetic white family when her par-
         ents are killed. Bob seems always to be in some kind of
         trouble: she refuses to learn her lessons in school, she steals
         things, she runs off into the forest, she has an illegitimate
         half-breed child, and so on. Eventually (in the early 1860s)
         she takes up with a hermit who, at the end, joins the army
         and accidentally kills Princess Bob.

342 Harvey, Jim. "Little Fox." Teen-Age Frontier Stories. Ed.
         A. L. Furman. New York: Lantern Press, 1958, pp. 231-
         41. Originally published in Twelve/Fifteen (Pierce and
         Washabaugh, 1955).
              Little Fox (Hopi) sneaks away from home early one morn-
         ing to find his family's small flock of goats in Apache terri-
         tory. A scuffle with the Apaches takes place in which Little
         Fox is injured, but he manages to save the goats and escape.

343 Haskell, Walter Scott. "The Grasshopper Trust." Overland
         Monthly, n.s. 49 (1907), 164-66.
              Dead-Snake-Come-to-Life discovers that the five hundred
         acres of "improved land" he has secured from the agent is
         only one foot wide--six inches on either side of a fence. The
         Indian quietly lays in a huge supply of locusts and awaits his
         chance for revenge. Soon the combination of a railroad strike
         and drought leaves the agent without supplies, so he approaches
         the Indian to buy locusts, the only food on the reservation.
         Dead-Snake-Come-to-Life sells the agent a bushel for a thou-
         sand dollars, then demands five thousand dollars for the second,

and finally coerces the agent into giving him a quarter section
of land for the food. The court later upholds this transaction
and the agent is discharged.

344 Hassler, Jon. "Smalleye's Last Hunt." Prairie Schooner,
46, No. 2 (Summer 1972), 128-42.
Smalleye, an eighty-four-year-old Indian guest at an old
folks' home, plans to shoot geese--as he had loved to do in
his younger days. He walks to town, steals his nephew's shotgun, and brings it home wrapped in an old rug. Although he
owns only one shotgun shell, Smalleye crawls to the roof and
waits for the flock. A friend, Nelson, is supposed to help
him; but Nelson forgets, and Smalleye at last fires his shot
to get attention. The roof collapses and the Indian falls to the
balcony with the chimney bricks. The next day Nelson finds
a dead snow goose in the yard.

345 _____. "Willowby's Indian." Prairie Schooner, 47, No. 4
(Winter 1973/74), 283-93.
"French" lives in the Morgan Hotel in the small town of
Willowby in the Minnesota "Lakes Region." During the summer, he dresses as a Chippewa Indian to have his picture taken
with tourists. (Actually, French has no proof of Indian ancestry.) The day before Christmas, in the hotel lobby, he sees
a boy stealing a pack of gum. When he goes to pick up his
unemployment check, he is coerced into dressing up as Santa
Claus for the Rialto matinee and, while handing out candy, he
recognizes the thief.

346 Hathaway, Jo. "In the Service of Love." Overland Monthly,
n.s. 35 (1900), 60-64.
Luria Starr, a young girl with a terminal disease (she
has only six months to live) hears about the discovery of an
old Modoc skull. She rushes out to acquire it: "I must have
it." She replaces it when she discovers that it is a squaw's
skull, not a brave's.

347 Havard, Aline. "Wanena's Choice." St. Nicholas Magazine,
53 (Oct. 1926), 1149-51, 1184-85.
Around 1670 most of the Ojibway tribes are friendly to
the French, except Chief White Otter and his band. White
Otter hates them because he had hated his French father. His
twelve-year-old daughter, Wanena, however, does not share
this hatred. When the French explorer, Greysolon Du Lhut,
and his scout are captured and sentenced to death by White
Otter, Wanena helps them to escape and has them hide on the
tribe's Holy Isle. Unfortunately, White Otter searches the island and recaptures the men. Du Lhut bargains for his freedom by claiming to be able to burn--without the use of fire--
a wooden image on the island. He does so with his watch
crystal, so he and his scout are freed. Du Lhut requests that
Wanena not be punished. Five years later he returns to marry
the Indian girl.

348   Hawkes, Clarence. "Some Painter Episodes." Overland
      Monthly, n.s. 49 (1907), 368-72.
          A hunting guide (non-Indian) tells his client of his ex-
      periences with painters (wild cats). One of these involves a
      pet painter he had tamed, which one day kills a half-breed who
      was trying to kill him. Iroquois Bill, "as mean a skunk as
      ever wore moccasins," had been stealing from the guide's fur
      traps.

349   Haycox, Ernest. "Dispatch to the General." Bar 3 Roundup
      of Best Western Stories. Ed. Scott Meredith. Freeport,
      N.Y.: Books for Libraries Press, 1954, pp. 107-25.
          A few days after Custer's last battle at the Little Big-
      horn, Sergeant Hounds and a guide, Gervaise, are sent by
      General Terry straight through the heart of Sioux and Cheyenne
      territory with a message for General Crook. Gervaise is killed
      along the way, but by surmounting hardship, danger, and close
      calls, Sergeant Hounds completes the mission.

350   _____. "A Question of Blood." Collier's, Jul. 17, 1937,
      44. Reprinted in By Rope and Lead (Boston: Little, Brown,
      1951). Also reprinted in Out West, ed. Jack Schaefer
      (Boston: Houghton Mifflin, 1955), pp. 143-46.
          About 1870 Frank Isabel buys a Crow woman from the
      reservation, paying a horse and a bottle of whiskey for her.
      Later, when she is pregnant, he marries her in the white
      man's way. He gradually comes to feel rejection and isolation
      from his fellow whites because of his having married an Indian.
      At the end, this "squaw man" brings his half-breed son to the
      table with him, while his wife stays on her blanket in the cor-
      ner, crying.

351   _____. "Stage to Lordsburg." The Old West in Fiction.
      Ed. Irwin R. Blacker. New York: Ivan Obolensky, 1961,
      pp. 427-39. Originally published in By Rope and Lead
      (Boston: Little, Brown, 1951).
          The stagecoach from Tonto to Lordsburg must travel
      through hostile Apache country, but withstands the expected
      attack.

352   Hayes, Anna Hansen. "Wah-Tis-Kee--Little Flame." Buck-
      skin and Smoke. San Antonio, Tex.: Naylor, 1971, pp.
      23-32.
          Wah-Tis-Kee is the beautiful daughter of a Shoshone
      chief. They live, long ago, beside the Snake River in Idaho.
      Wah-Tis-Kee wants to marry a handsome, young Blackfeet
      named Blackrock, who comes bravely to her father to request
      permission for the marriage, even though their tribes are tra-
      ditional enemies. Her father sends Blackrock away and orders
      Wah-Tis-Kee, instead, to marry a rich but old Shoshone man
      whom Wah-Tis-Kee does not like. Thus, Wah-Tis-Kee and her
      lover try to escape on the river in the middle of the night.
      Her angry father sees them paddling away and kills them both

with an arrow. In the morning a huge black rock stands in the middle of the Snake River, creating what the white men later called the Twin Falls.

353 Heard, John, Jr. "The Killing of the Captain." Cosmopolitan, 17, No. 4 (Aug. 1894), 440-50.
A young Mexican, Santana, loves a young Mexican girl named Orejana; she, however, loves the captain of the nearby fort. When Santana learns of this, he is furious. While tracking down some Chiricahua Apache renegades, the captain is shot by one of a number of newly-arrived Mexican irregulars. Both the captain and his murderer, Santana, die in the fracas.

354 Hemingway, Ernest. "The Doctor and the Doctor's Wife." The Short Stories of Ernest Hemingway. New York: Scribner's, 1938, pp. 99-103.
A white doctor lives near the Ojibway Indians. He hires Dick Boulton, a half-breed who owes him money, to cut some logs. Dick, who is lazy but clever, outsmarts the doctor and avoids doing the job.

355 _____. "Fathers and Sons." The Short Stories of Ernest Hemingway. New York: Scribner's, 1938, pp. 488-99.
Thirty-eight-year-old Nick Adams, driving along with his young son, remembers his own father, who taught him much about hunting and shooting but very little about love and sex. This he learned from an Ojibway girl, Trudy Gilby.

356 _____. "Indian Camp." The Short Stories of Ernest Hemingway. New York: Scribner's, 1938, pp. 91-95.
Young Nick Adams accompanies his doctor father to an Indian camp where an Indian woman needs help delivering her baby. The woman, in a lower bunk, is in great pain and her husband, in the upper bunk, has an injured foot. The doctor performs a Caesarian with a jack knife and no anesthetic. When the operation is successfully completed, Nick's father notices that the Indian in the upper bunk has slit his own throat.

357 _____. "The Indians Moved Away." The Nick Adams Stories. Ed. Philip Young. New York: Scribner's, 1972, pp. 34-36.
Nick Adams recalls some of the Indians who used to live around Grandpa Bacon's farm in Michigan. He remembers that "Indians all smelled alike" and none of them were "successful." One exception was an Indian named Simon Green, who had had a big farm and had made a success of it. When Simon Green died, however, his sons sold the farm: "That was the way the Indians went."

358 _____. "Ten Indians." The Short Stories of Ernest Hemingway. New York: Scribner's, 1938, pp. 331-36.
Nick Adams, a teenager, has an Indian girlfriend, Prudence Mitchell. One day Nick's father tells him that he saw

Prudence and another boy "threshing around" together in the woods that afternoon. Nick's heart is broken.

359 Hendryx, James B. "The Parson." Great Stories of the West. Ed. Ned Collier. Garden City, N.Y.: Doubleday, 1971, pp. 276-330.
A fighting missionary is brought to Halfaday (in the Yukon) after having been beaten by some cruel Siwash Indians. One of the Indians helps to have the wounded man's bones set and his cuts stitched. "Thanks to the doglike devotion of the Indian boy," the Parson recovers for more adventures.

360 Henry, O. "The Atavism of John Tom Little Bear." Rolling Stones. New York: Doubleday, Page, 1911, pp. 36-55.
John Tom Little Bear is an educated Cherokee who joins with two other men to put on a medicine show in Kansas, selling fake medicines to gullible townspeople. A little boy who has run away from home goes along with them, until he is retrieved by his mother. But when the estranged father kidnaps the boy from his mother, the now-drunk Indian reverts to type, rescues the boy, and returns him to the mother. At his belt he wears the scalp of the boy's father.

361 _____. "He Also Serves." The Complete Works of O. Henry, Vol. 1. Garden City, N.Y.: Doubleday, 1953, pp. 747-54.
High Jack Snakefeeder, a college-educated Cherokee who becomes a professional ethnologist, has a girlfriend named Florence Blue Feather. Shortly after Florence mysteriously disappears, High Jack and his friend (Hunky Magee) start off on a Central American expedition to study some Aztec ruins. In one of these they discover a stone statue of the ancient god Tlotopaxl. High Jack, interestingly enough, looks exactly like the statue, and decides he is the god reincarnated. Later he wanders into the jungle with a native girl who looks very much like Florence Blue Feather, and is never heard from again. Hunky Magee marries the real Florence Blue Feather.

362 Hibben, Frank C. "The Massacre in Peralta Canyon." In Other Days. Ed. Frances T. Hymphreville. Chicago: Scott, Foresman, 1956, pp. 154-65. Originally published in Argosy (Jun. 1952).
Four Pueblo Indians accidentally encounter four grizzly bears on a cliff. In the ensuing fight three of the Indians are killed before the survivor kills the last bear.

363 Hoch, Edward. "The Wolfram Hunters." The Saint Magazine Reader. Ed. Leslie Charteris and Hans Santesson. Garden City, N.Y.: Doubleday, 1966, pp. 141-56. Originally published in The Saint Mystery Magazine (Mar. 1964). Reprinted in Chronicles of a Comer and Other Religious Science Fiction Stories, ed. Roger Elwood. (Atlanta: John Knox, 1974), pp. 33-47.

A small band of Apaches lives in the upper valley of the
Rio Grande, some ninety years after the "Bomb" has destroyed
all the other people on earth. These Apaches have, like Noah
and his family, been given a second chance. They have grown
rather corrupt--they kill all criminals on crosses every Easter,
they spend time hunting useless wolfram (tungsten), and they
no longer practice Christianity. Father Legion, living alone
in a cave in the hills, remembers the true religion. He ap-
prehends a murderer, wins the respect of the Apaches again,
and begins to lead them back to the true ways.

364 Hoffman, Elwyn Irving. "Yat: A Digger Indian Story of the
     California Foothills." Overland Monthly, n.s. 26 (1895),
     489-93.
     Yat (a Digger Indian of the Pleasant Valley tribe) is
strong and well-liked--and in love with Maria of the Penn
Valley tribe; however, he has a rival, George, also of the
Penn Valley tribe. At a local celebration, Yat and George
compete in a foot race, after which Yat develops severe leg
cramps. Maria visits him the next day, mocks him, and informs him of her marriage to George. In anger Yat hurls
her from him, killing her. He is never able to walk again.

Hogan, Ray, and Gwynn Grady. "Bitter Sunset." (For com-
     plete bibliographical information and story summary, see
     Grady entry--# 305.)

365 Holland, Rupert Sargeant. "Drums in the Fog." Indians,
     Indians, Indians. Ed. Phyllis R. Fenner. New York:
     Franklin Watts, 1950, pp. 202-21. Originally published in
     St. Nicholas Magazine (Nov. 1937).
     Three Maine youths outwit the twenty Abnaki Indians who
are about to attack the fort.

366 Holt, Irene. "The Gift." Arizona Quarterly, 3 (Autumn 1947),
     207-12.
     Big Mud, a Navajo, wants to please his wife, Smiling
Woman, with a fine gift because they have not been getting
along together very well for over a month. He buys a stove,
and has some problems installing it. It works well by the
time Smiling Woman's relatives arrive, however, and Big Mud
can see that Smiling Woman is very proud of him and his gift.

367 Hooker, Forrestine C. "Her Indian Lover." Sunset, 20
     (Mar. 1908), 459-63.
     Natchez is an Apache scout for the cavalry. As such,
one of his jobs is to scout for the army against the renegade
Apache, Geronimo. He becomes infatuated with the lovely
daughter of Captain Carlton, and presents her with little gifts
which she scoffs at. He soon realizes, however, that she
loves Lieutenant Blake. So great is his love for the girl that
Natchez later sacrifices his own life (by intercepting the bullet
of an Apache "snake") to save the life of the brave lieutenant.

368 Horgan, Paul. "The Captain's Watch." <u>Figures in a Land-</u>
<u>scape.</u> New York: Harper, 1931, pp. 56-77.
An army captain and his troop are killed by Indians. One
lieutenant lives to bring back the tale, and to lead another troop
of civilians in an attempt to make a treaty with the Indians.
Their effort is successful because they use special lamps to
trick the superstitious Indians into thinking that they have
brought the stars down from the sky.

369 _____. "Comedy on the Plains." <u>Harper's</u>, 183 (1941),
641-46.
Clyde Binney helps greenhorn cavalry Lieutenant Pyne to
round up some renegade Apaches who are on a drinking and
stealing spree off their reservation. Binney, Pyne, and two
other men capture the forty Apaches in a basin where they are
hiding: "They were just simply pitiful, Mr. Binney remembered, like a whole flock of moth-eaten old hawks, not doing
anything."

370 _____. "Water in the Wilderness." <u>In Other Days.</u> Ed.
Frances T. Humphreville. Chicago: Scott, Foresman,
1956, pp. 212-37. Originally published in <u>Collier's</u> (Jan.
3, 1953).
Joe Dummy, in 1887, is an Apache scout for the United
States Army. Scouting with Lieutenant Matt Hazard to check
on the movements of some Apaches from Mexico, Joe is wounded
with a poisoned arrow. When Matt saves his life, Joe becomes
fiercely loyal to him. They report back to the fort, where soon
Matt's first baby is born. When the baby gets sick, Joe makes
a dramatic ride to get a doctor, who saves the baby. Matt's
wife, who had previously disliked and mistrusted the dirty,
smelly scout who always hung around her husband, now relents. She even lets him hold the baby--but not until after
she has given Joe a bath and has made him put on a new shirt.

371 Hough, Emerson. "Claxton, D. D.: A Story of the Northwest
Mounted Police." <u>Sunset,</u> 36, No. 4 (Apr. 1916), 16-18,
48, 50, 52-56, 58-60, 62.
Sergeant Claxton and Corporal Bray are stationed with
the Northwest Mounted Police at the remote Beaver Lake Post.
One day Claxton goes out to chop wood, but slips and badly
cuts his foot with the ax. He starts sewing it up as an Indian
man from the Woods Cree village seventy-five miles east comes
into the post. Using sign language, the Indian communicates
that smallpox has decimated his village.

372 _____. "The Wedding of Beaver Eyes." <u>Outing</u>, 38, No.
6 (Sep. 1901), 624-31.
Billy, a half-breed scout for the United States, has seen
a lot of Indian fighting. After one series of battles, he goes
with two homesick Crees to visit their Plains homeland, where
he falls in love with Beaver Eyes, a lovely Indian maiden.
Soon Billy must report for duty, and he takes Beaver Eyes

with him. At the fort, Billy kills an Indian, but he and Beaver
Eyes escape to the Northwest and live many happy years together. As white encroachment increases, priests visit Billy
and try to convince him to be married in the white man's
church. They finally agree, but wear their traditional tribal
dress for the ceremony.

373 Howard, Eric. "Indian Business." Story, 4, No. 20 (Mar.
     1934), 63-65.
     A young Navajo, Seganitso Begay, while riding his horse
to a sing, contemplates his possible future with an attractive
girl he knows. Two white government men in a car stop and
criticize him for wanting to take part in the sing rather than
tending crops. Seganitso rides on to the celebration, but now
his heart is troubled.

374 _____. "Indian Idyll." Prairie Schooner, 9, No. 3 (Sum-
     mer 1935), 205-11.
     Dancing Leaf returns home for the summer to her Tewa
Pueblo after four long years at a white school. She wants to
forget the identity she had there and resume the Indian way of
life. She becomes increasingly attracted to Butterfly Boy, who
promises to make her a beautiful string of turquoise. He gives
her the necklace on Fiesta Day. Dancing Leaf's white teachers
come to the celebration to remind her that she is to return to
school in the fall, but the girl remains at home and marries
Butterfly Boy.

375 _____. "Navajo Letter." Prairie Schooner, 9, No. 1
     (Winter 1935), 57-60.
     A young Navajo male writes to a white man, presumably
an old school friend, telling him about the poverty and problems on the reservation. He asks his friend to help him find
a job in the city so that he and his girlfriend can marry.

376 Huffman, Bert. "Ah-lo-ma." Overland Monthly, n.s. 45
     (1905), 491-93.
     Blanche Ramon, the apparently high-society daughter of
a wealthy Oregonian, comes from Oregon to Boston. All Boston is delighted with her beauty, intelligence, talent at music,
etc., until it is discovered by accident that she is one-quarter
Umatilla Indian.

377 Huggins, E. L. "Smohalla, the Prophet of Priest Rapids."
     Overland Monthly, n.s. 17 (1891), 208-15.
     The white narrator tracks down Smohalla, a prophet and
seer of Indians along the Columbia River. The two men discuss Indian and white ways. Smohalla expresses his resent-
ment and hatred of whites, the result of his own personal experiences.

378 Humphrey, William. "A Good Indian." A Time and a Place.
     New York: Knopf, 1968, pp. 29-46. Originally published

in The Saturday Evening Post (Aug. 1965) under another
title.
John, an Oklahoma Indian, sells his land for nine thousand dollars and spends part of the money on a yellow Cadillac.
John wrecks the car in a few hours and returns to buy a second yellow Cadillac with the rest of his money and an old wagon.
A couple of hours later he is killed when he wrecks that one
too. John's squaw comes back to the dishonest, prejudiced
car dealer to borrow a wagon--the one John traded earlier--
to carry her dead husband away for burial.

379 _____. "The Last of the Caddoes." A Time and a Place.
New York: Knopf, 1968, pp. 179-208. Originally published
in Esquire (Oct. 1968).
Jimmy Hawkins discovers that he is part Caddo Indian on
his father's side; he also learns that his mother hates that part
of him which is Indian. Partly to spite her, and partly to find
out about his ancestors, Jimmy goes to his grandfather's farm
and spends a summer digging into the Caddo grave mound in
the cotton field. He becomes so involved in his new identity
that he adopts a new name, "Snake-in-His-Mother's-Bosom,"
and his relationship with his mother deteriorates even further.
It seems that he thinks it will be his final duty to murder her.

380 Hunsinger, Ruth. "A Dakota Story." The Indian Historian,
6, No. 4 (Fall 1973), 5-7.
A young, slightly crippled Indian named Two Crows is
"one of the tribe's best arrow makers," but he is unhappy because of his twisted hips and his dependency on the family.
One day he rescues a beautiful wild horse trapped in a muddy
water hole. After he breaks the horse for riding, Two Crows'
father holds a feast and "customary 'oh to kon' or give-away,
in honor of his son."

381 Jackson, Edgar N. "Whimper." Teen-Age Frontier Stories.
Ed. A. L. Furman. New York: Lantern Press, 1958,
pp. 9-24. Originally published in Twelve/Fifteen (Pierce
and Washabaugh, 1956).
Matt Gates names his dog "Whimper" because it makes
only a whimpering sound and never really barks. Matt's father
feels that Whimper is worthless as a watchdog; but when the
boy is kidnapped by Coosuck Indians, the quiet dog follows
Matt and then returns to lead a rescue party.

382 Jackson, Penny. "Rites of Spring." Transatlantic Review, 7 (Fall 1961), 82-91.
A Northeastern Canadian Indian named Joe carries canoes
and is a guide for white fishermen and hunters so he can make
enough money for his son to go to the city. The boy decides
not to return to the Indian school that winter. One day Joe's
son finds his father mauled by a bear and carries him home.
Joe recovers slowly and acts as though he were in a dream
world. When spring comes Joe goes out to hunt bear and is
found lying still (but unmarked) on the ground.

383   Jacobs, Harvey. "The Girl Who Drew the Gods." Mademoiselle, 61 (May 1965), 174-75, 222-29, 236. Reprinted in
The Year's Best S-F: 11th Annual Edition, ed. Judith Mer-
rill (New York: Delacorte), pp. 295-318.
    Oliver August and Marilyn Mayberry meet while taking a
college course called "Know the Navajo II," a continuation of
"Know the Navajo I." They learn that Navajos never draw
pictures of their gods: "If the gods were drawn," the instruc-
tor says, "the image would leap up and devour the artist.
Crunch." When Marilyn does bring in pictures of the gods,
Oliver knows that he must "devour" her for the crime. After
six months of dating, Marilyn finally lets Oliver make love to
her--thus giving him (presumably) an opportunity for the proper
revenge.

384   Jerome, Lucy Baker. "The Return of Altoonah." Overland
Monthly, n. s. 42 (1903), 63-66.
    Altoonah, an Indian girl, is married to a white soldier
named Kirkham. She really, however, loves the Indian Eagle
Feather. Kirkham and a friend go hunting and accidentally
encounter Eagle Feather. Altoonah has followed them. Kirkham engages in hand-to-hand struggle with the Indian, then
grabs his rifle and takes aim. At the exact moment Kirkham
fires, Altoonah embraces Eagle Feather--so the bullet kills
them both.

385   Johnson, Alvin. "The Killing of Different Man." John Stuy-
vesant Ancestor and Other People. New York: Harcourt,
Brace, and Howe, 1919, pp. 72-81.
    Different Man is a lazy, freeloading, good-for-nothing
Indian who comes around to the storekeeper and begs for tobacco and molasses. He gets married, but his wife's mother
comes one day and takes the girl away. An enraged Different
Man follows them and murders the mother. He is tried by an
all-white jury and is sentenced to death. Because the sheriff
is a coward, the storekeeper actually conducts the hanging.

386   _____. "Squaw Man and Doctor." The Battle of the Wild
Turkey and Other Tales. New York: Atheneum, 1961,
pp. 226-41.
    A Cornell professor visits an Indian reservation to make
a study of Indian education. It is his theory that Indian children
become truly educated only if they are taught in white schools
off the reservation. But his talk with a pregnant Indian woman
on the train convinces him (or, at least, the reader) that white
education merely destroys Indianness and certain "superior"
Indian values.

387   Johnson, Dorothy M. "Flame on the Frontier." Indian Country. New York: Ballantine, 1953, pp. 1-19. Originally
published in Argosy.
    Mary Amanda, a thirteen-year-old girl, is captured by
the Indians when her father and brother are murdered. She

hates captivity, and resists learning the language and doing the
work of a squaw. She refuses the young men who court her,
but (to avoid an old man who seeks her for his second wife)
she finally accepts one named Snow Mountain. They marry,
have a child, and she grows to love him. When offered a
chance to be ransomed, she decides to stay with Snow Mountain and never sees her mother again. A sub-plot concerns her
sister, Sarah, who is much younger and grows up virtually as
an Indian girl. She forgets entirely the white ways and wants
to marry an Indian buck; but when offered the ransom, Sarah
returns to her white home.

388   . "Journal of Adventure." Bar 5 Roundup of Best
     Western Stories. Ed. Scott Meredith. New York: Dutton,
     1956, pp. 144-59. Originally published in Collier's (1954).
          Edward Morgan, visiting the West for a final adventure-
     some fling before returning to marry Vicky and become a clas-
     sics teacher, lives among the Crows for a time. When he is
     injured in a Cheyenne attack and is alone (with a broken leg
     and pneumonia), Blue Wind Maiden, a Crow, comes and saves
     his life. He dutifully marries her and they have two children.
     Later she dies in a blizzard. Edward reestablishes contact
     with Vicky and they finally marry.

389   . "Journey to the Fort." Indian Country. New York:
     Ballantine, 1953, pp. 67-81. Reprinted in Bar 3 Roundup
     of Western Stories, ed. Scott Meredith (Freeport, N.Y.:
     Books for Libraries Press, 1954), pp. 184-201. Originally
     published in Collier's.
          Mrs. Foster and her seven-year-old daughter (Mary) had
     been captured by Sioux when their wagon train was attacked.
     Mrs. Foster did not know what happened to her husband, and
     presumed him dead. She had secretly sent Mary away from
     the Indians in the hope that the child would be picked up by
     another wagon train. Now, after seven months of captivity,
     Mrs. Foster has been ransomed and is being escorted back
     to the fort. She learns that her husband and daughter are
     both alive and waiting for her at the fort.

390   . "Lost Sister." The Hanging Tree and Other Sto-
     ries. New York: Ballantine, 1951, pp. 91-102.
          Bessie was captured as a little girl and raised to be an
     Indian. She even had an Indian son who became a great chief-
     warrior. One day Bessie is recaptured by whites and sent to
     live with her sisters, who neither like nor understand her.
     She finally runs away and is never located. Years later, a
     nephew finds what he believes to be Aunt Bessie's bones in a
     canyon. Though he is fairly certain it is Bessie's remains,
     he "would not make her captive again" by burying her in the
     family plot.

391   . "A Man Called Horse." Indian Country. New York:
     Ballantine, 1953, pp. 164-79. Originally published in Col-
     lier's.

A young upper-class Bostonian goes out West to become
a dude, believing this will help him "find himself." Captured
by an Indian tribe, he is dragged to their dwelling place like
a horse (which accounts for his new name). At first he is a
slave to a family, but he eventually marries the pretty daughter
and becomes a warrior. When mother, daughter, and child die
he returns home a changed person, having learned from the
Indians how to be a man.

392 _____. "Scars of Honor." Indian Country. New York:
Ballantine, 1953, pp. 132-48. Originally published in
Argosy.
Charley Lockjaw is an old drunken Indian who represents
the last reservoir of the old ways. He teaches several younger
men how to get "pure" before a war, how to do a sundance,
etc. Then he dies, and one of his devotees kills a horse for
his journey to the afterlife--much to the annoyance of white
men who wanted to buy the animal.

393 _____. "The Unbeliever." Indian Country. New York:
Ballantine, 1953, pp. 20-34. Originally published in Collier's.
Mahlon Mitchell (called "Iron Head" because of his red
hair) used to live with the Crows and was "good medicine" for
them. Then one day the luck ran out; in a surprise attack he
left, after "mercy-killing" (?) his friend. Now a beaten and
unsuccessful older man, he volunteers to guide troops back to
the village for negotiations. Mitchell decides to stay, pick up
with his former wife, and be an old man among Indians. But
first he wants to return for his pay and to bring back some
supplies. The Indians don't want him to, but he insists. So
the tribe plans a feast before he goes. They poison Iron Head.

394 _____. "Warrior's Exile." Indian Country. New York:
Ballantine, 1953, pp. 51-66. Originally published in Argosy.
Smoke Rising, a Plains Indian disappointed with his
twenty-eight years of life, seeks a vision and death. On the
quest he discovers his old girlfriend and her baby in the snow.
Smoke Rising kills the warrior who had stolen her and from
whom she was running away.

395 _____. "War Shirt." Indian Country. New York: Ballantine, 1953, pp. 99-115. Originally published in Collier's.
A white man, shunned by a father who rejects him because of a red, hand-shaped birthmark on his cheek, joins an
Indian tribe. Years later his white brother attempts to locate
him. Old Bije Wilcox offers to reunite the two for a thousand
dollars but later decides, as a matter of principle, not to accept "Judas money" to betray the brother. The white-man-
turned-Indian does not want to return with his brother.

396 Jones, Carl P. "A War Chief of the Tontos." Overland
Monthly, n. s. 28 (1896), 528-32.
Jim Duffy, ex-scout and Indian fighter with the Fifth

Cavalry in Arizona, reminisces about an experience he had in
1873. One band of Apache braves led by Chief Delshay continually left the reservation to raid settlers. Delshay was arrested, but escaped. Lt. Schuyler offered a fifty-dollar reward for the Apache leader's scalp, then left with a tracking
party to try to find the Indian. After the lieutenant's departure,
Duffy is ordered to follow him and deliver a package which con-
tains--unknown to Duffy--Delshay's scalp.

397 Jones, W. Arthur. "Minnie-wah-wah." Overland Monthly,
n. s. 23 (1894), 195-97.
Minnie-wah-wah, a Spokane Indian girl and daughter of
Coyote Chief, is promised in marriage to a Flathead man. She
is a devoted convert of Dr. Whitman's mission at Waitipeii. A
few days before Minnie-wah-wah's wedding, some Flathead Indians murder the doctor and his wife. Because of the murders,
Minnie-wah-wah refuses to marry the Flathead man and commits suicide. The Flathead man soon sickens and dies, and
the "superstitious" Indians are more easily converted to Christianity.

398 Kantor, MacKinlay. "Dakotas Coming." The Saturday Evening
Post Reader of Western Stories. Ed. E. N. Brandt. Garden City, N. Y.: Doubleday, 1960, pp. 154-82.
Three white petty burglars are mistaken for an advance
party of Dakotas (Sioux), so the Iowa frontier settlers abandon
their homes and seek protection. In one cabin, however, a
woman is about to have a baby and cannot be moved. When
the three burglars discover there really are twenty-five Dakotas out there, they rush back to help the defenseless women,
and become heroes in the process. One of the burglars falls
in love with one of the women and "turns over a new leaf."

399 Kelenaka-Henuok-Makhewe. "The Sick Child." Harper's, 98
(Feb. 1899), 446-48.
A young Indian girl is sent to make an offering to the
Great Spirit. She returns to find that her little sister who
was ill has become much worse. The medicine women claim
that there is no hope, but when the medicine man arrives he
gives the child something that seems to make her feel better.
He says, however, that her spirit is gone. The next morning
the little sister's crib is empty--the young Indian girl has
learned what death means.

400 Kennedy, C. Justin. "The Gold of Sun-Dance Canyon." Overland Monthly, n. s. 50, (1907), 280-84.
Garvey Stewart, prospecting for gold, receives a letter
from his wife begging him to come home to relieve her loneliness. He starts home, but sees a Stoney Indian camp as it
is being ravaged by a landslide. He nurses Takaho, the one
squaw who survives the tragedy, back to health. She promises
to show him a large gold deposit if he will forget his white
wife and marry her. Though Garvey does not like Takaho,

greed prompts him to accept her proposal. Later he discovers
that the gold is really "fool's gold" and is thankful that he is
free to return to his wife.

401   Kent, W. H. B. "Drake Feeds the Buzzards." Great Stories
       of the West. Ed. Ned Collier. Garden City, N.Y.: Double-
       day, 1971, pp. 226-66.
            The Papago Indians (the last small, dying remnant of a
       once-great tribe) are bothered by some white fortune hunters
       out to get the "cursed" emeralds from the mouths of dead men
       at the old mine.

402   Kipling, Rudyard. "Brother Square-Toes." Rewards and
       Fairies, Vol. 21 of the Works of Rudyard Kipling. New
       York: Scribner's, 1920, pp. 171-99.
            A Frenchman tells of his experiences among the Senecas
       in 1793--especially Chief Cornplanter and Chief Red Jacket in
       Pennsylvania shortly after the revolution. The chiefs go to
       talk with Big Hands (General Washington) to seek his assurance
       that the United States will not get embroiled in the new war
       between France and England.

403   Kistler, Jessie R. "The Bloody Ax That Slew an Entire Fam-
       ily." Tales Tolled by the Mission Bells. Los Angeles:
       Research Publishing Co. , 1947, pp. 174-85.
            A specially made ax has a strange history of killing and
       maiming: one time accidentally in the hands of a woodcutter;
       then serving the murderous designs of Hooplah, the blood-
       thirsty Tulare Indian chief; later serving the selfish aims of
       robbers.

404   _____. "The Cats That Lived Like Kings." Tales Tolled by
       the Mission Bells. Los Angeles: Research Publishing Co. ,
       1947, pp. 186-97.
            Francisco is a lazy mission Indian who likes to take care
       of the cats, and to steal brandy and wine from the mission
       stores. When gold is discovered, he is even too lazy to want
       to dig it out.

405   _____. "El Oro, the Horse That Saved a Mission." Tales
       Tolled by the Mission Bells. Los Angeles: Research Pub-
       lishing Co. , 1947, pp. 26-37.
            El Oro, the swiftest horse around, saves the mission when
       José rides it to carry a message that savage Indians are at-
       tacking.

406   _____. "The First Popular Orchestra in California." Tales
       Tolled by the Mission Bells. Los Angeles: Research Pub-
       lishing Co. , 1947, pp. 149-59.
            Padre Duran teaches some Indian mission converts to
       play in an orchestra.

407   _____. "Gabriel, the Indian That Lived 150 Years." Tales

Tolled by the Mission Bells. Los Angeles: Research Publishing Co., 1947, pp. 14-25.
The first convert of Padre Serra, an Indian named Gabriel, lives to a great age among the California missions.

408 _____. "The Half-Breed Lad That Decorated the Grand Church." Tales Tolled by the Mission Bells. Los Angeles: Research Publishing Co., 1947, pp. 76-86.
Tofito (half-Mexican, half-Indian) paints the interior of the San Juan Capistrano mission church.

409 _____. "How a Rabbit Lured a Whole Tribe to Dolores." Tales Tolled by the Mission Bells. Los Angeles: Research Publishing Co., 1947, pp. 64-75.
Young Sanelan, chief of a small California tribe, is chasing a rabbit when he is drawn near the Dolores Mission in California. The Padre there feeds him and gives him clothes. Later, Sanelan returns to lead his tribe to the mission.

410 _____. "How a Russian Icon Disappeared from Solano." Tales Tolled by the Mission Bells. Los Angeles: Research Publishing Co., 1947, pp. 231-37.
Chief Sum-Yet-ho of the California Suisunes sees a depiction of the Virgin on a stolen Russian Icon, and he lusts after her. Later he tries to get a similar-looking blonde woman for his "white squaw," but is unsuccessful.

411 _____. "How Little Pedro Was Saved by the Royal Bell." Tales Tolled by the Mission Bells. Los Angeles: Research Publishing Co., 1947, pp. 1-13.
Digger Indians, having "round stupid faces," being "definitely inferior in intellect," and being "shiftless and dirty," should be pleased when the first mission is established in California. Some of the Indians, however, set fire to the church in an effort to drive out the padres. Little Pedro escapes the conflagration by crawling into the bell tower.

412 _____. "Ola, the Ox That Escaped the Barbecue Pit." Tales Tolled by the Mission Bells. Los Angeles: Research Publishing Co., 1947, pp. 160-73.
Luis has a pet ox. One of the mission padres saves its life when the animal is scheduled for the barbecue pit.

413 _____. "The Olive Oil Press That Caught a Thief." Tales Tolled by the Mission Bells. Los Angeles: Research Publishing Co., 1947, pp. 100-10.
Garcia is a "problem child" who steals olives, chews tobacco, and the like. But he shows that he is not all bad when he helps secure the mission against pirates.

414 _____. "Pasquala, the Indian Maid That Saved Her Mission." Tales Tolled by the Mission Bells. Los Angeles: Research Publishing Co., 1947, pp. 211-21.

Pasquala, a Tulare Indian girl, is converted by the California missionaries. Later she is kidnapped back to her tribe. When she learns that her tribe is about to attack the mission, she runs ahead to warn them, and so the attack is repulsed. Pasquala dies soon afterward.

415 _____. "The Royal Bell That Has Rung Every Eve for 150 Years." Tales Tolled by the Mission Bells. Los Angeles: Research Publishing Co., 1947, pp. 87-99.
    Padre Viader is attacked by an Indian resentful of the missions in California, but soon baptizes him "Marcello."

416 _____. "The Scarlet Serape That Caused an Indian Revolt." Tales Tolled by the Mission Bells. Los Angeles: Research Publishing Co., 1947, pp. 124-34.
    Manuel and his friends are eventually shot for their violent takeover of the mission.

417 _____. "Tavajo, the Indian Lad That Sailed to Spain." Tales Tolled by the Mission Bells. Los Angeles: Research Publishing Co., 1947, pp. 198-210.
    Tavajo is a Digger Indian who, distressed that the beloved Padre Peyri has been recalled to Spain, swims out to the ship and accompanies him to Spain.

418 Kittredge, William. "The Underground River." Atlantic Monthly, 227, No. 3 (Mar. 1971), 87-92.
    Cleve (Indian) remembers a recurring dream as he tries to decide upon funeral arrangements for his brother, Lonnie, who died the night before from what the coroner called "alcoholic poisoning." The sheriff becomes suspicious that the freshly-killed deer in the back room is illegal and attempts to investigate. Cleve kills him, then attempts to escape in the trunk of a friend's car. He is captured and killed--realizing that his dream of going down the river is now reality.

419 Kjelgaard, Jim. "The Fifth Friend." Buckskin Brigade. New York: Holiday House, 1947, pp. 214-42. Reprinted in Indians, Indians, Indians, ed. Phyllis R. Fenner (New York: Franklin Watts, 1950), pp. 252-78.
    John Colter, a fur trapper and trader, goes into hostile Blackfeet country to trap beaver. He is captured by the Blackfeet, but is given an opportunity to run for his life. He escapes by hiding in a beaver house.

420 _____. "Freight for Santa Fe." Buckskin Brigade. New York: Holiday House, 1947, pp. 244-80.
    Near the end of a wagon trip from Independence to Santa Fe, hostile Indians attack. They try to burn out the wagoneers, but the brave white men plow up a strip around the encircled wagons so that the fire cannot get to them. Finally the Indians give up and ride off.

421 _____. "The Medicine Bag." Buckskin Brigade. New
York: Holiday House, 1947, pp. 64-90.
In 1615 Father LeCaron goes up the Ottawa River to
bring Christianity to the Hurons, the Iroquois, and the Nipissings, because "these savages were unenlightened souls who
needed guidance." When he and his entourage are attacked by
Nipissings, half are killed outright and the others are taken
captive--to be tortured later by the Indian women. When the
Indians discover that Father LeCaron has brought them seeds
for planting crops, however, the Indians release the prisoners.

422 _____. "Savage Trek." Buckskin Brigade. New York:
Holiday House, 1947, pp. 92-124.
Two French fur traders set out with a small band of
Chippewa Indians in 1661 to explore potential new fur regions.
On the way they outwit a large war party of Hurons. Later
an escaped slave from the Hurons, a Cree Indian named Stemaw,
joins them and tells them of a huge inland sea to the north and
agrees to take them there. Arriving at the sea, they discover
the remains of Henry Hudson's old fort, and make tentative
plans for what is later to become the Hudson Bay Company.

423 _____. "The Tree." Buckskin Brigade. New York:
Holiday House, 1947, pp. 2-32.
Early Breton explorers are shipwrecked off Cape Breton
in 1506. They trade trinkets with the natives for valuable furs,
and are rescued by a fishing vessel from Normandy.

424 _____. "Wilderness Road." Buckskin Brigade. New York:
Holiday House, 1947, pp. 162-82. Reprinted in Indians,
Indians, Indians, ed. Phyllis R. Fenner (New York: Franklin Watts, 1950), pp. 15-34.
Crawling Cat, leading a band of fourteen Shawnee braves,
takes part in a massive Indian uprising in 1780 against white
settlers and soldiers at Fort Boonesborough, Kentucky. He
returns with only four braves still alive to find that his village
has been burned and most of his people are dead. He recognizes the inevitable, saying, "We will go to the west."

425 Knapp, Adeline. "The Overland Trail." Sunset, 14 (Apr.
1905), 565-70.
Mojaves attacking a wagon are frightened off when strange-
looking monsters appear in the American desert--domesticated
camels imported from the Middle East.

426 Knight, Eric. "My Navajo and the Bluebells of Yorkshire."
Story, 25, No. 108 (Jul./Aug. 1944), 2, 98-100.
A man reminisces about his early boyhood dreams in
Yorkshire, England. As he played there (in Middleton Woods)
he always wished to be an Indian, a Navajo. He remembers
how he grew up, came to America, and eventually went to the
Navajo reservation with his daughter. There he talked with
Santiago and Percy, two Navajos, who wanted little more than

that he bring them whiskey so that they might attract the best
women. The narrator later realizes that dreams are better
than reality simply because they are dreams.

427 Kosanke, Martha. "The Adventures of Snake Choke." Indian
Romances of the Western Frontier. New York: Exposition
Press, 1954, pp. 117-24.
     Young Chief Snake Choke is the son of Chief Shakum
Choke and Sea-sky-lea's sister. He saves a beautiful maiden
named Flag Lily from a big black turtle. He falls in love with
the girl, but a brave named Blue Pigeon also loves her. When
he sees Flag Lily with Blue Pigeon he is convinced that she
prefers Blue Pigeon over him, so he goes on a trip through
Blackfeet land. One day he saves an injured brave from a
huge snake and, discovering the brave to be Blue Pigeon, is
filled with jealousy. But Blue Pigeon has come to tell Snake
Choke that Flag Lily loves him and is sick because Snake
Choke has left. Snake Choke returns to Flag Lily.

428 _____. "The Babe in the Bark Basket." Indian Romances
of the Western Frontier. New York: Exposition Press,
1954, pp. 142-50.
     Barney Smith, known as "Honest Barney," is a good
white man who helps Indians with their fairs and races. He
has a son, Bill, who is married to Carlotta, a half-Indian.
One day, while leading in a canoe race, Bill spots something
afloat, leaves the race, and rescues the object--which turns
out to be a baby in a basket. The baby's Indian mother comes
forward and asks Bill and Carlotta to care for the baby. When
she dies a man named Larry Hawkins, a gambler, comes to
claim the baby as his. After an argument, it is decided that
Hawkins and the white man, Frank Williams, will play cards
to determine who should get the child. Hawkins cheats; Bill
and Carlotta take the baby.

429 _____. "The Big Round House." Indian Romances of the
Western Frontier. New York: Exposition Press, 1954,
pp. 199-205.
     As the years go by, more and more white settlers come
to Salishan territory. Some Indians worry, but Sea-sky-lea
trusts the white man to share with the Indian, taking only what
he needs from the land--as is the habit of the Indian. Sea-
sky-lea and all Indians have a sincere belief in the Great Spirit;
the chief recites a poem about the Great Spirit.

430 _____. "Blind Tom." Indian Romances of the Western
Frontier. New York: Exposition Press, 1954, pp. 50-58.
     A young blind Salishan man, Blind Tom, secretly loves
a kind maiden named Magola, who also secretly loves him.
One day he overhears Magola talking with a strong, rich brave,
Baldy, who tells Magola that he wants to marry her. When
Magola reveals her love for Blind Tom, Baldy points out that
the blind man cannot take care of her. Blind Tom, not want-

ing to stand in Magola's way, wanders off and goes to a white
man's camp. This white man brings Dr. Hanner to Blind Tom
and the doctor cures Tom's vision problem. Tom returns to
his people just in time to prevent Baldy from marrying Magola
--and he claims her as his own bride.

431 _____. "Buffalo Jack, the Lasso Man." Indian Romances
of the Western Frontier. New York: Exposition Press,
1954, pp. 172-79.
Buffalo Jack, a white man, befriends Chief Striped Horse
and his tribe. Chief Striped Horse tells Jack that a wildcat
has been sneaking into camp and taking away a brave each
night. Jack suspects foul play from Chief Spotted Tail; that
night Jack catches the "wildcat"--a Spotted Tail brave. They
go to the Spotted Tail camp to free all the kidnapped braves.
There they learn that the evil braves are attacking a wagon
train, but Jack and Chief Striped Horse go there and rescue
the only two (white) surviving children. Chief Striped Horse
decides to take care of them.

432 _____. "The Burning Bush." Indian Romances of the Western Frontier. New York: Exposition Press, 1954, pp.
110-16.
The Black Snake tribe attacks the Salishan people; however, a burning bush appears between the tribes and drives
the Black Snakes away. Father Chief Sea-sky-lea thanks the
Great Spirit. Soon a beautiful maiden, Princess Clonetta of
the Black Snake tribe, rides up to arrange peace between the
two peoples. A Salishan, High Buck, immediately falls in love
with her and she with him. Peace is made and, some time
later, High Buck asks to marry Princess Clonetta. After considerable discussion, the marriage is arranged.

433 _____. "Chain Lightning." Indian Romances of the Western
Frontier. New York: Exposition Press, 1954, pp. 59-68.
Camped in Arizona, Father Chief Sea-sky-lea of the Salishan tribe sees chain lightning in the sky and is afraid, believing it to be a bad omen. The chief calls his people together and they move to a new camp. Later three white men
ride into the new camp, telling the Indians that they have
avoided an earthquake.

434 _____. "The Crocodile." Indian Romances of the Western
Frontier. New York: Exposition Press, 1954, pp. 25-29.
Sea-sky-lea, a Salishan youth, goes with his tribe to the
Gulf of Mexico, where he makes friends with two white youths,
Richard Whitehead and Charlie Jones. While the three are
hunting crocodile, Charlie is badly hurt; he is saved by Sea-
sky-lea and Richard. As a matter of pride and friendship,
these two refuse money offered to them by Charlie's father.

435 _____. "Easter Lily and Red Oak." Indian Romances of
the Western Frontier. New York: Exposition Press, 1954,
pp. 100-08.

Red Oak, younger brother of Sea-sky-lea, sees a beautiful maiden in a canoe and falls in love with her. He learns that she is Easter Lily of the Crowfoot tribe, the daughter of the cruel Chief Black Crow. Although neither tribe will approve of their marriage, Easter Lily tries to join Red Oak's people; but Father Chief Sea-sky-lea sends her home. Red Oak later goes to the Crowfoot tribe, and Chief Black Crow threatens to torture him. When the chief's squaw begs her husband to show mercy, Chief Black Crow relents. The two chiefs smoke the peace pipe and arrange the marriage of Red Oak and Easter Lily.

436 _____. "Happy George, a Paleface." Indian Romances of the Western Frontier. New York: Exposition Press, 1954, pp. 157-63.
    A wounded white man stumbles into Salishan Sea-sky-lea's camp and falls unconscious. When the man recovers he cannot talk. Since he is agreeable and helpful around the camp, they call him Happy George. One day Happy George leaves the Indian camp and returns with a small, white, female baby. He cares for her and the Indians name her Fairy Queen. Some time later, a stranger comes into camp and recognizes Fairy Queen as his daughter. So that the kind Indians will not lose Fairy Queen, the man decides to make his home with the Indians.

437 _____. "Mariam." Indian Romances of the Western Frontier. New York: Exposition Press, 1954, pp. 164-71.
    Chief Black River and his son, Round Jack, live in Iowa with their people. Another member of the tribe is a good and kind (but plain) maiden named Mariam. Round Jack and Mariam are close friends. One day Chief Itasca and his many braves visit the camp. Among the group is a brave named Roulette, who falls in love with Mariam. This makes Round Jack realize that he, too, loves Mariam. One night the two braves save Mariam from a pack of wolves. After the incident, Mariam announces her love for Round Jack; Roulette goes away to forget her.

438 _____. "Mountain Pink." Indian Romances of the Western Frontier. New York: Exposition Press, 1954, pp. 187-98.
    Chief Black Horse and Chief Gray Eagle are chiefs of two Salishan bands. Chief Black Horse has a beautiful (but spoiled) daughter, Princess Ginny, who loves Chief Gray Eagle's son; however, Young Gray Eagle loves a maiden of his own tribe, Mountain Pink. Princess Ginny employs a deceitful scheme to secure a marriage to Gray Eagle. As a result, all are unhappy. One day Ginny's stallion throws her, crushing her to death. At last Gray Eagle and Mountain Pink can be together.

439 _____. "The Orphaned Twins." Indian Romances of the Western Frontier. New York: Exposition Press, 1954, pp. 17-24.

Princess Patika (older sister of Sea-sky-lea) of the Salishan tribe marries Harry, a white man. They have twins, Princess Patika and White Chief Harry. One day a roving Indian accidentally shoots young Harry, and later Patika dies to join him. After some years the wandering Indian turns himself in to receive his due punishment, but Christian principles prevail and he is forgiven and welcomed into the tribe.

440 _____. "The Phantom Ship." Indian Romances of the Western Frontier. New York: Exposition Press, 1954, pp. 133-40.

Cherry Red is a young brave who has had a sacred visionary experience about a White Ship, after which the White Ship becomes sacred to him. Cherry Red loves the maiden Thornapple, and is friendly with the strong brave Quick Shoot and his loved one, Tiger Lily. When the four youths are canoeing, a storm arises, almost causing Cherry Red and Thornapple to drown; but Quick Shoot saves Cherry Red, and he, in turn, calls upon his sacred White Ship to save Thornapple. Thereafter Cherry Red grows ill and delirious. Thornapple goes to his side. When Cherry Red weakens and dies, his White Ship comes for him.

441 _____. "Princess White Eagle." Indian Romances of the Western Frontier. New York: Exposition Press, 1954, pp. 85-90.

Two Indian tribes, the Crowfoot and the Gray Eagle, live close to one another. Chief Black Crow is an evil man, but his son (Young Chief Crowfoot) is good and kind. Young Chief Crowfoot loves Princess White Eagle, daughter of Chief White Eagle, but when his father objects to the match, the young man leaves his people and goes to live with the Gray Eagle tribe. Crowfoot warriors capture the young chief and the father burns his son at the stake; Princess White Eagle soon dies of grief. The two tribes eventually make peace.

442 _____. "The Redwood Tree." Indian Romances of the Western Frontier. New York: Exposition Press, 1954, pp. 91-99.

Whiteskin, son of White Chief Harry, loves the Indian maiden, Bluebell. During a tornado Bluebell is swept into Lake Sach, but Whiteskin saves her. One day Chief Red Blanket asks Whiteskin to lead some braves into battle against the Roanokes. During the battle Whiteskin is severely wounded and left for dead; however, Bluebell follows the Lighted Darts in the sky, finds Whiteskin, and saves his life. Whiteskin becomes a chief and marries Bluebell.

443 _____. "Rivera." Indian Romances of the Western Frontier. New York: Exposition Press, 1954, pp. 180-86.

Rivera is the beautiful granddaughter of the Salishan Chief Sea-sky-lea. One night at a dance, the Indians notice a white man watching the proceedings. Sea-sky-lea, worried that this man might do evil, orders that the intruder be tied to a stake and burned if he will not reveal the reasons for his being there. The white man is defiant; however, when a rainstorm quenches the flames, he is freed. This man, Samuel Simpson, approaches Sea-sky-lea, asks to join the Indian tribe and to marry Rivera, whom he loves. After wrestling with two strong braves and capturing a white stallion, he is permitted to do so.

444 _____. "Sea-sky-lea." Indian Romances of the Western Frontier. New York: Exposition Press, 1954, pp. 13-16.
Sea-sky-lea, a Salishan youth, is the son of a chief. He marries White Fawn. While he is off at battle proving his right to succeed his father as tribal head, White Fawn dies-- apparently giving birth to a daughter, also named White Fawn.

445 _____. "Sea-sky-lea Learns the Ways of the Frontiersmen." Indian Romances of the Western Frontier. New York: Exposition Press, 1954, pp. 69-77.
When the Salishan Sea-sky-lea is about eighteen, a rich white man named Harrison lives near the Indian camp; he is generous with the Indians and becomes friendly with Sea-sky-lea. The young Indian learns that three white men are plotting to rob "Chief" Harrison, so he warns his white friend. One robber, named Bill, is really not very devoted to the task and agrees to give up his plans and live in peace with the Indians; another thief, Black Jim, is chased away. Sea-sky-lea and Bill become good friends. Later they find out that Black Jim has been hanged.

446 _____. "The Spider Web." Indian Romances of the Western Frontier. New York: Exposition Press, 1954, pp. 41-49.
A young Salishan girl, Onetta, watches a spider spin a web and wants to do the same, so she gets colored threads from her mother and spins a most beautiful web. A white trader sees it and wants to buy it, but Onetta refuses. He returns when the camp is empty and takes the web, leaving money in its place. Hearing Onetta's screams, Yoko and Rebo come running. They catch the white man, and Father Chief Sea-sky-lea orders a lashing for him; however, Onetta saves him from this punishment, and the white trader apologizes for his actions.

447 _____. "The Striped Arrows Make Peace." Indian Romances of the Western Frontier. New York: Exposition Press, 1954, pp. 78-84.
Potika, the favorite granddaughter of Salishan Father Chief Sea-sky-lea, prefers activities of the braves to those of the squaws. She sees a bad omen indicating the approach of danger and tells her grandfather. Striped Arrow's evil tribe soon sets fire to the grasslands around the Salishan camp. The fire is extinguished and the two tribes battle; however, the fight ends when brave Potika, carrying a tomahawk, rides her

horse into the battle and knocks Chief Striped Arrow off his horse. The humiliated aggressors leave. At Potika's insistence the Salishan women heal the wounded Striped Arrow's men and send them home (except one in whom Potika has a special interest). Peace is made between the tribes.

448 _____. "The Surprise Attack." Indian Romances of the Western Frontier. New York: Exposition Press, 1954, pp. 125-32.

White Fern, a grandniece of Salishan Sea-sky-lea, warns the tribe of an attack--the Shawnees are coming. The battle is fierce, but soon a Light (the Great Spirit) appears in the sky and the Salishans win the battle. Among the wounded Shawnee braves is one called Sake, who is nursed back to health by White Fern. Sake then decides to remain with the Salishans and take the tribe's vows. One day he is captured by the Shawnees, but White Fern and some of Sea-sky-lea's braves follow and rescue Sake. Later Sake and White Fern are married.

449 _____. "Young Chief Great Oak." Indian Romances of the Western Frontier. New York: Exposition Press, 1954, pp. 151-56.

Three Salishan tribes have three chiefs: Chief White Feather (whose beautiful daughter is Princess White Wing), Chief Blue Feather (whose beautiful daughter is Princess Blue Wing and whose son is Brave of the Forest), and evil Chief Black Feather (whose good son is Young Black Feather). Princess White Wing and Brave of the Forest love each other and plan to marry. Young Black Feather loves Princess Blue Wing, but she cannot love one of an evil tribe. When Chief Black Feather learns of his son's love, he kidnaps Princess Blue Wing for the boy; but Young Black Feather returns the Princess to her tribe. Learning the true virtue of Young Black Feather, Princess Blue Wing falls in love with him. Later, after much trouble, Young Black Feather joins Chief Blue Feather's tribe and becomes Chief Great Oak.

450 _____. "Young Chief Lost in the Redwoods." Indian Romances of the Western Frontier. New York: Exposition Press, 1954, pp. 30-40.

At age ten, Sea-sky-lea, a Salishan youth, and his friends, Young Joe and Willow, get lost in the forest. A white man, Thomas Wilder, befriends them, giving them food and a place to sleep. The next day they go into the white settlement and meet Wilder's wife and beautiful little girl, Lily. Young Joe develops a youthful "crush" on her. On the way home the boys discover that the evil Shehang Indians are about to attack the white settlement, so Young Joe runs back to warn them. After several years Joe learns that Lily is very sick; he sends the tribal medicine mother, who heals the girl. A grateful Wilder gives gifts to Young Joe and others at the Indian camp.

451 Kroll, Francis L. "A Warrior's Work." Young Readers' Indian Stories. New York: Lantern Press, 1951, pp. 9-22.

Little Bear, a twelve-year-old Sioux, helps to rescue a
small Sioux hunting party from a much larger force of enemy
Pawnees by shooting flaming arrows into the dry grass around
the Pawnee camp.

452 LaFarge, C. Grant. "Sintamaskin: A Midwinter Fairyland."
Atlantic Monthly, 78, No. 466 (Aug. 1896), 180-87.
The story is narrated by one of two hunters near the
close of the caribou season. The narrator has nothing to show
for his effort; his partner, George, has one caribou. The narrator is fascinated by the name of Lake Sintamaskin, and he
insists upon going there. His two Abnaki guides, Pierre Joseph
and Peter, lead him to the lake; he and George find and kill
three caribou.

453 LaFarge, Oliver. "All the Young Men." All the Young Men.
Boston: Houghton Mifflin, 1935, pp. 31-43.
Old Singer (an old Navajo man) argues with Wesley, his
granddaughter's husband--a "school Indian" more white than
Navajo. The old man gets drunker and drunker at Wesley's
urging and finally leaves, only to be arrested by police. Old
Singer dies in jail.

454 _____. "Dangerous Man." All the Young Men. Boston:
Houghton Mifflin, 1935, pp. 127-33. Originally published
in Scribner's Magazine (1930).
Walter Mather, a white gold prospector, has been captured by Navajos. Badger Killer, eager to keep such men as
Mather away, boasts of being a dangerous man. As he escorts
Mather out of Navajo country he seizes the white man's six-
shooter and kills him. Badger goes back with his new gun and
new horse, hoping to win the hand of the girl he has been
courting.

455 _____. "The Happy Indian Laughter." A Pause in the Desert. Boston: Houghton Mifflin, 1936, pp. 175-92. Originally published in New Yorker.
A white girl has met an Indian when he was an airman
in the war, and now comes to visit him at his home on the
reservation. They plan to see if they love each other and if
she can bear to live like an Apache among his people. Their
relationship seems to be going well, but when he tells a humorous typical Indian story she becomes upset and decides she
must leave and never see him again.

456 _____. "Hard Winter." All the Young Men. Boston:
Houghton Mifflin, 1935, pp. 3-28. Originally published in
The Saturday Evening Post (Dec. 30, 1933).
Tall Walker, an Apache, is seduced by a white woman
who wants to know about Indians, and likes the idea of buying
one for her own amusement. He lives with her for a time,
goes to New York with her, but eventually has to return to care
for his sheep. His sheep die in a big storm. His son dies,

too. The white woman comes to buy him away from his wife,
but he finally asserts his Indianness and rejects her.

457   . "Higher Education." All the Young Men. Boston:
        Houghton Mifflin, 1935, pp. 81-110. Originally published
        in The Saturday Evening Post.
        At the age of ten, Wind Singer's daughter had been sent
away to school in California and now, six years later, she returns to her tribe--the Navajos. She is "kind of lost." Her
name is both Running Girl and Lucille (given her by whites).
She spurns Strong Hand, the Navajo boy, preferring the fancy
make-up and white man's fine clothes to those of the Navajo.
She has an affair with the only white man around, the trader
Show-Off, but when Show-Off refuses to marry her she jumps
off a cliff. The narrator, a Mr. Fayerweather, refuses to
lend Strong Hand a gun to kill Show-Off.

458   . "Little Stone Man." New Yorker, 36 (Jun. 25, 1960),
        32-38.
        Twenty-year-old Charlie Bond (white) has grown up near
San Leandro Pueblo where his father is a medical doctor. He
has been friendly for years with many of the Indians, including
Agapito Rael, the Turquoise Cacique. Agapito and some other
Indian men tell Charlie that a sacred figurine has been stolen
and asks for his help. When Charlie finds the figurine, the
Indians perform a ceremony to protect him from its power.
Charlie returns to college in the fall and, at a party, discusses
pueblo anthropomorphic figurines with a Dr. Sorenson. Back at
the pueblo the following June, Charlie is rebuffed by his old Indian friends because they think he had revealed their secrets.
Puzzled and hurt, he discovers in his mail a copy of an article
by Dr. Sorenson, naming Charlie as informant.

459   . "Love Charm." All the Young Men. Boston:
        Houghton Mifflin, 1935, pp. 137-50.
        Generous Man, a Jicarilla Apache, finds himself hope-
lessly in love with Conchita, a white (Spanish) woman. He gets
a powerful love charm from an old medicine man, one designed
to make Conchita fall in love with him. It seems to work, and
before long Conchita agrees to join Generous Man in the cottonwood grove at night. Torn between love and hatred for him,
Conchita stabs him in the shoulder with a knife; Generous Man
then shoots her with his rifle.

460   . "North is Black." All the Young Men. Boston:
        Houghton Mifflin, 1935, pp. 63-77. Originally published in
        The Dial (Jan. 1927).
        A young Navajo man falls in love with a white girl whom
he names Northern Maiden. She encourages him, hires him
as her guide, gives him a bracelet, and invites him to her
brother's place to hunt. While there, he discovers many things
about white people and their way of life; he also discovers that
Northern Maiden loves Charlie, a white man. The Indian returns home sadder but wiser.

461 _____. "Women at Yellow Wells." All the Young Men.
Boston: Houghton Mifflin, 1935, pp. 153-83.
During a heavy rainstorm Jane is stranded with two Navajo women. Her husband, with whom she runs the trading
post, is caught out on the other side of the flooded wash. A
young white couple seeks refuge at the post also, and later a
Navajo man with a newborn baby. This man asks Jane to return and cover up his dead wife because he (like most Navajos)
is afraid of dead bodies. Jane and the white couple do as he
asks.

462 _____. "The Young Warrior." Bar 5 Roundup of Best
Western Stories. Ed. Scott Meredith. New York: Dutton,
1956, pp. 124-30.
Apaches attack whites, killing first a young couple, then
two others who search for them, and then the remainder of the
now poorly-manned wagon train. (This is one of the very few
such stories told from the Apache point of view.)

463 Lafferty, R. A. "All Pieces of a River Shore." Orbit 8:
An Anthology of New Science Fiction Stories. Ed. Damon
Knight. New York: Putnam, 1970, pp. 69-85.
A rich Indian collector, Leo Nation, accumulates many
things, including long paintings of the Mississippi River shore.
These pictures are on reels and run for hundreds of yards.
He and his friend, Charlie Longbank, try to determine where
the pictures come from. Their answers frighten them, for
the ancient pictures appear to have come from another race
in another world.

464 _____. "Continued on Next Rock." Orbit 7: An Anthology
of New Science Fiction Stories. Ed. Damon Knight. New
York: Putnam, 1970, pp. 79-106.
A team of archaeologists is digging around an Indian
mound and a magical rock shaped like a chimney. Among them
is an undergraduate, Magdalen, who has the ability to see in-
visible things, including the ancient past and the distant future.
Also helping them is a mysterious man, Anteros Manypenny,
who claims to be an Indian and who has magic powers. The
dig produces an astonishing variety of Indian artifacts from a
variety of time periods--including the future. The chimney
rock falls, killing Magdalen (as she knew it would) and reveal-
ing an ancient statue of Anteros.

465 _____. "Narrow Valley." SF 12. Ed. Judith Merril.
New York: Delacorte, 1968, pp. 256-70.
In 1893 land allotments are made to the Pawnee Indians,
each one receiving 160 acres on which he will then have to pay
taxes. Clarence Big-Saddle selects a pleasant valley for his
allotment, but wants to avoid paying taxes on it. He prays to
the gods that his valley will remain green and lush, but that
it will appear as no more than a narrow ditch to outsiders.
Down through the years several whites consider buying the land

for the amount of unpaid taxes, but they always find only the
little gully, and so leave. There are further complications in
the 1960s when the Ramparts buy the land, but Clarence Little-
Saddle and his son (Clarence Bare-Back) repeat Clarence Big-
Saddle's earlier incantations, and the Ramparts are driven away.

466 L'Amour, Louis. "The Gift of Cochise." Bar 3 Roundup of
Best Western Stories. Ed. Scott Meredith. Freeport, N.Y.:
Books for Libraries Press, 1954, pp. 142-61.

Angie Lowe, her husband Ed, and their two children start
a little farm deep in Apache country. Ed goes to town, where
he takes part in an unfair gunfight involving Ches Lane; Ed is
killed, but in the process saves Ches's life. Ches heads out
to repay the debt by trying to find Angie in the wilderness; but
no one knows where she lives, or even if she is still alive.
She does live, though, because Cochise, respecting her bravery
and her ability to ward off attacks by his men, orders his warriors not to bother her. Later Cochise captures Ches Lane
(out on his search for Angie) but is so impressed with the man
that he decides against killing him, and instead delivers him to
Angie.

467 Lane, Carl. "River Dragon." Indians, Indians, Indians. Ed.
Phyllis R. Fenner. New York: Franklin Watts, 1950,
pp. 172-87. Originally published in River Dragon (Boston:
Little, Brown, 1948).

Eagle Feather, a Cheyenne youth, is astonished to see
the enormous horned, smoke-belching dragon coming up the
Missouri River. Ben Cutts, the steamboatman, tells him
about the boat and speaks of trading with the Cheyenne tribe.

468 LaPointe, Frank. (Sioux). "Millie's Gift." An American Indian Anthology. Ed. Benet Tvedten. Marvin, S.D.: Blue
Cloud Abbey, 1971, pp. 14-17.

Millie White Rabbit, an elderly Sioux grandmother, having
sold her allotment of 160 acres, comes in on a Greyhound bus
to live out her days with her son, a struggling farmer. When
her grandson goes off to college, she gives him her last one
hundred dollar bill. She does not live long enough to see him
graduate, "but she would live on in his memory as long as he
lived."

469 Larsen, Eric. "Feast." South Dakota Review, 9, No. 3
(Autumn 1971), 82-92.

Christine Cutter, a white sixth-grade teacher, arranges
to have a group of Eskimos visit the class so that her students
can learn something about their culture. On the appointed day
no one shows up until the last minute, and then it is one lone
woman. Miss Cutter has the Eskimo sit on a chair and open
her mouth to display teeth worn smooth from chewing skins;
the children file past and take one quick look before going
home for the day.

470 Larsen, Marie. "Fiddlin' Joe." Young Readers' Indian Stories. New York: Lantern Press, 1951, pp. 145-58.
Joe and Milda are alone in a cabin one night when a band
of hostile Indians prepares to attack. Joe plays his fiddle and
calms, or perhaps enraptures, the Indians. They come up
close to listen, then quietly slip away into the forest.

471 Lawrence, D. H. "None of That." The Woman Who Ran
Away and Other Stories. New York: Knopf, 1928, pp.
283-307.
A Mexican/Indian bullfighter, Cuesta, is taken in tow by
Ethel, a wealthy American woman. She is fascinated by him;
he is slightly contemptuous of her but nevertheless fascinated,
too. They are brought together by the narrator. She commits suicide, and leaves Cuesta a half million dollars.

472 Lawrence, Lars. "The Hungry Ones." Arizona Quarterly,
12, No. 3 (Autumn 1954), 211-16.
Ben Joe Nezzy (an old Navajo) with his wife, daughter,
and grandchildren, on their way to Reata to buy and sell goods,
are stopped by the State Police. The Belicanos tell them they
cannot go into town that day. That evening Joe relates a story
about Nayenezgani (He-who-destroys-alien-gods) to his grandchildren. He reflects upon and speaks to his wife about the
ways of the whites as opposed to the more fulfilling ways of
Navajo life. He falls asleep with the thought that he will build
a hogan as far away from the whites as possible.

473 _____. "Ukehe, Hago-oneh." Arizona Quarterly, 15, No. 4
(Winter 1959), 341-48.
Frank and Ham (white men), stranded in the desert by
some "bad whites" in Reata, meet Nez Bigay (son of Ben Joe
Nezzy), who invites them into his hogan to rest and eat. They
learn that Ben and Nez think they must be very good white men
to have received such poor treatment from other whites. The
next morning Nez offers to aid the two men. Frank leaves the
hogan overwhelmed with gratitude and good feelings for these
people.

474 Leahy, Jack Thomas. "Hanging Hair." Kenyon Review, 23
(1961), 671-86.
An Indian trader, living in an Indian village on the Pacific coast, goes on a drunken spree down along the ocean.
Hanging Hair, who the Indians think is a "spirit" of some sort,
comes along and helps the trader, then begins beating and
chasing the waves. She chases one wave way out. It comes
back as a tremendous tidal wave and flattens the Indian village.

475 _____. "The Marriage of Jack Clam." Prism, 3 No. 1
(Fall 1961), 35-41.
While Sally Smashrocks is digging for clams, Jack Clams
runs up to her and demands that she fix his supper. She ignores him. Jack approaches Lupin Tobin and explains his sit-

uation: Jack and Sally had lived together for many years; she has just found out that she is pregnant, and refuses to take care of him until he marries her. Lupin, who owns all the businesses on the reservation, does not have the authority to furnish marriage licenses but sells Jack a Raleigh Coupon for five dollars and tells him that a preacher will be coming the following week to perform the ceremony. Some members of the Queen's Black Guard are vacationing on the reservation, so Lupin enlists the aid of a drunken Black Guard to pose as a preacher. Sally and Jack, at least, are satisfied that they have been married.

476 Leather, Fitzherbert. "Kooswap: A Tale of Red and White Civilization." Outing, 38, No. 1 (Apr. 1901), 40-45.
A Nez Percé named Kooswap is gambling and drinking heavily in the rough gold-seekers' town of Shando. Having lost his money at gambling, he rides his favorite horse through glass doors of the gambling parlor, then heads back toward the reservation with the sheriff and the Indian agent close behind. In the dark, Kooswap's dying horse stumbles down a steep hill, falling to rest in a thicket, where Kooswap promptly goes to sleep. The sheriff and his men assume that Kooswap is dead.

477 _____. "Moosuk: A White and Red Christmas of the De-batable Ground." Outing, 45, No. 3 (Dec. 1904), 273-81.
Moosuk discovers a bear in a white man's trap, kills it, and takes its skin. When the "voyageur," Jules Perrin, dis-covers the theft, he finds and robs Moosuk of all his beaver traps. Unhappy at the reprisal, Moosuk follows Jules to Fort Okinakane, intending to kill him and take all his furs. When Moosuk realizes that Jules is snowblind, he leads him to the fort.

478 Lewis, Edward. (Pima). "A Cowboy's Last Ride." Arrows Four: Prose and Poetry by Young American Indians. Ed. T. D. Allen. New York: Pocket Books, 1974, pp. 149-51.
In his first day on the professional rodeo circuit, a young cowboy does well on his first two "go-'rounds" in the saddle bronc event. In his third go-'round he draws a mean roan named Dead End. The cowboy dies after Dead End crashes into the fence.

479 Lighton, William R. "Big-Governor-Afraid." Atlantic Monthly, 88, No. 527 (Sep. 1901), 409-18.
Big-Governor-Afraid is a naive Easterner who is governor of the Nebraska Territory. His eloquent talk about being kind to the Pawnees and Sioux amuses the Nebraska settlers, who know that the only way to treat Indians is to exterminate them. The settlers play several tricks on Big-Governor-Afraid in order to show him what Indians are really like.

480 _____. "Billy Fortune and the Rainbow's End." Sunset, 31 (Nov. 1913), 964-77.

Some white adventurers mix up a washtub full of "fire-water" and sell it to the Sioux, eventually cleaning out all the money on the reservation.

481 Lincoln, Victoria. "A Necklace for a Saint." Desert Water:
Seven Stories. Boston: Little, Brown, 1954, pp. 5-71.
Charlie Tissthalnos, a ten-year-old Indian orphan, is raised by his Apache grandmother. (Charlie's father had been her son; his mother had been a Pueblo girl.) When the grandmother dies Charlie is taken to the Santa Maria Pueblo to live with his Pueblo aunt and uncle. There he attends school and learns about the Catholic Church. Torn between three cultures --Apache, Pueblo, and white--Charlie has a difficult time. At the end it appears that he will go the white man's road, because he heads for Washington where his uncle has a job with the Department of the Interior.

482 Lindsay, Batterman. "Abandoned: A Tale of the Plains."
Atlantic Monthly, 78, No. 468 (Oct. 1896), 538-42.
Kobeh, an old man decrepit with rheumatism, and his younger but blind wife, Sinkavata, are outcasts of the Ishmaelitish group. They move from the reservation to the open plains, where they settle in the brush outside a white rancher's home and survive by receiving scraps of food in exchange for doing odd jobs. When the rancher and his wife must leave for a few days to take their cattle to market, Kobeh and Sinkavata realize they too must move on. They do not get very far, however, because Kobeh catches pneumonia and later dies of heart failure. After performing her dutiful wailing, Sinkavata weights herself down with stones and drowns herself in the river.

483 _____. "Kwelth-Elite, the Proud Slave." Overland Monthly,
n. s. 33 (1899), 534-39.
Some Indians go by canoe to the Snoqualmie Falls Hop Ranch to earn money "hop-picking." Among them is a striking young Indian woman named Kwelth-Elite (which means "proud slave"). She belongs to an old woman, T-semakeine, whose dwarf grandson, Okinakeine, is enamored of the slave girl. Kwelth-Elite hates the dwarf, who unceasingly makes her life miserable, so she obtains a magical ritual from a powerful shaman to get rid of her tormenter. Okinakeine dies and Kwelth-Elite eventually marries a half-breed rancher on the Puyallup Reservation.

484 Link, Virgil Curtis. (Apache/Navajo). "Remember Yesterday."
Sun Tracks, 1, No. 2 (Fall 1971), 7-15.
Benny, an Indian college student, goes to visit his grandmother on her deathbed at a white nursing home. She is unhappy because the old Indian way is gone and all her sons have taken the new way instead--in their education, in their church, and in their willingness to put her in a nursing home.

485 _____. (Apache/Navajo). "The Turquoise Beads." South

Dakota Review, 7, No. 2 (Summer 1969), 126-29. Reprinted in The American Indian Speaks, ed. John R. Milton (Vermillion, S.D.: Dakota Press, 1969), pp. 126-29.

Cyrus, a young Apache, talks with his old grandmother who is weaving baskets. He asks why it only rains on the Apache Mountains and not in their valley. She answers that it is because the gods deserted the valley when the whites took over. Suddenly, as rains fall on the mountains, an excited Cyrus sees a double rainbow. His grandmother tells the boy how those with good hearts may find turquoise beads at the feet of rainbows.

486 Little, Joseph. (Mescalero Apache). "Whispers from a Dead World." The Man to Send Rain Clouds: Contemporary Stories by American Indians. Ed. Kenneth Rosen. New York: Viking, 1974, pp. 27-31.

Walter, out looking for his wife, gets drunk at the tribal bar. He hears that she is at his brother's house, and goes there. The brother hits him. Walter then goes to the cliff and, imitating an eagle, apparently leaps to his death.

487 Lockwood, John A. "The Paymaster's Escort." Overland Monthly, n.s. 33 (1899), 109-11.

A mysterious early morning visit to Lieutenant Smith by Minola, a young Indian maiden, is the gossip of Fort Carlin, Wyoming. Actually she has come to warn him of an attack to steal gold he will be transporting to the Indian agency later the same day. Smith successfully defends against the planned theft.

488 London, Jack. "The Faith of Men." Sunset, Jun. 1903, 114-21.

Because of an inaccurate wedding announcement in a newspaper, Lawrence Pentfield believes his girlfriend back home has married his friend. He hastens out to marry Lashka, an Indian girl, in a kind of misdirected revenge.

489 _____. "The God of His Fathers." The God of His Fathers and Other Stories. New York: McClure, Phillips, 1901, pp. 1-33.

Baptiste is a half-breed, part-English and part-Indian. Because of several unhappy and unfortunate experiences with missionaries (who refuse to perform a marriage ceremony for him and his white sweetheart, and who protect the white man who murdered his daughter) Baptiste vows to keep all missionaries away from his people. When he becomes chief of his tribe (in Canada) he forces a missionary to forsake his God or die. The cowardly missionary forsakes God.

490 _____. "Keesh, the Son of Keesh." Children of the Frost. New York: Regents Press, 1902, pp. 163-80.

A white missionary converts Keesh, convincing him that killing is evil. Later, when Keesh wants to marry a neighboring chief's daughter, she and her family reject him because he is afraid to kill. Conflict seethes within Keesh, and he finally does what she asks. To prove his bravery, he brings her four heads, as a token of his not being afraid to kill. They are heads of her father, her two brothers, and her new lover. At the end she also bares her neck for his knife.

491 _____. "The League of the Old Men." Children of the Frost. New York: Macmillan, 1902, pp. 233-61.
An old Indian (Imbere) turns up in Dawson one day and surrenders himself to the white man's law, confessing to having murdered "scores" of white men. Then he tells a story of how he did so (with the help of several of the old men of his Whitefish tribe) in an unsuccessful effort to stem the flow of whites.

492 _____. "Lost Face." The Best Short Stories of Jack London. Garden City, N.Y.: Garden City Books, 1953, pp. 59-70.
A Polish patriot (Subienkow) and some associates, after years of cheating the Nulato Indians (in Canada) of their furs, are captured and held for torture in what appears to be just retribution for similar tortures the Indians had earlier suffered at the hands of the whites. Subienkow is scheduled to die last. Sure that he cannot possibly escape, and desperate to avoid the torture, he devises a plan to receive a quick death. He cons the Indian chief (Makamuk) into believing that he can make a special medicine which, when applied to his body, will prevent physical harm. Subienkow bargains to exchange his life for the secret potion. When the chief renders the first of three planned ax-blows to the white man's medicine-covered neck, Subienkow's plan succeeds and he is beheaded. Makamuk loses face before all his people.

493 _____. "The Son of the Wolf." Overland Monthly, n. s. 33 (1899), 335-43. Reprinted in The Son of the Wolf: Tales of the Far North (Boston: Houghton Mifflin, Riverside, 1900), and in Atlantic Monthly.
Scruff Mackenzie, a tough white man, decides that he wants to marry the chief's daughter, Zarinska, whom he will then name Gertrude. To do so he has to outwit and outfight the Indian men, including a shaman, and so proclaim the superiority of the white over the Indian. Mackenzie wins the fight and Zarinska.

494 _____. "Where the Trail Forks." Outing, 37, No. 3 (Dec. 1900), 276-82.
Hitchcock, Hawes, Welse, and Sigmund pan for gold in Alaska. One day Sipu, a Chinook Indian girl, comes into camp to say goodbye to Hitchcock, her friend. She announces that she, the chief's daughter, has been chosen as a human sacrifice so that the poor hunting will improve. The witch doctor comes to the gold-seekers' camp and takes Sipu away. Hitchcock wants to save the girl, but the others argue against his

plan; so he collects his gear and helps Sipu to escape. The next day, the three other men are murdered and the camp is looted.

495 _____. "The White Silence." The Son of Wolf: Tales of the Far North. Boston: Houghton Mifflin, 1900, pp. 1-20.
This is the story of Mason, his Indian wife Ruth, and Malemute Kid: Ruth is attracted to Mason in part because he is "the first man whom she had known to treat a woman as something better than a mere animal or beast of burden." Mason is killed by a falling tree.

496 _____. "The Wife of a King." Overland Monthly, n. s. 34 (1899), 112-19.
Cal Galbraith, while recovering at a northern mission, meets Madeline (formerly Chook-ra), a half-breed Siwash Indian. With Madeline as his wife, Cal goes north and eventually strikes a rich gold claim near Circle City. After a number of happy years, Cal grows restless, goes south, and becomes involved with Freda, the "Greek dancer." Meanwhile, Madeline travels north to Malemute Kid's cabin, where she stays for some time learning about dress, dance, etc. The Kid takes a more refined Madeline--under the guise of a "Russian Princess"--to Cal. He immediately becomes infatuated with the "Russian Princess." Then, recognizing Madeline, Cal tries to woo her back.

497 _____. "The Wisdom of the Trail." Overland Monthly, n. s. 34 (1899), 541-44.
Sitka Charley, an Indian knowledgeable about both white and Indian ways, leads a small expedition to the Yukon. The trek is painful and cold, and the party is almost out of food. Captain and Mrs. Effingwell, Joe, Kah-Chucte and Gowhee (two Siwash Indians), are all exhausted and near starvation. Sitka Charley shoots Kah-Chucte and Gowhee when they feebly attempt to run away with a few remaining supplies. A moment later, the survivors hear rifles of the "Men of the Yukon."

498 _____. "The Wit of Porportuk." Sunset, 24 (Feb. 1910), 159-72.
El-Soo, the lovely full-blooded daughter of a Yukon Indian chief, has spent a number of years in the care of missionaries before returning to her father, who is near death. He has incurred large debts to Porportuk, an old Indian capitalist. To pay them off, El-Soo auctions herself off to the highest bidder; Porportuk is the purchaser, paying well over twenty thousand dollars. Then she runs off with a younger Indian lover, but the old man catches up with his "property." After giving El-Soo to her lover, he shoots her ankles so she can never run--or walk--again.

499 Loomis, Noel M. "Grandfather Out of the Past." Spurs West. Ed. S. Omar Barker. Garden City, N. Y.: Doubleday, 1960, pp. 215-45.

Tuchubarua is a 126-year-old Comanche who is still able
to make arrows but who, otherwise, has become mostly a beg-
gar in his tribe. He gets involved in the marriage arrange-
ments of his great-great-granddaughter. She is courted by
Black Antelope, who loves her, and also by Quahuahacante, an
evil man who wants her for his fifth wife and who claims to
have taken her virginity. Tuchubarua reveals the truth about
Quahuahacante--that as a youth he had committed incest with
his sister. Incest is one of the most serious crimes among
the Comanches so, now that his secret has been revealed, Quahuahacante commits suicide.

500 _____. "The Twilighters." Bar 3 Roundup of Best Western
    Stories. Ed. Scott Meredith. Freeport, N.Y.: Books for
    Libraries Press, 1954, pp. 184-251.
        Claydon brings a message to Krudenier about a rich wagon
    train scheduled to pass through Krudenier's territory. Kruden-
    ier makes plans for an attack on the train, in which he will
    use the services of ten Choctaws, as well as assorted other
    disreputable folk. Krudenier has two Indian friends, Gomez,
    a part-Apache lieutenant, and Nikaakibuno, an Osage woman he
    has bought from Comanches for five horses, and who parades
    around his cabin entirely nude and who satisfies his wants.
    Claydon lusts after Nikaakibuno, and finally defeats Krudenier
    to win the prize temporarily. Gomez, however, who also lusts
    after the woman, defeats Claydon, feeds him to an alligator,
    and himself claims the nude beauty.

501 Loughead, Flora Haines. "In the Shadow of the Live-Oak."
    Overland Monthly, n.s. 34 (1899), 14-19.
        Richard Davenport and his wife (Mary) live in an isolated
    cabin in the Sierra Madre Mountains. One day Richard goes
    into town for supplies, leaving Mary alone at the cabin. In
    town he learns that a half-breed, José Gomez, is on the loose
    after having massacred an entire family. Richard rushes home
    to protect his wife and arrives in time to shoot José who is
    just outside the cabin.

502 Luce, Grace. "The Passing of Tomas." Overland Monthly,
    n.s. 34 (1899), 444-47.
        Tomas, a seventy-year-old Indian, and his ancient wife
    (Anita) live with their dogs in a shanty near a graveyard. One
    day Tomas finds a silver whiskey flask from which he drinks.
    He passes out and is later awakened by a white man accusing
    him of theft. He is taken to jail and Anita follows him to
    await his release. The next morning he finds his wife dead
    outside the jail; he stumbles home, sits on a grave, and dies.

503 Lucero, Margaret. (Santo Domingo Pueblo). "A Necklace for
    Jason." Arrows Four: Prose and Poetry by Young Amer-
    ican Indians. Ed. T. D. Allen. New York: Pocket Books,
    1974, pp. 43-46.
        Egged on by Aunt Netty, who says that the drunken youth
    Jason is not man enough to shoot himself, he grabs a rifle and

puts a bullet through his neck. When Jason returns from the hospital two months later, the narrator puts a bead necklace she has made around his neck.

504   Lucey, James D. "Hell at Helio Three." With Guidons Flying: Tales of the U. S. Cavalry in the Old West. Garden City, N. Y.: Doubleday, 1970, pp. 113-28. Originally published in Giant Western (1951).
Lieutenant O'Neil is assigned to take charge of a heliograph station in Arizona. He is expected to reestablish discipline among the demoralized soldiers at the station and also to deal with the hostile Apaches in the area. O'Neil accomplishes both these objectives. He avoids an attack by the Apaches by convincing them that the heliograph has magical powers. The soldiers are impressed with his cleverness.

505   Ludlum, Evelyn Mosse. "A Little Indian Nursemaid." Out West, 27, No. 1 (Jul. 1907), 70-73.
Felicity, a thirteen-year-old Indian girl, becomes a nursemaid for Tomsy, the young son of a rancher and his wife. They believe she is lazy, but keep her because the youngster seems attached to the girl. Felicity proves her worth by saving Tomsy from a wildcat.

506   Lummis, Charles F. "The Comanche's Revenge." A New Mexico David and Other Stories and Sketches of the Southwest. New York: Scribner's, 1920, pp. 94-100.
The Spanish inhabitants of Tomé in New Mexico are afraid of the Comanches, but one of them promises a marriage between his daughter, Maria, and the Comanche chief's son. Years later, when the children are grown and the time comes for the wedding, the girl's father hides her and tells the Comanches she has died of the smallpox. Eventually the Comanches find out about the lie, enter and massacre a church full of people, and carry off Maria and others. The chief's son gets the girl in the end.

507   _____. "The Enchanted Burro." The Enchanted Burro and Other Stories as I Have Known Them from Maine to Chile and California. Chicago: A. C. McClurg, 1912.
A Comanche dresses as a burro, murders his enemies, and scalps them. He is finally discovered when Lelo, a New Mexico Isleta Pueblo man, shoots the burro and kills the Indian inside.

508   _____. "A New Mexico David." A New Mexico David and Other Stories and Sketches of the Southwest. New York: Scribner's, 1920, pp. 1-11.
Lucario, the last survivor of many Indian raids on his family, is determined to get even or die. In a massive attack that New Mexicans make on a large troop of Utes, a seven-foot Ute Indian offers to settle the score in single battle with any one from the opposing side. Lucario (short of stature and

seated on a small horse) volunteers, and throws his knife right
between the eyes of the charging Ute who attempts to use an
unfairly acquired lance.

509 _____. "Poh-hlaik, the Cave-Boy." The King of the Bron-
cos and Other Stories of New Mexico. New York: Scribner's, 1897, pp. 75-94.
    While out hunting wild turkeys, Poh-hlaik and his young
friend, Kah-be, accidentally discover that one of their tribesmen, Enque-Enque, has betrayed their Pueblo tribe to the
hated Navajos. The ambush takes place, but the wounded Poh-
hlaik becomes a hero by killing the traitor.

510 McCord, Jean. "Bitter Is the Hawk's Path." Bitter Is the
Hawk's Path. New York: Atheneum, 1971, pp. 131-49.
    Sam Joe Falcon and Billy Joe Reed are high school
friends. Sam Joe, an Indian, is strong and tall and poor.
Billy Joe is small and afraid, but has plenty of money. One
day, jealous of Sam Joe's superior knowledge of French, Billy
Joe steals some money from him. After this, their friendship
is spoiled.

511 McLennan, William. "P't'i Barouette." Harper's, 85 (Jun.
1892), 71-75.
    Some French explorers are in the North, and one of them
(Phinee) begins to tell a story: One night their dog started
barking at something outside. It turned out to be an Indian
youth carrying a rifle. They took the taciturn boy in from
the harsh cold night. He was a Windego, and they nicknamed
him P't'i Barouette. The boy was very distrustful of his hosts,
and as a result he slept restlessly. The next day they headed
for the Great River, but the cold sent them back to the cabin.
On the way they learned that the young man was the son of de
Canard Noir, apparently an Indian chief. Later the two Indians
(father and son) go hunting, and in the woods P't'i Barouette
kills de Canard Noir.

512 McMurry, James. "The Children of Kinderhook." The Catskill Witch and Other Tales of the Hudson Valley. Syracuse,
N.Y.: Syracuse Univ. Press, 1974, pp. 129-43.
    The early Dutch settlers of Kinderhook, New York, be-
come acquainted with a neighboring group of Indians. These
Indians are friendly and happy, and their life is simple and
joyful. The settlers marvel at this beautiful way of life, but
they realize it is their duty to teach the Indians about Christianity and about the white man's superior, civilized ways.
The Indians politely reject this "progress." The Dutch minister finally gives up and asks the Indians to leave the area
so that there will be no more contact between the Dutch and
the Indians, whose presence would surely corrupt the Chris-
tians. The Indians understand and are never seen again.

513 _____. "Pokepsie." The Catskill Witch and Other Tales

of the Hudson Valley. Syracuse, N.Y.: Syracuse Univ.
Press, 1974, pp. 19-24.
A Pequot Indian family discovers a spirit in the forest
who plays magic music on his flute. His music has the power
to help any person who can hear it. One night when a Pequot
man and his wife are trying to escape from pursuing Huron enemies, the flute music gives them the strength to swim across
the river to "a safe, pleasant harbor" on the other side. This
spot is still called Poughkeepsie, which means "a safe, pleasant harbor. "

514 _____. "The Saranac Wizard." The Catskill Witch and
Other Tales of the Hudson Valley. Syracuse, N.Y.: Syracuse Univ. Press, 1974, pp. 41-49.
An evil spirit (wizard) takes the shape of a Saranac Indian. He is jealous of two brothers, Wolf and Eagle, who are
strong and brave and are loved by all the tribe. Wizard tries
several times to sow discord between the brothers. Finally
he succeeds and the tribe is divided. They stop warring against
each other, however, when the Wizard's wicked plan is exposed,
and they imprison the Wizard in a hollow tree.

515 McNichols, Charles L. "The Buck in the Brush." Harper's,
189, No. 1130 (Jul. 1944), 126-28.
Miss Daisybelle Stacey is an idealistic young missionary
woman who tries to bring the "Word" to the Indians of southern
California. One day, while bathing in the river, she is swept
away by the current and is rescued by Yammum, an Indian
"buck" who had been cutting brush near the river bank and who
had heard her calls for help. Later Yammum claims, as his
rightful reward for saving her life, the right to sleep with
Miss Daisybelle; but she decides that this kind of missionary
work is not for her, and she quickly heads back to Los Angeles
with her well-worn copy of Longfellow's Hiawatha.

516 MacQuigg, Gertrude E. "The Lure of the Hills." Out West,
27, No. 5 (Nov. 1907), 463-68.
A young Indian, Manuel, repairs a roof while a pretty
white woman, Triste, repairs a bundle. The two get caught
up in a rabbit chase with some Indian youths, and, out on the
desert, Triste meets and talks with a white horseman, Trevo
Spaulding. Triste rides away and Trevo is thrown from his
horse as he tries to follow her. She later returns, discovers
the injured man, and they declare their love for each other.

517 Madden, David. "Love Makes Nothing Happen." Southwest
Review, 53, No. 3 (Summer 1968), 266-75.
Belle, an acculturated Eskimo, lives close to a military
station near Anchorage with her nine-year-old son, Jimmy (il-
legitimate, by a military man who left Belle) and her lover,
Walt (also a military man). Jimmy is a sensitive boy who
has had difficulties growing up (prejudice, rejection, etc.), but
he has a half-wolf dog named Mike whom he dearly loves.

Their neighbor constantly complains that the dog should be tied up. One afternoon while Jimmy is gone, the neighbor's baby toddles outside. Mike attacks the baby and is subsequently shot.

518 Mahon, John E. "Van Lennep's Cowardice: An Incident of a Frontier Army Post." Overland Monthly, n. s. 27 (1896), 17-21.
Richard Wainwright is fresh from West Point at Fort Yankton with Troop D of the Twelfth Cavalry. He asks Lieutenant Beardsly why Major Van Lennep is shunned by the soldiers, and Beardsly replies that Van Lennep had once exhibited cowardly behavior in an attack on a Cheyenne camp. Later, Van Lennep explains to Wainwright that he had been fearful not for his own life, but for his family, because paying off a brother's debt had left him financially insecure. Van Lennep soon gets a chance to prove that he is not really a coward during a Geronimo-led Apache attack on the fort.

519 Maloy, Lois. "Swift Thunder of the Prairie." Indians, Indians, Indians. Ed. Phyllis R. Fenner. New York: Franklin Watts, 1950, pp. 103-18. Originally published in Swift Thunder of the Prairie (New York: Scribner's, 1942).
Little Star-Brother races "Swift Thunder" every day on his pony, but the railroad train always wins. During a time of hunger, Star-Brother's tribe cannot find buffalo because the animals have been frightened away by the train. Red Arrow tries to wreck "Swift Thunder" by placing a big boulder on the track, but Star-Brother races ahead to stop the train. Mr. Pennypacker (the Indian agent) talks to the chief, convincing him that the Indians must learn to accept the ways of the white man.

520 Manfred, Frederick. "Blood Will Tell." Apples of Paradise and Other Stories. New York: Trident, 1967, pp. 141-58.
Dawn is a lovely half-Sioux, half-white girl who lives in the village of Wodan with Ira Barber (whose ancestry nobody quite knows). Ira beats Dawn and is jealous of her because he thinks she likes Doc Chalmers. Ira breaks Dawn's leg before he goes on a trip to sell some furs; when he returns a month later, he is feverish with a rattlesnake bite. The doctor attends Ira, just as he had nursed Dawn while Ira was gone. When his health improves, Ira seems changed. In St. Louis he had found out that his own mother was half-black and half-Sioux. Ira won't be a wife-beater any more, and will consent to marry Dawn.

521 Marriott, Alice L. "Allotments." The Ten Grandmothers. Norman, Okla.: Univ. of Oklahoma Press, 1945, pp. 216-21.
In 1900 Hunting Horse, Spear Woman, and Bow Woman (all Kiowa) are attracted to the "Jesus road" of the Christian missionaries because the missionaries preach beliefs the Kiowas have always espoused anyhow: do good, help each other, be

generous, be peaceful. But the missionaries tell Hunting
Horse that he can have only one wife. At this same time the
government is allotting the land. Spear Woman solves the marriage problem by saying that she will live alone on one allotment, so Bow Woman and Hunting Horse can live married on
the next one.

522 _____. "Back to the Blanket." The Ten Grandmothers.
Norman, Okla.: Univ. of Oklahoma Press, 1945, pp. 238-50.
In 1929 Leah returns to the Kiowa reservation from school in
Pennsylvania. She finds that she has to face new problems:
how to eat food and water she has been taught are probably full
of germs; how to get along with her sister who did not go away
to school; how to handle the missionaries who do not want her
to visit her family or wear "Indian clothes"; how to help her
people if she is no longer one of them.

523 _____. "The Bear." The Ten Grandmothers. Norman,
Okla.: Univ. of Oklahoma Press, 1945, pp. 3-14.
In 1847 Kiowas and Comanches join forces for a raid on
the Utes--to take women captives and to get revenge for the
death of one of their men. The raid, however, is not successful, and the Utes drive them off.

524 _____. "Breaking Camp." The Ten Grandmothers. Norman, Okla.: Univ. of Oklahoma Press, 1945, pp. 251-57.
In 1930 Eagle Plume, now old and growing blind, moves
with the sacred Kiowa "Grandmother bundle" to live with his
niece. The bundle is put into a special tipi.

525 _____. "Buffalo Grass." The Ten Grandmothers. Norman, Okla.: Univ. of Oklahoma Press, 1945, pp. 285-89.
Spear Woman (Kiowa), now very old in 1944, is taken by
her granddaughter, Leah, to visit the buffalo park. She sees
the buffalo but realizes that they, like her own grandchildren,
were born inside the fence, and so cannot really know what it
was like to roam free over the country.

526 _____. "Dangerous Man." The Ten Grandmothers. Norman, Okla.: Univ. of Oklahoma Press, 1945, pp. 173-87.
In 1883 the Kiowa Snapping Turtle tells Prickly Pear that
he is going to use his power to kill him when the sun's rays
reach him the next morning. Prickly Pear prepares for death.
Even though he is a Christian, he is sure that Snapping Turtle
has the power to kill him. The missionary sisters tell Prickly
Pear to have faith in Jesus, and that they will pray for him.
The next morning Prickly Pear is still alive; Snapping Turtle
dies, choking on peyote.

527 _____. "Favorite Son." The Ten Grandmothers. Norman,
Okla.: Univ. of Oklahoma Press, 1945, pp. 101-11.
In 1870 Young Sitting Bear, the favorite son of the Kiowa
chief Sitting Bear, goes on a raid against the whites. He is

killed. When word comes back Sitting Bear mourns deeply, then goes out to find the body of his son and brings it back to camp. He announces that he will give his "Grandmother bundle," and its power, to Eagle Plume, his oldest son.

528 _____. "First Fight." The Ten Grandmothers. Norman, Okla.: Univ. of Oklahoma Press, 1945, pp. 31-40.
In 1862 the Kiowas go on a raid against white men, stealing their horses. Young Hunting Horse helps chase the horses from the barn, then kills a white man with a stone club.

529 _____. "The First Tipi." The Ten Grandmothers. Norman, Okla.: Univ. of Oklahoma Press, 1945, pp. 64-71.
In the winter of 1865 Spear Girl (Kiowa), with the help of her friends, makes her own tipi, so that she and her husband can move out of her mother's tipi.

530 _____. "The Give-away." The Ten Grandmothers. Norman, Okla.: Univ. of Oklahoma Press, 1945, pp. 77-83.
In 1869 the Kiowa warrior Stone in the Pool is killed on a raid in Ute country. His two wives, at the next Sun Dance, are given away by their brother to new husbands. One of them is pleased; the other runs away and picks her own man.

531 _____. "Going Away." The Ten Grandmothers. Norman, Okla.: Univ. of Oklahoma Press, 1945, pp. 155-61.
In 1883 the Kiowa Hunting Horse decides that his favorite son must learn how to live in the new world, so he and Spear Woman take the boy, Grass Stem Hunting Horse, to the Indian school at Ft. Sill. They stay long enough to see him in his new school uniform, with his hair cut short, and to learn his new name, Stanley Hunt. They leave after watching their son run off to play with the other children.

532 _____. "Hanging the Red Blanket." The Ten Grandmothers. Norman, Okla.: Univ. of Oklahoma Press, 1945, pp. 142-54.
In 1881 the Kiowas have a difficult time finding enough food now that the buffalo are gone. Even deer and rabbits are scarce. The Indians are temporarily hopeful when Buffalo Coming Out has a vision that the white men will go away and the buffalo will return. They dance and hope, but nothing comes of it.

533 _____. "Healing Power." The Ten Grandmothers. Norman, Okla.: Univ. of Oklahoma Press, 1945, pp. 222-29.
In 1910 Middle of the Heart Woman comes to Eagle Plume to get help for her back pain. He uses his Kiowa medicine power to help her, but tells her that if the pain continues she must go to the white doctors. She does, and they remove two handfuls of kidney stones. Middle of the Heart Woman is finally cured.

534 _____. "The Household." The Ten Grandmothers. Norman, Okla.: Univ. of Oklahoma Press, 1945, pp. 72-76.
In 1866, after her baby is born, Spear Woman (Kiowa) finds that she has too much work to do. She is pleased when Hunting Horse suggests that--to provide her with companionship and help--he should take her younger sister as his second wife.

535 _____. "Hunting." The Ten Grandmothers. Norman, Okla.: Univ. of Oklahoma Press, 1945, pp. 26-30.
The young Kiowa Eagle Plume goes on his first buffalo hunt in 1861. His teacher is Lone Bear, an experienced hunter, and his prey is a buffalo calf. When the arrows he shoots into the calf fail to kill it, Eagle Plume cuts the animal's throat with his knife.

536 _____. "Hunting for Power." The Ten Grandmothers. Norman: Univ. of Oklahoma Press, 1945, pp. 41-49.
In 1863 Eagle Plume, eldest son of Sitting Bear, chief of the Kiowas, goes out alone to seek his "medicine" or "power." After sitting for nearly a week atop a mesa, he receives his medicine through what is, or appears to be, a talking lizard. Sitting Bear, hearing about the experience, is pleased to know that one of his sons will be able to receive the "Grandmother bundle" when he dies.

537 _____. "Indian Sketches: The Power Goes On." Southwest Review, 29, No. 1 (Autumn 1943), 67-69.
On a July night several Indians gather deep in the woods. One young man has been called away to fight, and his mother wants to know if he will return. An old man beckons her and she gives him a yarn bag from which he withdraws two wooden dolls. The dolls are cleverly manipulated by the old man and made to move as if they were puppets. The old man says that the actions of the puppets indicate that the young man will return from the fight.

538 _____. "The Interpreter." The Ten Grandmothers. Norman, Okla.: Univ. of Oklahoma Press, 1945, pp. 233-37.
In 1912 Spear Woman's granddaughter, Leah (Kiowa), goes to the store and interprets for the older people.

539 _____. "New Power." The Ten Grandmothers. Norman, Okla.: Univ. of Oklahoma Press, 1945, pp. 165-72.
In 1884 Eagle Plume (Kiowa) learns from Quanah Parker, the Comanche half-breed, about the new kind of power to be achieved through peyote. Eagle Plume is pleased because he achieves a vision when he uses it.

540 _____. "Plains Painter." The Ten Grandmothers. Norman Okla.: Univ. of Oklahoma Press, 1945, pp. 268-73.
An earlier version of this story appeared in Southwest Review, 27, No. 3 (Spring 1942), 357-63.

In 1938 Phillip (Kiowa) is hired to paint some murals in the post office at the new Agency building. He is torn between making the painting an accurate replica of Big Bow's camp and making it artistically balanced, as his art professor had taught him.

541 _____. "Playing Camp." The Ten Grandmothers. Norman, Okla.: Univ. of Oklahoma Press, 1945, pp. 95-100.
In 1869 some Kiowa children, playing war, build a wall across the peninsula where they are camped. That night a returning warrior blows a captured white man's bugle, and the sleeping Kiowas think they are being attacked. In their hurried attempt to escape they forget about the wall, and some horses are injured.

542 _____. "Playing Indians." The Ten Grandmothers. Norman, Okla.: Univ. of Oklahoma Press, 1945, pp. 274-77.
In 1941 some Caddoan school children are taken to the state museum and are shown the bones and artifacts of ancient Caddo Indians. This is all part of a dubious plan to make them "proud to be Indians."

543 _____. "Power Given." The Ten Grandmothers. Norman, Okla.: Univ. of Oklahoma Press, 1945, pp. 84-92.
During the Sun Dance in 1869, Kiowa chief Sitting Bear's favorite son, Young Sitting Bear, achieves his "power," but he later gives it to his brother, Eagle Plume.

544 _____. "Running Away." The Ten Grandmothers. Norman, Okla.: Univ. of Oklahoma Press, 1945, pp. 188-95.
Three Kiowa boys get restless in the winter of 1890 and run away from Ft. Sill, just before a heavy blizzard. The next spring, as he returns home from Ft. Sill with his parents, Stanley Hunt accidentally finds the bodies of the three school boys. Spear Woman thinks: "This is what sending boys to school did. It made them so restless they ran away, and it took away knowledge of how to care for themselves."

545 _____. "Searching to Know." The Ten Grandmothers. Norman, Okla.: Univ. of Oklahoma Press, 1945, pp. 196-205.
In 1890 Wooden Lance (Kiowa) makes a journey north to see if Wovoka's prediction--that the dead people and the buffalo will return--is realistic. On his way he visits Cheyenne, Sioux, Arapaho, Shoshone, and Piute Indians, noting the reactions of each to Wovoka and his Ghost Dance. Wooden Lance decides that the predictions cannot work for him, and that he does not believe.

546 _____. "Shut Inside." The Ten Grandmothers. Norman, Okla.: Univ. of Oklahoma Press, 1945, pp. 134-41.
The winter of 1874 is a terrible one for Eagle Plume's band of Kiowas, shut up inside the horse corral at the fort.

When Hunting Horse's second wife, Bow Woman, gives birth
to a baby, however, Hunting Horse and Spear Woman manage
to make a cradle for it.

547 _____. "Strength of Power." The Ten Grandmothers.
Norman, Okla.: Univ. of Oklahoma Press, 1945, pp. 258-
63.
In 1936 Fred (Kiowa) receives a head injury in an automobile accident and loses the use of part of his brain. The
white doctor thinks an operation can help, but Fred's father,
himself a Kiowa healer, will not give permission for the operation.

548 _____. "The Sun Dance." The Ten Grandmothers. Norman, Okla.: Univ. of Oklahoma Press, 1945, pp. 50-63.
In 1865, during the big Kiowa Sun Dance, Spear Girl
elopes with Hunting Horse. He is young and not wealthy
enough to pay for her with horses, but she decides she would
rather marry him than follow her mother's instructions to become the second wife of Crow Necklace.

549 _____. "That Woman." Southwest Review, 52, No. 3
(Summer 1967), 250-61.
At a rehearsal for an Indian celebration, an anthropologist
notices a middle-aged white woman sketching the events, and
asks a local Indian (Jeannette Looking Glass) about her. The
artist is Daphne Wrightson, who lives with Joe Arrow Maker
but does not marry him because of a promise she has made
to her grown white children. Both the Indians and whites of
the community disapprove of the arrangement. When Joe has
a heart attack at the celebration, only Jeannette seems to sym-
pathize with and accept Daphne.

550 _____. "They Do Come Back." The Ten Grandmothers.
Norman, Okla.: Univ. of Oklahoma Press, 1945, pp. 264-
67.
In 1937 the dead Kiowa girl Mary comes back in the
shape of an owl to claim her blankets that had not been given
away after her death.

551 _____. "Things That Die." The Ten Grandmothers. Norman, Okla.: Univ. of Oklahoma Press, 1945, pp. 126-33.
After burying Kiowa chief Sitting Bear in 1871 with two
of his horses, the new chief, Eagle Plume, ponders what to
do with his people. After several years of thinking about it
and weighing the alternatives, he decides to take them to the
fort, where the soldiers are to teach them farming. The soldiers shut the Indians in the horse corral for the winter.

552 _____. "The Traders." The Ten Grandmothers. Norman,
Okla.: Univ. of Oklahoma Press, 1945, pp. 16-25.
In 1861 some white traders come to the Kiowa camp.
They bring cloth, bells, coffee, and beads to trade for buffalo
hides. One young man has candy for the children.

553 _____. "The War Party." The Ten Grandmothers. Nor-
man, Okla. : Univ. of Oklahoma Press, 1945, pp. 278-84.
In 1942 a Kiowa artist, Phillip, enlists for service in the
Second World War. He gets to ride in a jeep in the annual
Kiowa fair.

554 _____. "War Song." The Ten Grandmothers. Norman,
Okla. : Univ. of Oklahoma Press, 1945, pp. 112-25.
In 1871 some Kiowa raiders kill a white man and capture
two of his children. The mother and another child escape.
Three old men eventually confess to the killing, one of them
Sitting Bear. As the three are taken to jail in a wagon, Sitting
Bear stabs a soldier, is shot himself, and dies.

555 _____. "Winning Horse Race." The Ten Grandmothers.
Norman, Okla. : Univ. of Oklahoma Press, 1945, pp. 206-
15.
In 1894 Red Stone (Kiowa) wins a horse race against the
Comanche Quanah's best horse, but he is drunk and kills the
horse. Red Stone returns to find that he has shamed his sister and that his wife has killed herself; Red Stone is banished
from the tribe.

556 _____. "Woman's Place." Southwest Review, 49, No. 4
(Autumn 1964), 353-65.
A devoted Indian couple, Wilma and Elmer, had been
married when still in their teens and had spent their lives in
hard work and self-sacrifice. They had even taken in and
raised Elmer's brother's ten children when his wife had died.
One day Wilma finds out that Elmer has taken a girlfriend; she
forces him to leave, and she files for divorce. Later, at a
summer powwow, Wilma explains to the narrator that, although
she and Elmer had gradually grown apart and had both needed
a fresh view of life, they are now near reconciliation--Elmer
is back courting Wilma, and the "old way" again seems best
to both of them.

557 Marsh, George T. "Land of His Fathers." Scribner's, 65,
No. 6 (Jun. 1919), 751-61.
The old Ojibway, David Makwa (Bear), is hired by McDuff
and John Gordon (whites) of the Transcontinental Railroad as a
guide into Flaming River country. They are surveying the land
to determine the best possible route for the railroad. David
tells them that the map they have is wrong; however, it is discovered that David lied to save his Gwanatch Tawadina (Beautiful Valley) from the destruction that the railroad would surely
bring. David resigns himself to the inevitable, but kills himself and McDuff by capsizing their canoe in swirling waters.

558 Marshall, Emma Seckle. "An Infusion of Savagery." Out
West, 28, No. 4 (Apr. 1908), 321-25.
Estelle (white) ends her association with Robert when she
learns that he is part-Apache. Years later, at an Indian sports

event in an Arizona railroad town, Chaska--a mysterious half-breed--saves a white baby (child of a white woman tourist) from certain death on the railroad tracks, losing his own life in doing so. The implication is that Chaska is Robert and the baby's mother is Estelle.

559   Martin, Helen A.   "Indian Kate."   Overland Monthly, n. s. 47 (1906), 29-30.
      Kate, a Wahula Creek Indian, works as a servant for a white family in California.   She squanders her salary on items such as peppermint lozenges and calico dresses.   A circus comes to town at the same time as a large group of Wahula Indians.   Kate marries her "uncle" and gambles away her dresses, leaving clean white ways behind.   "Truly, 'Once an Indian, always an Indian.' "

560   Mason, Nettie.   "A White Soul."   Out West, 29, No. 6 (Dec. 1908), 459-62.
      Near the San Gabriel mission lives a boy named Gabriel Dumar; his mother is a half-breed Indian and his father a French fur trapper.   The boy is very quiet, but develops a close friendship with Father Garcon, who starts training Gabriel for the priesthood.   When picking flowers for the altar, Gabriel notices a dust cloud.   He knows that cattle have escaped and could trample them to death.   He sends the unaware priest off on his own horse, thus saving the older man's life while sacrificing his own.

561   Masters, Charlie.   "The Silver Fish."   Arizona Quarterly, 16, No. 2 (Summer 1950), 124-29.
      Dr. Gillian, the brusque new director of the Laboratory for Ethnological Studies, speaks to Dr. Wiley about firing the Indian janitor, Manuel.   The Indian is supposedly lazy and inefficient.   The next day, Gillian and Wiley notice a particularly graceful Indian perform in the pueblo Green Corn Dance.   Realizing that the dancer is Manuel, they decide to "give the fellow another chance."

562   Matchett, William H.   "The Anasazi Skull."   Arizona Quarterly, 12, No. 2 (Summer 1956), 213-23.
      Ed and Marie, who visit the Navajo reservation to conduct a survey of Indian attitudes toward education, go to the hogan of Tall Hat's woman to ask questions.   Tall Hat's woman enthusiastically presents her opinions of white schools.   Tall Hat interrupts and asks if Ed and Marie would like to hunt for potsherds at a nearby location.   Marie stumbles upon a skull and wants it, but Ed wisely says they must leave it because the Navajos are very fearful of such things.   Suddenly they discover that they've been deserted and must find their way back alone.   They reassure their interpreter that they do not have the skull.   Tall Hat comes to the camp the next day, admits his inability to understand white men, and reveals that he doesn't care whether or not they have the skull--as such "crazy

acts" are typical of white people--but he indicates that his wife
had talked too much the day before, and he now wants to express his own opinions about the schools.

563 _____. "The Chipping Sparrows." Arizona Quarterly, 12,
    No. 1 (Spring 1956), 36-47.
    Ed and Marie travel to the Navajo reservation to survey
    Navajo attitudes toward education. On the way, Ed stops to
    pick up two dead birds along the road. He has a great love
    of birds and skins dead ones he finds for a school museum.
    Once at the trading post, the proprietor (Vernon Black) intro-
    duces them to Laura (a middle-aged Navajo woman) so that she
    may show them a good place to camp. Laura is accompanied
    by her two sons, who are fascinated when they watch Ed skin
    the two birds. Later, the older boy brings Ed a freshly killed
    pinyon jay. Ed tries to express thanks for the gift, but also
    his disapproval of the killing. That evening, when Ed returns
    to camp, he finds the boy proudly waiting for him with two
    sparrows he has unsuccessfully tried to skin himself.

564 Meigs, Cornelia. "The Buffalo Dance." Indians, Indians, In-
    dians. Ed. Phyllis R. Fenner. New York: Franklin Watts,
    1950, pp. 81-102. Originally published in St. Nicholas
    Magazine (Sep. 1929).
    The Ojibways and the Dakotas have long been tribal en-
    emies, but an Ojibway youth nurses back to health a Dakota
    boy who had been badly hurt by a wounded moose. Later that
    boy saves the Ojibway's life when he comes to spy on the Da-
    kota village.

565 Melton, James. "Religion Comes to Pocatello." Stanford Short
    Stories 1957. Ed. Wallace Stegner and Richard Scowcroft.
    Stanford: Stanford Univ. Press, 1957, pp. 127-45.
    Joe Pocatello is Shoshone Indian on his prostitute mother's
    side and white on his unknown father's side. Neglected by his
    mother, he is adopted by Bill Two-horse, who becomes a sub-
    stitute father for him. After being valedictorian in his high
    school class, then joining the Marines and winning numerous
    decorations, he returns to the reservation to find old Bill Two-
    horse, now nearly a hundred years old, on his deathbed. Joe
    decides he is ready to grant the old man's final wish, so he
    participates in the Sun Dance. When it is almost over, and
    Joe has been dancing for seventy-five hours, Bill Two-horse
    dies. Joe Pocatello seems to have asserted, finally, his In-
    dian heritage.

566 Menard, Josette Gertrude. "An Indian Lover." Canadian Mag-
    azine, 5 (1895), 242-49.
    Liza Boisjoli, a white girl who lives with her father in
    Ste. Therese, secretly loves a young Indian named Gabriel.
    Gabriel wants to marry Liza, but she knows that her father
    would disapprove. Feeling rejected, Gabriel suggests that they
    "end it all"--and they paddle downstream in a canoe toward the

rapids. Liza's father follows, but his awkward handling of
his canoe causes it to overturn. Gabriel ignores Liza's pleas
to save her father, but the lovers successfully "shoot the rapids." Realizing the latent savageness of the Indian, Liza ends
the relationship and vows to enter a convent.

567 Mendoza, Durango. (Creek). "Summer Water and Shirley."
American Indian Authors. Ed. Natachee Scott Momaday.
Boston: Houghton Mifflin, 1972, pp. 96-105. Originally
published in Prairie Schooner (Fall 1966). Reprinted in
Literature of the American Indian, ed. Thomas E. Sanders
and Walter W. Peek (New York and Beverly Hills, Calif.:
Glencoe, 1973), pp. 498-505.
   Shirley is a ten-year-old Indian girl who makes the mis-
take of pointing at and talking to a "stiginee" (or witch) named
Ansul Middlecreek. Later Ansul puts a spell on her and she
gets an intense fever, sees dwarfs, and nearly dies. Her
brother apparently saves Shirley with some counter-magic.

568 Mercein, Eleanor. "The Prior Claim." Mixed Company.
New York: Harper, 1936, pp. 212-48.
   Polly, a white girl captured by Indians in frontier Kentucky at the age of ten, is later recaptured by white settlers.
One of them, Ezra Todd, decides he will marry her, and takes
her to live with him in a cabin he has built near the woods.
They have a child. Polly's heart, however, remains with Gray
Eagle, the young Indian chief she had married a month before
the white settlers kidnapped her. When Gray Eagle comes for
her, she reluctantly leaves the baby, but willingly joins him
and returns to the Indians.

569 Michelson, Charles. "The Lame Coyote's Lone War." Cosmopolitan, 30, No. 6 (Apr. 1901), 631-37.
   The padre of San Carlos baptizes the baby of an ugly
Apache woman; he names the male baby Jesus. When Jesus
is twelve, the padre is murdered in an Indian raid. Jesus
thereafter gleefully participates in many raids with other Apaches. When his foot is badly wounded he is renamed Coyote-
that-drags-his-foot. The lame Coyote spends three years in
the Sierra Madres as a lone renegade, killing prospectors and
sheepherders. Finally, a shrewd colonel who has been sent
specifically to rid the hills of the lame Coyote, ambushes and
kills the Indian.

570 Middleton, Elizabeth H. "Four Eagle." Mid Country: Writ-
ings from the Heart of America. Ed. Lowry C. Wimberly.
Lincoln: Univ. of Nebraska Press, 1945, pp. 269-79.
   Four Eagle, a proud old Assiniboin, is accused of making
a bad home for his three grandchildren. The reservation nurse,
the agent, and the superintendent agree that the children must
be sent to a boarding school, claiming that Four Eagle is an
incompetent parent. To prevent this, Four Eagle agrees to
marry Lizzie Bearcub, an enormously fat woman whom he de-

spises, to keep house for him so that the children can stay at home.

571 Mighels, Phillip Verrill. "Barney Doon, Braggart." Harper's, 108 (Jan. 1904), 219-29.
Barney is a cook out West. When a papoose is dropped off at the town, Barney wants to care for the baby and try to return him to his family. He sets off in the wrong direction and stubbornly keeps going despite a sandstorm. Sally, in whom Barney is romantically interested, rescues them; the child's mother later comes for her papoose.

572 Millard, Frank B. "Coyote-That-Bites." Overland Monthly, n. s. 18 (1891), 471-74.
Coyote-That-Bites is a cruel, bloodthirsty, child-killing Apache. One morning he "gets his fill of blood" early by murdering a Mexican family and drinking their mescal. Later, as he sleeps it off in a drunken stupor, two white children (aged three and six) come and play with his knife and rifle, thinking him a harmless Yaqui. After they go home he wakes up, too late to murder them also.

Miller, Siyowin, and Juanita Platero. "Chee's Daughter." (For complete bibliographical information and story summary, see Platero entry--# 633.)

573 Milton, John R. "A Small Betrayal." Western Review, 5, No. 2 (Winter 1968), 22-35.
John Freeman asks at the Martinez General Store in Peñasco (northern New Mexico) about a ring of stone he has discovered off the road outside of town. The shopkeeper evades his question, but Lupe Martinez, a young Indian girl, asks Freeman to return the next day. That night in Taos he asks other people, including some police, about the site. The next day he learns from Lupe that an old man, one of the three remaining Penitentes (a masochistic religious group) was buried under the stones after having been accidentally killed. Taos police question Lupe's father about the ring of stones and the long-missing man. Rather than remain to help clear up the trouble his questions have brought to the sleepy little town, John Freeman drives away.

574 Momaday, N. Scott. (Kiowa/Cherokee). "The Bear and the Colt." American Indian Authors. Ed. Natachee Scott Momaday. Boston: Houghton Mifflin, 1972, pp. 119-24.
An Indian youth tracks and kills his first bear, and thus proves his manhood: "He was a man, then, and smeared with the blood of a bear."

575 Montana, David. (Papago). "Day Dawns on an Old Night." An American Indian Anthology. Ed. Benet Tvedten. Marvin, S. D.: Blue Cloud Abbey, 1971, pp. 32-37.
The narrator, an Indian, has comes from "the distant

desert" in Oregon to live in Los Angeles. There he is befriended by Rafael, a carefree youth who welcomes him as
"one of us. We all came here to make it big, but for the
time being we're just taking it easy." The narrator enjoys
this life of leisure for a time, but becomes more and more
restless: "We're just like all the other rats, striving to find
our cheese." Finally he decides he must leave and return to
the desert and to the songs of his people. His decision is con-
firmed when Rafael commits suicide.

576 Moore, Lucia. "The Proud." They Opened the West. Ed.
     Tom W. Blackburn. Garden City, N.Y.: Doubleday, 1967,
     pp. 26-45.
          Joe Meek traps in the mountains until the market for furs
     wanes, then sets out for Oregon to begin a new life as a farmer
     and politician. Along the way he acquires three Indian squaws
     --the third being Virginia, a Nez Percé who goes with him to
     Oregon.

577 Morrow, Honore Willsie. "Fighting Blood." The World's
     Best Short Stories of 1925. New York: George H. Doran
     Co., 1925, pp. 312-30. Originally published in Delineator
     Magazine (1924).
          Old Tom, a Deerfoot Indian, is forced to run liquor to
     supplement his meager rations on the reservation. He is
     caught and shot by a dishonest revenue agent who is in cahoots
     with the organizers of the liquor-hauling ring. Ruth, a "saint-
     like" Quaker who is there to help the Indians, acts on the ad-
     vice of Susy, Old Tom's wife, and temporarily puts aside her
     peaceful nature to fight for what she believes.

578 Mott, Lawrence. "Follette." Harper's, 113 (Sep. 1906),
     567-72.
          Brisbois Briere and his wife, Lisette, are fur trappers
     in northern Canada. One day Brisbois becomes lost when he
     goes out to check his traps; however, his dogteam leader (Fol-
     lette) finds the way home. With money received from selling
     both a trapped fox and Follette, Brisbois plans to buy a special
     gift for his wife. But hearing of the plan infuriates Lisette,
     so he hesitates. Then an Indian named Osasquinini comes to
     their lodge seeking his wife who, according to Indian legend,
     is supposed to return as an animal. The Indian mentions his
     wife's gray eyes, prompting Lisette to bring in Follette.
     Osasquinini and the animal seem to know each other; he leaves,
     and Follette follows.

579 Mulford, Clarence Edward. "The Vagrant Sioux." Outing,
     48, No. 1 (Apr. 1906), 68-78.
          The white men of the Bar 20 Range (Hopalong Cassidy,
     foreman Buck Peters, Lanky Smith, Pete Wilson, Billy Wil-
     liams, Red Conners, and Johnny Nelson) go into the small town
     of Buckskin, Texas, to drink at Cowan's bar and have "fun."
     Part of their fun consists of teasing a vagrant Sioux Indian,

known only as "By-an'-by," and getting him drunk. Later, a
badly wounded Johnny is brought into the ranch. The other
men start out to trail those responsible, and find the culprits
to be four Sioux--one of whom is By-an'-by. All four Indians
are killed in the ensuing gun fight.

580 Munn, H. T. "Zinto: An Episode of Great Slave Lake."
Outing, 29, No. 3 (Dec. 1896), 256-63.
When Zinto, a handsome Couteaux Jaunes Indian, has bad
luck in hunting, Ateachili tries to convince pretty Gloona,
Zinto's woman, that bad medicine is in Zinto's lodge and that
she should come to live with him. Despite her superstitions,
Gloona refuses to leave her beloved Zinto. One day, when the
three are out together in a canoe, Ateachili strands Zinto on
an island and leaves with Gloona. Zinto survives the winter
on eggs and birds, then destroys all nesting places. When
Ateachili returns the following spring, expecting to find Zinto
dead, he is outwitted and abandoned by Zinto--who returns to
Gloona.

581 Neal, Della R. "A Strife in the Blood." Overland Monthly,
n. s. 46 (1905), 195-203.
Rachel Carleton, a half-breed girl, runs away from a
party at her home, the Merton Ranch, because she is upset
when she overhears comments about her Indian blood. Her
husband, Walter, goes after her, but she refuses to tell him
what is wrong. When Walter visits the city, she refuses to
go along. Just before Walter returns, Rachel disappears and
cannot be found. Five years later, Walter sees a dirty, aging
Rachel in an Indian camp, but she runs from him again.

582 Neihardt, John G. "The Alien." Indian Tales and Others.
New York: Macmillan, 1926, pp. 116-35.
A half-breed, Antoine, is rejected by whites as an "Injun" because he is half-French and half-Osage. He runs away
from a "hanging party" by whites, and seeks refuge in a wolf
cave. Antoine loves the wolf (he names her Susette) and lives
with her. Then even Susette rejects him, preferring her own
kind; she brings a male wolf to the cave and together they kill
Antoine.

583 _____. "The End of the Dream." Overland Monthly, n. s.
46 (1905), 253-59.
A plains Indian tribe is visited by a terrible sickness.
Nu Zhinga goes out to get a tuft of hair from a white bison
to drive out the plague from his village, but returns to find
his mother dead and the village deserted.

584 _____. "The Fading of Shadow Flower." Overland Monthly,
n. s. 41 (1903), 145-50.
Shadow Flower, an Omaha maiden, secretly loves Big
Axe, so her heart is broken when he marries an enemy Ponca
woman. Later, after bearing a child, the Ponca murders Big

Axe in his sleep and escapes. Shadow Flower takes the child and runs off to join her lover's spirit.

585 _____. "The Last Thunder Song." Overland Monthly, n. s. 44 (1904), 431-36. Reprinted in Indian Tales and Others (New York: Macmillan, 1926).
Mahowari, an old Omaha medicine man, tries unsuccessfully to bring rain by dancing. A white reporter, a white minister, and a white doctor all make comments about Mahowari and about Indians in general.

586 _____. "Little Wolf." Overland Monthly, n. s. 38 (1901), 461-64.
Little Wolf is a "runt" in the Omaha tribe, destined (because of his small size) never to be a "brave." One day when all the braves are off raiding the Sioux, some Otoe Indians attack the unprotected Omaha village and carry off the horses and women. Little Wolf follows and, dressed as a wolf, frightens off the Otoes--but not before they kill all the Omaha women, including the girl Little Wolf had hoped to marry. Ironically, the Omaha braves later shoot what looks to them like a "wolf."

587 _____. "Mignon." Indian Tales and Others. New York: Macmillan, 1926, pp. 105-15.
Yellow Fox has been taken as a "wild man" in the circus to Europe where, in Paris, a young woman named Mignon befriends him. They fall in love but do not marry. He returns and sadly takes an Indian girl for his wife. Mignon later comes to him and they go off to set up a new tepee; after a time, the Indian wife comes and cuts Mignon's throat.

588 _____. "A Prairie Borgia." Overland Monthly, n. s. 42 (1903), 49-62.
An old Omaha chief, Wazhinger Saba, is insanely jealous of the young Wazadi, an unselfish young healer and leader. The old chief tries in several ways to humiliate and then to murder his rival. He finally succeeds with some strychnine he gets from white traders.

589 _____. "The Singing of the Frogs." Overland Monthly, n. s. 38 (1901), 226-30.
Wabishaha, a young Omaha warrior, loves his horse so much that he has no interest in women. When his horse is captured by enemy Pawnees, he follows and is taken captive himself. He is to be killed, but is saved by Umba, a Pawnee "daughter of the prairie" who loves him. Refusing the offer to take her as his squaw, he is eventually killed. Umba kills the horse, and then herself, to be Wabishaha's companions in the spirit world.

590 _____. "The Smile of God." Overland Monthly, n. s. 39 (1902), 544-47.
A tribe of Omahas, unable to find buffalo, is starving.

They expel Shanugahi (a cripple) thinking that he has somehow displeased Wakunda, who they believe has sent the famine on the tribe. Shanugahi finds a great buffalo herd and returns, a hero, to lead his people to the food supply which will ensure their survival.

591   . "The Spirit of Crow Butte." Overland Monthly, n. s. 38 (1901), 355-57.
A small group of Crow Indians is besieged on a lonely butte by a more powerful group of Sioux. One young Crow volunteers to stay as a decoy--and die--to give the others a chance to escape on foot.

592   . "The Triumph of Seha." Overland Monthly, n. s. 38 (1901), 282-84.
Seha, a young Indian, envisions his "medicine" and successfully receives the power of thunder; later he brings rain to the maize fields of his people. Old Ebahami, the village medicine man, is jealous and tries to work his magic against Seha. Seha, however, is more powerful.

593   . "Vylin." Indian Tales and Others. New York: Macmillan, 1926, pp. 77-87.
An Indian girl marries a white fur trapper and travels with him. Gradually the fur trapper seems to like the "song box" (the "Vylin") better than his wife. She becomes jealous of the "violin," thinking it is a girl. When she stabs it, he kicks her out.

594   . "When the Snows Drift." Overland Monthly, n. s. 38 (1901), 103-06.
Mun-choe, ejected from the Omaha tribe for murdering a tribesman, is forced to leave his loved one, Wa-te-na, behind. Later he is discovered frozen in the snows near the village--along with Wa-te-na, who has heard his cry and has joined him in death.

595   . "The White Wakunda." Indian Tales and Others. New York: Macmillan, 1926, pp. 29-48.
An Indian "Christ" is born to an old virgin (?). He goes off to the white man's land, and then returns on a steamboat to convert the other Indians. They reject him, throwing stones, etc. He preaches kindness, but finally they tie him to a post and lash him to death.

596 Neuman, E. Howell. "The Mahala of 'Dandy Jim.'" Overland Monthly, n. s. 52 (1908), 476-79.
Tutochanuca and his squaw, both Mono Indians, find two white outlaws; they kill one and capture the other. The captive, Jim Dann, is told that his life has been saved so that he can marry Tutochanuca's daughter, Tepiwa, who attends a white school. Tepiwa agrees to the marriage in order to protect her father, and Jim agrees in order to keep his former

crimes a secret. Though Jim is enthralled with the beautiful
Tepiwa, the feeling is not mutual, so Tepiwa runs away. Some
months later, while returning to white civilization, Jim sees
Tepiwa with a baby, two squaws, and a huge Indian man.

597   Newton, D. B. "Chain of Command." With Guidons Flying:
      Tales of the U.S. Cavalry in the Old West. Garden City,
      N.Y.: Doubleday, 1970, pp. 129-49.
         Tom Swenson, a new army recruit, is on his first mis-
      sion with an experienced company of Oregon Volunteers. Al-
      ready disillusioned with the army, he complains constantly as
      they follow the trail of Snake Indians who have stolen some
      livestock. Sergeant Colbrook hears Tom's fault-finding and
      takes an interest in helping Tom "shape up." During the suc-
      cessful battle against the Snake Indians, Tom and the sergeant
      become friends and Tom feels better about the army.

598   Norris, Frank. "A Memorandum of Sudden Death." A Deal
      in Wheat and Other Stories of the New and Old West. New
      York: Doubleday, Page, 1903, pp. 101-27.
         Four white men, alone on the desert of western Arizona,
      are attacked by nine Indians and ultimately destroyed. The
      story is a transcription of the manuscript written by one of
      them, the wounded Karslake, who writes in the saddle during
      breaks in the fighting. He is the last survivor and his final
      sentence is never completed: "It will...."

599   North, Arthur. "San Vincente." Sunset, 23 (1909), 381-88.
         Friendly Cahuilla Indians rescue two officers from enemy
      Indians in Mexico. The two officers later meet on opposite
      sides in the Civil War.

600   O'Hagan, Howard. "The Teepee." New Mexico Quarterly,
      15, No. 3 (Autumn 1945), 304-12.
         A white man precedes his partner, Bruce, into the Rock-
      ies to look over the timber and choose a camp site. The two
      men plan to float cut timber down the river to a railroad camp.
      One morning he notices tracks of unshod horses and sees a
      Cree woman ride away. He locates her teepee, learns she is
      alone, and spends the night there. The woman, Marie La-
      pierre, informs him that her husband, Felix, will soon return
      with supplies--so he quickly leaves. Although the white man
      fears Indian reprisal, he is surprised when Felix visits his
      camp and offers his wife's services any time he is away from
      the teepee.

Ohiyesa see Charles A. Eastman

601   O'John, Calvin. (Ute/Navajo). "Basket Lady." An American
      Indian Anthology. Ed. Benet Tvedten. Marvin, S.D.: Blue
      Cloud Abbey, 1971, pp. 66-68.
         The narrator, a child, is afraid of the "Basket Lady" who
      lives in the mountains and who will "come out someday to get

all the little children. " When the narrator is one day carried in a huge basket to where Basket Lady waits to cook him, he is given a hat by an old Indian and told to hit her with it. The narrator does so, and the Basket Lady dies. But there are still a "whole bunch of them in the Grand Canyon," so little children must still beware.

602 Older, Mrs. Fremont. "Amatil and Olna." Love Stories of Old California. New York: Coward-McCann, 1940, pp. 37-47. [See "Matilija," by Mrs. A. S. C. Forbes, which uses the same or similar characters, setting, and plot.]
Matilija is chief in Ojai Valley (the "Nest," a canyon in Chumash country). His daughter, Amatil, is in love with Olna, of a neighboring group. Meanwhile, priests have established Mission San Buenaventura, a day's walk away, and Padre Antonio visits Ojai several times bearing gifts. One day soldiers on horseback come into Ojai, taking people away to the mission. A terrified Amatil, who had been married to Olna the night before, is carried off. At the mission she is taught many new things. One day Olna and some Indian men attack the mission, but must retreat. Amatil escapes; Olna is killed; Amatil buries her beloved husband and jumps off a cliff.

603 _____. "California's First Princess." Love Stories of Old California. New York: Coward-McCann, 1940, pp. 151-68. [See "The Story of Rossiya," by Mrs. A. S. C. Forbes, which uses the same or similar characters, setting, and plot.]
On their wedding day, Russian Princess Helena Gagarin and her new husband, Baron Alexander Rotchef, make a strange request of Czar Nicholas I: to go to California to take command of Fort Ross. Once there they learn that neither the Indians led by Solano, nor the Mexicans led by General Vallejo, are very happy about their presence. However, the two native leaders engage in a few formal meetings with the Russians, and social life at the fort prospers for a time. At the first visit, Solano is intrigued by Helena. After some time has passed, Solano tries to capture her, but the attempt is thwarted by General Vallejo. Eventually the fort is sold and the two Russians return to their homeland.

604 _____. "The First Lady's Divorce." Love Stories of Old California. New York: Coward-McCann, 1940, pp. 19-36.
In 1769 Don Pedro Fages arrives in the California wilderness and helps to tame it, becoming its fourth governor. He had left a wife, Doña Eulalia Celis, and a son, Pedro, in Barcelona, and wants them to come to the New World. Eulalia is reluctant but finally agrees; once arrived, however, she hates California. When she finds out that her husband has an Indian lover, Dolores, Eulalia attempts to get a divorce. Failing to do so, she sees to it that he loses his governorship. When they sail back to Spain in 1790, loyal Dolores swims after the boat and drowns.

605 _____. "Hugo Reid's Indian Wife." Love Stories of Old
California. New York: Coward-McCann, 1940, pp. 111-18.
In the 1830s, Scotsman Hugo Reid goes to California to
set up a trading post near Mission San Gabriel. One day Doña
Eulalia and her Indian friend, Bartolomea (always called "Victoria" by Hugo), come to the post for supplies. Hugo is struck
with Victoria's beauty, but learns that she has been married
since she was thirteen. He visits with Doña and Victoria;
Hugo and Victoria fall in love, but she insists on being faithful to her husband. When Victoria's husband dies, the two
lovers are married--but their life together is not very happy.

606 _____. "Yoscolo and Perfecta." Love Stories of Old California. New York: Coward-McCann, 1940, pp. 92-101.
A Franciscan friar, Padre José Viader, is attacked by
a young Indian, Yoscolo, whom he subdues and brings back to
the Santa Clara mission. Yoscolo soon becomes an enthusiastic
convert. Once, when gathering people to bring to the mission,
he finds a lovely young Indian girl--who is later christened
Dolores of Perfecta. She is a joy to the mission. When Yoscolo goes to the padre for permission to marry Perfecta, he
learns that Corporal Antonio has already asked for her hand.
The padre will not reverse his decision. An enraged Yoscolo
goes berserk, killing whites, and leading attacks on all the six
northern missions. After a time, he is killed and decapitated
by Antonio. Perfecta mourns.

Oledoska, and Daugahnogae. "The Warclub That Killed the
White Captain." (For complete bibliographical information
and story summary, see Daugahnogae entry--#194.)

607 Olsen, T. V. "A Kind of Courage." With Guidons Flying:
Tales of the U.S. Cavalry in the Old West. Garden City,
N.Y.: Doubleday, 1970, pp. 151-66.
Two Sac warriors, Tyeema and his brother-in-law Musketabah, are hunting in the woods. They are followers of Black
Hawk, who is at war with the whites. Musketabah is a mighty
hunter, respected by all his tribe as strong and fearless. He
scornfully calls Tyeema, who is a dreamer and a thinker,
"Rabbit." Tyeema endures this humiliation until one day Musketabah is captured and about to be tortured by some white
militiamen. With a brave and clever plan, Tyeema rescues
him. Thereafter, Musketabah no longer calls Tyeema "Rabbit."

608 _____. "The Strange Valley." Alfred Hitchcock's Super-
natural Tales of Terror and Suspense. New York: Random
House, 1973, pp. 20-29. Also printed in Great Ghost Stories of the Old West, ed. Betty Baker (New York: Four
Winds Press), pp. 13-25.
Three young Sioux discover a strange valley where they
see a huge, roaring monster that almost runs them down. As
they flee in terror, Young Elk throws his ax at the monster.

A century later a truck driver, traveling through this same valley, sees a ghostly Sioux warrior on horseback throw an ax at his truck. The truck driver stops and finds a decaying stone ax beside the road.

609 O'Neill, Bucky. "The Requiem of the Drums." Cosmopolitan, 30, No. 4 (Feb. 1901), 401-04.
In 1861 at Fort Buchanan, a young infantry drummer bids farewell to the young Papago girl he has lived with for a year and to their baby. She pleads to go with him, but he refuses because he is going into battle. The soldiers set fire to their quarters and leave. Soon Indians creep up to pillage the burned buildings. The first husband of the young Indian girl sees her and demands fulfillment of an ancient Papago law which governs those guilty of adultery. The young girl and her baby are promptly stoned to death.

610 Ortiz, Simon J. (Acoma Pueblo). "The End of Old Horse." The Man to Send Rain Clouds: Contemporary Stories by American Indians. Ed. Kenneth Rosen. New York: Viking, 1974, pp. 145-48.
When Tony's dog (Old Horse) chokes to death, two boys show their grief in different ways, one by weeping and the other by running so hard that he gets sick.

611 _____. (Acoma Pueblo). "Home Country." Howbah Indians. Tucson: Blue Moon Press, 1978, pp. 7-9.
When her mother dies, a Pueblo girl moves away to take a job in the dormitory at Keams Canyon on the Hopi reservation. As she leaves, her grandmother gives her a silver dollar.

612 _____. (Acoma Pueblo). "Howbah Indians." Howbah Indians. Tucson: Blue Moon Press, 1978, pp. 3-5.
The narrator recalls some ghost stories about Eagle, a Pueblo Indian veteran of the Korean War, who became manager of a Whiting Brothers gas station at San Fidel. He put up an enormous yellow and red sign saying, "WELCOME HOW-BAH INDIANS," a welcome to "you all" Indians. It was visible for miles, and it pleased many Indians. One day Eagle was found in a dry wash, bruised and dead, but local Indians still remembered him and laughed fondly because of the famous sign he had made.

613 _____. (Acoma Pueblo). "Kaiser and the War." The Man to Send Rain Clouds: Contemporary Stories by American Indians. Ed. Kenneth Rosen. New York: Viking, 1974, pp. 47-60. Originally published in New Mexico Quarterly, 38, No. 4 and 39, No. 1 (Winter/Spring 1969).
Kaiser is a Pueblo Indian who refuses to be drafted into the U.S. Army. The sheriff and his deputies try to find him, but Kaiser is well-hidden on Black Mesa. Later Kaiser decides to join the army after all; however, when he goes to sign

up he is arrested and put in jail. Eventually his sentence is extended when he tries to kill a man in the penitentiary. When he finally is released and returns to his village he seems very subdued; he wears a gray American suit until he dies.

614 _____. (Acoma Pueblo). "The Killing of a State Cop."
The Man to Send Rain Clouds: Contemporary Stories by American Indians. Ed. Kenneth Rosen. New York: Viking 1974, pp. 101-08.
Filipe and Antonio are kicked out of Winslow by Luis Baca, a state policeman of Mexican descent. Later, when Baca follows them out of town, Filipe leads him up into the hills near Black Mesa on the reservation and shoots him. Filipe is later arrested.

615 _____. (Acoma Pueblo). "Men on the Moon." Howbah Indians. Tucson: Blue Moon Press, 1978, pp. 11-19.
An old, old Pueblo Indian named Faustin receives a television set for Father's Day. His grandson, Amarosho, explains to him about the programs. First they see a wrestling match between an Apache and a white man. Then they watch a series of shots of a rocket ship taking off. Amarosho explains that the Apollo spacecraft is taking men to the moon to get rocks and knowledge about where everything began. "Hasn't anyone ever told them?" Faustin wonders. At night, Faustin dreams that a strange machine on metal legs smashes its way through the trees, crushing flowers and frightening animals. Flintwing Boy waits for the machine with a bow and arrow.

616 _____. (Acoma Pueblo). "The San Francisco Indians."
The Man to Send Rain Clouds: Contemporary Stories by American Indians. Ed. Kenneth Rosen. New York: Viking, 1974, pp. 9-13.
A seventy-year-old Indian goes to San Francisco in an attempt to find his granddaughter, who had attended business college there but had dropped out. None of the "Indians" he finds in San Francisco have seen her, but one of them wants him to teach her how to practice the Peyote religion. The old man does not know much about that, so he leaves for the bus station.

617 _____. (Acoma Pueblo). "Something's Going On." Howbah Indians. Tucson: Blue Moon Press, 1978, pp. 23-42.
Jimmo, a nine-year-old Pueblo boy, is frightened when he learns that his father, Willie, has probably murdered his white employer and run toward the mountains. Wounded in World War II and having now only one leg, Willie appears to have struck the man with his crutch, later found bloody and broken. Jimmo stays home, listening and watching as the evidence against his father accumulates and as an angry mob gathers to track him down. Then, before dawn, Jimmo sets out to find his father. He had remembered the night before about his great-grandfather who had also had trouble with the

white man and had refused to succumb to their soldiers or
their influences. When Jimmo finds the place where his father
had "replanted" his second crutch in the grove from which he
had cut it, he determines to keep on after his father: "Knowing where his father was going, Jimmo took a deep breath.
He knew that he was to follow. "

618 _____ . (Acoma Pueblo). "A Story of Rios and Juan Jesus. "
The Man to Send Rain Clouds: Contemporary Stories by
American Indians. Ed. Kenneth Rosen. New York: Viking,
1974, pp. 79-81.
    The unnamed narrator is an Indian who tells of how José
Rios gets himself committed to the psychiatric ward of the
hospital so he can listen to the screams of one of the inmates,
Juan Jesus.

619 _____ . (Acoma Pueblo). "Woman Singing. " South Dakota
Review, 7, No. 2 (Summer 1969), 34-44. Reprinted in The
American Indian Speaks, ed. John R. Milton (Vermillion,
S. D. : Dakota Press, 1969), pp. 34-44, and in Literature
of the American Indian, ed. Thomas E. Sanders and Walter
W. Peek (New York and Beverly Hills, Calif. : Glencoe,
1973), pp. 506-14.
    At the close of the season, Willie and Clyde (Navajos)
are working in Wheeler's potato fields in Idaho. While Willie's
main interest is securing liquor, Clyde's is a longing to be
home in Arizona among The People. After being paid, Willie
convinces Clyde to go into town with him and some friends--
Joe Shorty, Joe's pretty wife Emma, and their two children.
They see a movie, eat, and drink at the Elkhorn bar. A disgusted Clyde leaves and starts walking the five miles back to
the shacks. On the way he overtakes Emma and the children.
Both Shorty and Willie intend staying in town until morning.
Wheeler, the white boss, approaches them in his truck, stops,
and gives them a ride. Wheeler lets Clyde out and then follows Emma into her shack. Though Clyde is angered by the
incident he takes no action. The next day, a naive and hung-
over Willie remarks about how early he'd seen Wheeler among
the shacks. Clyde leaves Idaho by bus.

620 Overholser, Wayne D. "Beecher Island. " With Guidons Flying: Tales of the U. S. Cavalry in the Old West. Garden
City, N. Y. : Doubleday, 1970, pp. 167-76.
    Sam Burdick and his fellow civilian scouts are besieged
by hundreds of Cheyennes and Oglala Sioux. The scouts have
repelled one attack and now Roman Nose is leading another
attack. The scouts are frightened, but they weather this attack also. Many Indians are killed, including Roman Nose.
Without their leader, Sam knows, the Indians cannot win.

621 Oyen, Henry. "The Man Who Would Not Be Saved. " Overland Monthly, n. s. 40 (1902), 24-26.
    A cavalry lieutenant and a young maiden are trapped

in an adobe house, surrounded by about-to-charge Apaches.
As the soldier prepares for the final charge, the girl makes
him promise to kill her rather than let her become the wife
of an Apache. As the Indians charge, he shoots her, only to
discover immediately after she dies that the cavalry has arrived at that very moment to defeat the Apaches. He kills
himself.

622   Paige, Harry W. "The Summer of the Sweet Return." South
      Dakota Review, 7, No. 3 (Autumn 1969), 74-84.
         One August, in the Sioux community of White Thunder,
      alcoholic Ruben Black Bear has a vision of a young woman.
      He sees her standing in a tree saying, "Do what is right. Be-
      lieve in me and the people shall live." Ruben stops drinking.
      Frank High Pine, a medicine man, believes Ruben has had a
      vision of White Buffalo Woman; the local Catholic priests are
      convinced it was a vision of the Virgin Mary. Spontaneous
      rituals and worship occur around the tree, and the community
      splits into two factions based on their viewpoint of the visionary
      experience. In late September, a storm destroys the tree.

623   _____. "The Vision Quest." South Dakota Review, 9,
      No. 3 (Autumn 1971), 61-72.
         Jack Yellow Cloud (Lakota Indian) is half-nude at night on
      Eagle Butte, out on a "Hanblecheypi," a vision-seeking quest.
      He is there only to please his old grandfather. Jack is wish-
      ing he had stayed at Dartmouth for the summer session, when
      Tom Hawkman, an old childhood friend, drives up the butte.
      Tom asks him to go into White Clay to meet some old friends
      at a bar; Jack agrees, but once at the bar is disgusted with the
      people and the place. He returns to Eagle Butte, this time
      serious about his quest.

624   Paul, Nina Howard. "The Purple Boundary." Sunset, 57,
      No. 3 (Sep. 1926), 24-26, 56, 58, 60, 62, 64.
         Ede Sundell awakens in the night to find her husband,
      Kemp, gone; she also finds a note explaining that he needs a
      few weeks away in the desert wilderness, and that he has left
      with Indian Willie Mike. She decides to search for Kemp, with
      Indian Jim Mike as her guide. When she arrives at Kemp's
      camp, he is irritated at the intrusion, warning that she might
      have been harmed by a half-breed renegade named "Squint"
      Lopez. Ede decides to leave; Kemp, however, follows because
      he is worried about her. After many days, he spots Ede
      through binoculars just as Lopez attacks her. When Kemp ar-
      rives at the scene, an unexpectedly tough Ede has tied up the
      attacker. Ede and Kemp are reconciled.

625   Paulding, James Kirke. "A Night Adventure During the Old
      French War." America through the Short Story. Ed. N.
      Bryllion Fagin. Boston: Little, Brown, 1936, pp. 29-39.
      Originally published in 1831.
         Timothy Weasel, whose wife and eight children had been

murdered by Indians, decides to devote his life to getting revenge by killing Indians. On a mission to assess the strength of Indian forces near Fort Ticonderoga, he must use considerable will power not to murder a mere half-dozen Utawas.

626 Payne, Viola M. "The Comanche Arrowmaker." Scurry Country Style: Stories from Below the Cap Rock and Beyond. Austin: Univ. of Texas Press, 1967, pp. 181-84.
    An old, old Comanche continues to make arrows in the old way. He is not sure why, but he thinks perhaps it is because he wants to leave something permanent behind, something which would "show to all men who walked the earth that there once lived a man who did one thing well."

627 Peake, Elmore Elliott. "Flying Crow." Harper's, 116 (Mar. 1908), 546-52.
    Flying Crow, an Assiniboin who has left his people, lives in a Western town. He is a beggar and a drunk, yet he harms no one. The mayor gives him some chickens and a pig, in the hope of making Flying Crow self-sufficient. The Indian takes good care of the animals, but one day someone steals the pig. He follows the thief's trail and finds Blueskin Diggery to be the culprit. Later the chickens are stolen, and Flying Crow kills the thief--according to Indian custom. Flying Crow offers no resistance when arrested; he pleads guilty and is a model prisoner while awaiting execution.

628 Peattie, Margaret Rhodes. "Red Fox." Indians, Indians, Indians. Ed. Phyllis R. Fenner. New York: Franklin Watts, 1950, pp. 222-40. Originally published in St. Nicholas Magazine (Mar. 1937).
    A white boy, off to take care of his sick father in a Civil War hospital, meets up with a doctor. Both are captured by a band of Indians, even though most Indians have moved West and those who remain in the East are considered "as unimportant as dinosaurs." After the doctor removes cataracts from the eyes of the blind old medicine man of the tribe, however, the two whites are released.

629 Peterson, Martin Severin. "Indian." Prairie Schooner, 4, No. 4 (Fall 1930), 230-40.
    Skookum Charlie (a Plains Indian), Windy Burke, Doc Michaud, and Fred Mathis often play poker together at the Hotel Grand in Arlington, Oregon. There is no love lost between Charlie and Windy because Charlie had once embarrassed Windy by bulldogging a steer Windy had failed to conquer at a well-attended rodeo. One night Windy loses everything to Charlie in a poker game and, believing Charlie has cheated, Windy reaches for his gun. Charlie, however, quickly buries his knife in Windy's heart and slips away.

630 Petrakis, Harry Mark. "The Victim." The Waves of Knight and Other Stories. New York: David McKay, 1969, pp. 119-27. Originally published in U.S. Catholic (May 1966).

Lenny, a middle-aged Sioux who lives in the white man's city, is successful according to the white man's standards. His father, Charley Hawk, has just arrived from the reservation to attend the funeral of Lenny's brother, Jim, who died a drunk. Lenny misunderstands his father, who comes to mourn Jim in the old way. The old man feels he has lost both his sons: one is dead and the other has become a white man.

631   Philpy, Jane Flower. "The Pearl-Handled Knife." Young Readers' Indian Stories. New York: Lantern Press, 1951, pp. 175-89.
    Two Navajo boys, Kitzie Gorman and Billy Mariano, want to buy pearl-handled knives for themselves, but they realize that it is better to sacrifice their own wishes to save human lives.

632   Pitts, Mabel Porter. "The Legend of Lake Washington." Overland Monthly, n.s. 41 (1903), 339-45.
    Having been defeated and displaced by the white man, the Chinook Indians are now mostly gone. One Chinook guide, however, tells the friends of a murdered white man about how the ghost of the old chief rules the lake--killing, scalping, and carrying off the bodies of white men.

633   Platero, Juanita (Navajo), and Siyowin Miller. "Chee's Daughter." Literature of the American Indian. Ed. Thomas E. Sanders and Walter W. Peek. New York: Glencoe, 1973 pp. 471-81. Earlier published in Common Ground, 8, No. 2 (Winter 1948), 22-31, and in American Indian Authors (Boston: Houghton Mifflin, 1972), pp. 81-94.
    When Chee's wife dies, his in-laws come to take away his little girl--for that is Navajo tradition, it seems. Old Man Fat and his wife are indolent pseudo-Indians who work for a trader. The mother weaves rugs for the tourists to see, and they sell tours of their "real Indian hogan"--with its door facing north, not east, its brass bed, and its "garish pseudo-Navajo designs" painted on the roof. These two want the daughter selfishly, and refuse to let Chee have her back. When a new road goes through, however, the trader's business fails and Old Man Fat and his wife become poor. They finally return the girl to her father.

634   Poe, Edgar Allan. "The Man That Was Used Up: A Tale of the Late Bugaboo and Kickapoo Campaign." Complete Stories and Poems of Edgar Allan Poe. Garden City, N.Y.: Doubleday, 1966, pp. 350-57.
    This is a satire about General John A. B. C. Smith, who returns a hero from the Indian wars in the South, almost totally disabled. He needs new arms, legs, teeth, hair--among other parts--because the vicious Indians had cut him almost to shreds.

635   Pollough-Pogue, Marstyn.   "The Back Track."   Outing, 41,
         No. 1 (Oct. 1902), 41-45.
         At Wauboconk, the body of a half-breed is buried and his
      mysterious story is told: He is the Reverend John Paton, son
      of a white man and an Ojibway woman, who had spent nine
      years at Presbyterian University in Kingston, earned degrees
      in art and theology, and then accepted a missionary position
      with his mother's people on the Shegaugawa Lake Ojibway Indian
      Reservation in Ontario.   There he soon fell in love with the
      head chief's daughter, Meem-waum.   John ran away with Meem-
      waum in the night, and for weeks they lived happily together in
      a shanty on Cheemaung Creek; but one night, Meem-waum's
      father found them and killed John.   Meem-waum, in turn, killed
      her father, then lost her sanity.   She transported the body of
      her lover to a shack near Wauboconk, believing in her crazed
      mind that he was only sleeping.   She left him and went to pick
      berries, only to fall into the deep deserted mine shaft of the
      Dream of Avarice gold mine.   John's body was discovered and
      given a proper burial.

636   Popkes, Opal Lee.   (Choctaw).   "Zuma Chow's Cave."   The
         Man to Send Rain Clouds: Contemporary Stories by Amer-
         ican Indians.   Ed. Kenneth Rosen.   New York: Viking,
         1974, pp. 109-27.   [This short story is a chapter from a
         novel-in-progress.]
         Chowt is a small, lone, California Indian who, seeking
      drinking water, follows some rats into a small cave in the
      cliffs overlooking the Pacific Ocean.   He makes his home there
      for many years, eventually taking (at age seventy-five) a young
      bride to live with him.   As the story ends his daughter, then
      fifteen, discovers an army deserter floating in the water.   It
      appears that this Private Nelson will become her husband and
      will stay with them in the cave--which has become a kind of
      haven for refugees from the American mainstream.

637   Prescott, John.   "Winter Harvest."   Rawhide Men.   Ed. Ken-
         neth Fowler.   Garden City, N.Y.: Doubleday, 1965, pp.
         197-215.   Originally entitled "Uneducated Leather" and pub-
         lished in Street and Smith's Western Magazine (Aug. 21, 1943).
         Amos, setting up a new farm in northern Arizona, is
      having a bad winter.   There is no rain, and all of his white
      neighbors have moved away.   Some starving Indians come to
      winter by the creek, begging grain, and finally killing one of
      his oxen for food.   They make up for it, however, when one
      of their young squaws wet-nurses his famished newborn baby.

638   Prodan, Mario.   "The Indians of the Colorado River."   Har-
         per's, 199 (Sep. 1949), 80-82.
         The narrator, from the Far East but visiting friends in
      the United States, stops to see the Grand Canyon in Colorado.
      While there he is able to see the Indians of the Colorado River.
      At first he sees three Indians--man, woman, and child.   He

attends a Sun-Worship ceremony in which the same three Indians are dancing; next, he goes to an Indian hut where these
three Indians appear to be quite clever with figures; that evening, the same Indians perform another dance. When he arrives in New York he sees a newsreel in which three Indians
watch U.S. jets flying overhead.

639   Reed, Kenneth. "My Name Is Joseph." People Pieces. Ed.
        Merle Good. Scottsdale, Pa.: Herald Press, 1974, pp.
        24-33.
        Joseph Hochstetler has grown up as an adopted Delaware
Indian. A proud young warrior, he is about to marry the beautiful daughter of a Delaware chief when she is raped and killed
by white strangers. Joseph kills the strangers. Then, remem-
bering how the Delawares had earlier attacked his family and
captured him, he returns to his white father's cabin and becomes Joseph again.

640   Reed, Verner Z. "The Bruja Bonita." Tales of the Sun-land.
        New York and London: Continental, 1897, pp. 197-250.
        In the Santa Clara Pueblo, twin half-breed (Mexican/In-
dian) girls are born to the widow, Po-tseh. Carmelita and
Alicia grow up to be happy, beautiful girls. Carmelita falls
in love with a Mexican boy, Faustino Lucerno; Alicia falls in
love with a white cowboy, Mike Wentworth. The community
comes to believe that Carmelita is a "bruja," a witch. While
the medicine men are planning torture and death for the "bruja,"
Mike and Alicia help Faustino and Carmelita escape the pueblo.
They are pursued, but eventually escape and are married.

641   _____. "The Caverns of Ulo." Tales of the Sun-land.
        New York and London: Continental, 1897, pp. 109-58.
        A half-breed (Castilian on his father's side and Ulo In-
dian on his mother's) unsuccessfully searches for many years
for the lost land of the vanished Ulo tribe. He then unexpectedly finds it after being forced to leave a ship he is working
on. An old man in a strange masked costume claims to be
one in a line of kings, chooses the half-breed to be his suc-
cessor as king of the hidden cliff dwellers, teaches him the
things he will have to know as the pueblo leader, then dies.
The new king falls in love with Lo-Zeenah, a young Ulo maiden.
The Indians' growing suspicions about their new leader prompt
the lovers to attempt an escape. Lo-Zeenah is killed and the
half-breed is never again able to locate the Ulo land.

642   _____. "A Civilized Heathen." Tales of the Sun-land.
        New York and London: Continental, 1897, pp. 183-94.
        One-eyed Petra ("Sayla" is her Indian name) relates to
a white man this story of her sad life: After having attended
a white school, she was discontented living at the pueblo. Much
to the disapproval of her people, she loved and lived with a
young white ethnologist who was staying at the pueblo and who
had promised to marry her. When she discovered a letter

from his wife, however, she chopped off his hand as he was
sleeping, and ran away. Petra turned to whiskey and prosti-
tution. She lost her eye when a drunken man whom she had
cut with a knife tore it from her face.

643 _____. "The Herald of the Great White Christ." Tales of
the Sun-land. New York and London: Continental, 1897,
pp. 61-92.
    In 1540 Francisco Casca, a devout Christian, is with
Coronado's expedition in search of Cíbola, but is exiled into
the desert when he protests the cruel murder of a Yuma Indian. Near death, Casca is discovered by Lo-Eetah, daughter
of Es-tah, chief of the priests in the isolated Pueblo of the
Strangers. It is love at first sight for Casca and Lo-Eetah,
who teaches him her language before he enters the pueblo.
Once there he preaches the life of Christ, first converting Es-
tah and then eventually the whole Pueblo. Casca marries Lo-
Eetah and spends his life at the Pueblo of the Strangers.

644 _____. "An Indian's Revenge." Adobeland Stories. Boston: Richard G. Badger, 1898, pp. 114-30.
    San Antonio, the trouble-making second son of Mah-kotch-
ah-wuh (chief of the Spotted Fawn people), plays pranks on a
man who, in turn, threatens the boy and insults his father.
The boy runs to tell his father, and though Mah-kotch-ah-wuh
has little respect for this son, he is obligated to avenge the
insults. He warns the man that one day he will kill him, and
eventually fulfills his promise.

645 _____. "The Last Man of a Nation." Tales of the Sun-
land. New York and London: Continental, 1897, pp. 95-
105.
    A white man discovers an ancient Indian man in the crum-
bling Pueblo of the Exiles. The Indian relates his story: Years
earlier, Lo-Lah-Koita (born in another pueblo) grew up to be a
beautiful woman. Men fought over her, and when she chose a
husband there was much disappointment and discontent. One
unhappy suitor tried to implicate her in witchcraft. To avoid
a fight, Lo-Lah-Koita talked her clan into secretly leaving and
making a fresh start in a new pueblo. Thus the Pueblo of the
Exiles was founded. But inbreeding caused the population to
dwindle until finally only the old man is left.

646 _____. "The Law of Seh-now-wuff." Adobeland Stories.
Boston: Richard G. Badger, 1898, pp. 166-79.
    An old Ute chief named Te-Aguen is sad and lonely be-
cause he had once enforced a law of Seh-now-wuff, which states
that death should come to a Ute woman who sinned with a man
of another color. Once Te-Aguen had been in love with young
Keahnatch (The Light-Hearted One) and, after she returned from
the white school, he had married her. Their days of happiness
had been numbered, though. When Keahnatch confessed that she
was carrying the child of a white man, Te-Aguen murdered her.
He had loved her dearly, but he loved Seh-now-wuff even more.

647 _____. "Lost Pueblo." Tales of the Sun-land. New York
and London: Continental, 1897, pp. 161-79.
Hak-ki relates the history and the sad end of Lost Pueblo:
Once, six hundred years earlier, another pueblo was plagued
with blights, Apache attacks, and disease. Looki realized, as
a result of a vision, that the trouble was due to overpopulation
and that he should take part of the people away to found a new
pueblo. He did so--in a valley surrounded by steep cliffs. For
six hundred years no one left the valley. Finally, an excep-
tionally strong, brave, and inquisitive man, also named Looki,
scaled the cliffs and was gone for five years. He returned
with wondrous tales of white civilization, but he soon fell ill
and died of smallpox. The population was subsequently decimated, leaving only Hak-ki, the chief and priest, alive. He
mourned, then scaled the cliffs and left as the valley was flood-
ing.

648 _____. "Lo-to-kah and the Witch." Overland Monthly,
n. s. 24 (1894), 585-603.
Lo-to-kah tells of his experiences with Raymeya, the
witch. Alone one night in the forest, Lo-to-kah suddenly sees
a beautiful lady who asks him to become her husband and to
share her kingdom. Lo-to-kah refuses because he is very
much in love with his wife, Zeetah. Raymeya sadly disappears.
Many years and many adventures pass. As an old man, Lo-
to-kah seeks Raymeya's kingdom in the Sierra Madres. He
finds a paradise-like place and Raymeya, who has not aged.
He learns that she is being punished with the curse of immor-
tality for an evil deed she had done two hundred and fifty years
earlier.

649 _____. "The Tale of Burnt-Foot Maiden." Adobeland Stories. Boston: Richard G. Badger, 1898, pp. 77-95.
Mean, the son of Mah-kotch-ah-wuh (Chief of the Moache
Utes), is a brave youth. His father wants Mean to succeed
him some day as the tribal leader. Mean loves and marries
Kah-noon-i-patch (Burnt-Foot Maiden) and they are very happy
together. However, in his ambition for the son to be a great
warrior, Mah-kotch-ah-wuh convinces Mean to take a second
wife. Kah-noon-i-patch is enraged with jealousy and leaves
Mean to live alone in a yellow tent with their baby.

650 Rees, Gilbert. "The Rod of God." Sextet: Six Story Discoveries in the Novella Form. Ed. Whit and Hallie Burnett.
New York: David McKay, 1951, pp. 119-43.
Indians invade the early Massachusetts town of Dexter,
killing most of the inhabitants. They carry off a few women,
one of them a twenty-year-old girl. After a frightening stay
among the Indians, the girl is ransomed by old Mr. Hoar, who
later courts her. She is afraid of him, but does not know how
to refuse his advances.

651 Regli, Adolph. "Bow 'n Arrow Cowboy." Young Readers'

Indian Stories. New York: Lantern Press, 1951, pp. 126-
44.
Bert Ward, son of the Comanche reservation agent, had
learned to speak the Comanche language and to shoot arrows.
When Apaches attack the Cee Cee Ranch herd, Bert goes out
to help get the animals back. He and Little Wolf, one of five
Comache prisoners taken by the Apaches, stampede the herd
and drive off the Apaches.

652 _____. "Fiddler on Horseback." Young Readers' Indian
Stories. New York: Lantern Press, 1951, pp. 74-90.
Neil Webster is captured by Sioux Chief Crazy Horse and
a band of Cheyennes. Neil saves his life by playing guitar
music to them. He later escapes to carry an important message from General Crook to General Marquard.

653 Remington, Frederic. "The Great Medicine Horse." Harper's,
95 (Sep. 1897), 512-17.
The narrator, a white man who has come to the Asarokee
village, hears an old Indian's tale. The old man (named Paint)
claims personal knowledge of the "Great Medicine Horse." According to legend, this horse had earlier brought the Asarokees
good fortune but had not recently been seen. Paint claims to
have been in contact with the horse, and says that it would return only when the Indians went back to their "old ways." The
narrator is unsure whether or not to believe the story, since
he does not understand the old warrior's language and must
hear of the "Great Medicine Horse" through an interpreter--
the half-breed Sun-down Leflare.

654 _____. "How Order No. 6 Went Through (as Told by Sun-
down Leflare)." Harper's, 96 (May 1898), 846-52.
The half-breed Sun-down Leflare remembers an incident
in which he was to carry an order from his lieutenant. On
the way he found some dead Indian scouts; he recognized them
and, although it was cold enough for someone to freeze to death,
Leflare realized that they had been murdered. He was afraid,
but he finally reached his destination. After several days' re-
cuperation he was ready to return. When asked if he would
carry another message back he agreed, but asked for a new
horse to replace his own, which had succumbed after the earlier trip.

655 _____. "How the Law Got into the Chaparral." Crooked
Trails. New York and London: Harper, 1898, pp. 1-20.
Colonel "Rip" Ford of the Texas Rangers tells about
fights with Mexicans and Indians. In 1851 his lieutenant, Ed
Burleson, skirmished with Apaches as he was trying to trans-
port an Indian prisoner; at another time Ford used some friendly
Tahuahuacan Indians in a battle against the Comanches.

656 _____. "Massai's Crooked Trail." Harper's, 96 (Jan. 1898),
240-46. Reprinted in Crooked Trails (New York and London: Harper, 1898), pp. 79-91.

Massai (a Chiricahua) has been accused of murdering many people, kidnapping women, and killing horses. Because of these alleged offenses Massai is sought by the scouts, but somehow he is very hard to find--no matter how slim his chances to elude the authorities seem to be, he always manages to escape.

657   . "Natchez's Pass." Harper's, 102 (Mar. 1901), 437-43.
Marshall East is a white agent who issues "passes" to Indians who, in turn, murder innocent people off the reservation. Captain Sumners and his scout, Peaches (an Indian), try to prove East's complicity. One day they come across a group of dead herders and, next to them, a few dead Indians with passes in their belts. They confront East with their evidence and the agent flees when Peaches shows him the decapitated head of one of the Indians.

658   . "A Sergeant of the Orphan Troop." Harper's, 95 (Aug. 1897), 327-36. Reprinted in Crooked Trails (New York and London: Harper, 1898), pp. 33-51.
Sergeant Johnson is with the Third Cavalry (the Orphan Troop) which is stationed at Fort Robinson, Nebraska. A band of Cheyennes led by Dull Knife is engaged in a battle with Sergeant Johnson's men, and the cavalry chases the Indians away. One soldier heroically jumps over the barricade and kills White Antelope. In the final showdown, all the Cheyenne braves are either dead or wounded. A trumpeter plans to kill a little Indian girl, but Sergeant Johnson stops him because he has already seen too much senseless bloodshed.

659   . "A Sketch by MacNeil." Harper's, 98 (May 1899), 863-65. Reprinted in Out West, ed. Jack Schaefer (Boston: Houghton Mifflin, 1955), pp. 223-26.
MacNeil, an old army scout, reminisces: The Crow Indians had approached MacNeil, seeking help to catch Piegans who had raided the Crows. They never caught the Piegans, however, because the Crows interrupted their chase to dance in a snowstorm. MacNeil is amused by his memory of the Crows, clad only in G-strings, jumping around in the freezing snow.

660   . "The Spirit of Mahongui." Crooked Trails. New York and London: Harper, 1898, pp. 52-62.
Extracts from the memoirs of le Chevalier Bailloquet, a French fur trapper in Canada, reveal how, when on a voyage between Quebec and Montreal, he was captured by Iroquois and suffered a forced march to their camp. Later he was accepted and trained by the Indians. Eventually he escaped to the Dutch.

661   . "The Strange Days That Came to Jimmie Friday." Harper's, 93 (Aug. 1896), 410-19.
Jimmie Friday (an Indian scout) accompanies three New

York businessmen on a canoeing, camping, and hunting trip.
They appear quite ridiculous to Jimmie because of their inex-
perience. The trio almost collapse under the strain of their
packs, but Jimmie assists them. Later Jimmie kills a moose
with his hatchet. After the trip, the three are looking at Jimmie as the boat leaves him behind, and they all agree that
Jimmie is a "lovely Injun."

662 _____. "Sun-down Leflare's Money." Harper's, 97 (Jul.
1898), 195-99.
Sun-down Leflare is a half-breed who earns a living by
trading horses. Because he usually loses it in a crooked poker
game, however, he learns to cheat to win back his money.
Sun-down and his teacher cheat some white men and win a
livery stable. Later on, when Leflare learns that his teacher
has gambled it away, he sets out after the teacher.

663 _____. "Sun-down Leflare's Warm Spot." Harper's, 97
(Jul. 1898), 588-93.
Half-breed Sun-down Leflare discusses his girlfriends,
among them an Indian woman he had once fought Snow Owl for.

664 _____. "Sun-down's Higher Self." Harper's, 97 (Nov.
1898), 846-51.
The half-breed Sun-down Leflare explains to a white friend
what his "medicine" is. Sun-down uses his "medicine" to find
horses and directs his fellow Indians to capture them. They
think his "medicine" is wonderfully magical. Eventually he
confesses that he is able to spot horses from greater distances
by using field-glasses. Sun-down further claims that his "medicine" protects him from harm, but, knowing that Leflare is
a Roman Catholic, his friend finds the whole story unbelievable.

665 _____. "When a Document Is Official." Harper's, 99 (Sep.
1899), 608-13.
Billy Burling has just been commissioned a lieutenant.
Despite Burling's wish to celebrate, his commanding officer
orders him to deliver a message through dangerous Indian territory. Arriving at his cabin, Burling notices that the order
is missing. Inside are a few buffalo hunters and some traders,
who Burling assumes have taken the order, so he threatens to
kill them if it is not returned. A half-breed gives it to Burling, and the young lieutenant flees as the buffalo hunters give
chase. When they kill Burling they find only ashes of the order
he was carrying.

666 Reynolds, F. A. "Punch Choisser's Ride." Overland Monthly,
n. s. 30 (1897), 456-58.
In 1878 Lafayette "Punch" Choisser saves convicted Indian Willie, a half-breed, from the self-appointed vigilantes
known as the "Chowchilla Rangers." Choisser is chosen to
accompany Indian Willie to the San Quentin penitentiary where
he is to serve a life sentence. "Punch" is portrayed as a

"brave and generous" hero for outsmarting the vigilantes and
delivering Willie to the jail.

667   Reynolds, Mack. "Good Indian." Analog II. Ed. John W.
       Campbell. Garden City, N. Y. : Doubleday, 1962, pp. 46-
       54.
            Mortimer Dowling, head of the Department of Indian Af-
       fairs for fifteen years, is not very busy because the last In-
       dian has been dead for ten years and the last of a series of
       treaties had been signed a hundred years earlier. One day,
       much to Mortimer's surprise, his secretary announces that
       three Seminole Indians have come to see him. The three men,
       Charlie Horse, Fuller Bull, and Osceola the Eighteenth, claim
       that a few of their tribe had gone into hiding when the last
       treaty was signed--planning to return one hundred years later
       to seek better terms. They demand the State of Florida.
       Mortimer gets them drunk and has them sign a treaty with
       more reasonable terms.

668   Rhinehart, J. B. "A Story of the Oregon Trail." Overland
       Monthly, n. s. 23 (1894), 176-79.
            In May of 1851 a wagon train led by Captain Clark leaves
       Sangamon County, Illinois, for Oregon. The trip seems to be
       going well, without hostile Indian incident, but one day Mrs.
       Clark notices some Snake Indians moving in on her horses.
       She awakens their sons, Jim and Archie, to prevent their cap-
       ture. The Indians kill Mrs. Clark and Archie, and wound sis-
       ter Grace; Jim, however, makes a narrow escape. Some men
       unsuccessfully try to recover the horses.

669   Rhodes, J. A. "Lolita Lavegne: A Tale of Yokio Rancho."
       Overland Monthly, n. s. 33 (1899), 552-57.
            Old Lolita Lavegne, whose father was a violent Frenchman
       and whose mother was the daughter of a cruel Yokio (California
       tribe) chief, is the subject of a shocking story about her early
       days of courtship. Over a period of time she has had three
       suitors, Moran, Cheno, and Bolan, all found murdered, stabbed
       through the heart. The felon is never found. After a number
       of suitorless years, two men, Chiparo, a Modoc warrior, and Pa-
       jero, a Mexican soldier, fall in love with Lolita at the same
       time. A fist fight between the two wins Lolita's favors for
       Chiparo and leaves Pajero the jealous loser. Pajero plots to
       kill the lovers and awaits them in night ambush. But, to his
       surprise, he sees Lolita stab Chiparo to death.

670   Richardson, Alfred Talbot. "An Episode from the Reserva-
       tion." Out West, 25 (1906), 518-24.
            A white man steals an Indian's horse, and a conscientious
       marshall brings the case to trial. The Indian (Chickamin) is
       humiliated by the sharp defense attorney and the white thief is
       acquitted on the Supreme Court ruling that "a white man is not
       to be convicted on Indian testimony." Later, Chickamin burns
       down the court house.

671 Richter, Conrad. "The Iron Lady." The Saturday Evening
    Post Stories, 1957. New York: Random House, 1957,
    pp. 3-17.
    Andy Sloan is taken captive by Indians who had killed his
    parents; Mary Harris and her baby girl are also captured. To-
    gether they all escape to freedom and, in the process, Andy
    learns from Mary Harris about "iron in a man's soul." He
    later marries the girl.

672 Rinckwitz, Richard L. "The Circe of Lahonton Basin." Over-
    land Monthly, n.s. 52 (1908), 61-65.
    A prospector and his friend, Chester, are journalists
    from the East who have come to the gold strike in Sands Springs,
    Nevada. The prospector stops a half-breed girl (daughter of
    a white general and a Piute squaw) known as "Princess," and
    asks Chester's whereabouts. She does not answer the prospec-
    tor, but he reads a letter from Chester that is being carried
    by Princess's dog. In the letter, he describes his incarcera-
    tion and probable drugging. When Chester is found, he has
    gone mad.

673 Robie, Sargent. "The Stage-Driver's Story." Outing, 25, No.
    1 (Oct. 1894), 81-83.
    A cross-country stagecoach stops at a cabin to pick up
    a package from a blue-eyed woman. Jim, the driver, relates
    a story of how this woman, Belle Jackson, saved his life and
    the lives of his passengers twenty years earlier. The stage
    had been attacked by Bannock Indians and Jim, having been hit
    by two arrows, was unable to drive; however, Belle took con-
    trol of the horses and got the stage to safety.

674 Robinson, Gertrude. "Winged Feet." Indians, Indians, In-
    dians. Ed. Phyllis R. Fenner. New York: Franklin Watts,
    1950, pp. 119-39. Originally published in St. Nicholas
    Magazine (Dec. 1938).
    Squando, a young Kennebec Indian, skates swiftly down the
    frozen river to carry a vital message to General Washington
    concerning the whereabouts of the British forces.

675 Robinson, Will H. "Waiting for Tonti: A Story of the Cliff-
    dwellers." Arizona in Literature. Glendale, Calif.: Ar-
    thur H. Clark, 1935, pp. 74-91. Originally published in
    The Witchery of Rita (Berryhill Co., 1919).
    Stuart is a reincarnation of an Indian chief of a hundred
    years earlier, and Tonti is a Hopi maiden, also of an earlier
    era. Both had died when a Navajo brave had killed the chief
    (Tonti's lover). Now, on an archaeological dig at "Montezu-
    ma's Well" in Arizona, the whole story is re-enacted, and
    Stuart and Tonti head off into the sunset.

676 Roe, Vingie E. "The Little Boy of Panther Mountain." Sun-
    set, 39, No. 1 (Jul. 1917), 19-21, 50, 52-54, 56, 58.
    A thin, sickly, white man and his son arrive in Oregon

after much traveling and build a cabin in the mountains. Soon
they meet Snamishta, an ancient Indian who teaches the boy
many things about woodcraft and Indian lore. He also tells
tales of the Ghost Horse. One day the boy spies an old ema-
ciated white horse carrying rain-warped saddle bags. The boy
slowly makes friends with what he believes to be the Great
Horse and brings the animal home for his failing father to see.
Opening the saddle bags, the old man finds them full of gold.
With anxiety about his son's future now eased, the man dies.
The boy follows his father's last instructions (to seek old Sna-
mishta--who, it is discovered, has also died), then bravely
leaves for Conniston to find a preacher friend of the family.

677 _____. "Surrender." Sunset, 40, No. 3 (Mar. 1918),
    17-20, 67-70, and 40, No. 4 (Apr. 1918), 27-28.
    Hal Hayward, his sister Bryce, and others travel to Na-
vajo country to look over the land for the Reclamation Service.
Bryce is an accomplished, intelligent, lovely woman who is
enjoying the exploration immensely. They meet their two Navajo guides, Fighter and Chuska, and their Navajo interpreter,
Black Eagle. From the first, Bryce is fascinated with the
handsome, mysterious Black Eagle. One day he expresses his
love for her in a moving speech and she responds. The journey
ends and Black Eagle rides away. Bryce rides after him. He
expresses great joy over her love for him, but laments that
neither could she be happy in a hogan, nor he in a big city.
Black Eagle embraces her, then steps back over a sheer
cliff. Bryce faints.

678 Rollins, W. E. "The Medicine of Thunder Cloud." Overland
    Monthly, n. s. 47 (1906), 222-27.
    Thunder Cloud is a fine Crow chief who seeks good medi-
cine; he prays to E-saac-Kawar-te, the Great Spirit, to show
him how to obtain it. When the rising sun gleams on a distant peak, Thunder Cloud goes there. The journey itself is
exhausting and once at the mountain Thunder Cloud performs
the Sun Dance, cutting and tearing his flesh. He then has a
vision indicating that he has obtained good medicine together
with peace and plenty for his tribe.

679 Rolson, Jennie S. "The Last of Her Race." Out West, 42,
    No. 1 (Jul. 1915), 9-12.
    In ancient times, people of the Toltecs lived in what is
now the San Francisco area. Traditionally, the medicine men
of the tribe had the ability to prophesy disasters, especially
earthquakes. The medicine men were of one ancestry, passing their gift of prophecy from generation to generation. In
1778 one of the gifted Indians warned two Catholic mission
monks of impending disaster, but they did not heed him. In
1906 a girl with mostly white blood, but whose grandfather had
been one of these medicine men, warns her husband of impending danger as they are honeymooning, but he will not listen.
Thus, the last person with this gift of prophecy dies.

680 Rossiter, Kensett. "Nepa." Out West, 30, Nos. 2-3 (Feb. /
    Mar. 1909), 180-85.
    An Indian named Nepa, jailed for killing a man, is given
    a chance to secure his freedom in exchange for trapping a lone
    wolf that has been killing cattle in the area. On the last day
    of his allotted time, he finds the wolf in one of his traps, but,
    for some reason, lets it go. As he returns to town, expecting
    to be hanged, he learns that a man's gold had been stolen.
    Nepa goes after the thief and kills him, losing his own life in
    the process.

681 Rothschild, Michael. "The Price of Pine." Rhapsody of a
    Hermit and Three Other Tales. New York: Viking, 1973,
    pp. 43-58.
    A Christian Bagog Indian named Wassus George saves
    the life of a freezing white man, Urian Driver. As Driver re-
    cuperates in George's home, he lusts after George's daughter,
    Ona. George's wife, however, hates all white men and refuses
    to let Ona marry Driver. It is widely believed, though never
    proved, that Driver later murders George's wife and rapes Ona.
    George and his daughter leave the area, while Driver grows
    rich and prosperous in the new Northwest.

682 Rowe, W. P. "A Night Ride in Apache Land." Overland
    Monthly, n. s. 19 (1892), 142-47.
    Jack Burns is talking about a nearby band of raiding
    Apaches. Soon the men hear sounds of a horse and discover
    Frank Stanton's little girl on it. A letter pinned to her dress
    tells them that Apaches are near Frank's home and he needs
    help to defend it against attack. Jack and four men ride the
    twenty miles to Stanton's, manage to get into his cabin, and
    help hold off the Indians. With the morning comes the cavalry,
    and the Apaches speedily retreat.

683 Russell, Charles M. "Dad Lane's Buffalo Yarn." Outing, 51,
    No. 5 (Feb. 1908), 529-32.
    Dad Lane tells Long Wilson a tale about an incident in
    1862 when he and Joe Burke (also known as Bad Meat), a white-
    raised full-blooded Piegan, left the "Writin' Stone tradin' post"
    to get supplies. They had to cross some recently burned-over
    grasslands, where Bad Meat noted signs of Indians on foot, so
    they feared for their lives and their horses. Eventually they
    out-distanced these Indians, but had to travel without food for
    three days. Spotting a few old buffalo bulls, Bad Meat planned
    an animal kill. He and Dad Lane dressed in wolf skins, fol-
    lowed the buffalo, and finally secured the badly needed food.

684 _____. "Finger-That-Kills Wins His Squaw." Outing, 52,
    No. 1 (Apr. 1908), 33-36.
    "Squaw" Owens, a white old-timer, relates a tale told
    him by an old Blackfeet buck, Finger-That-Kills, about how
    he lost three fingers on his right hand. As a youth, Finger-
    That-Kills had been in love with a squaw who cost fifteen pon-

ies. Since he owned only five, he headed toward Crow country
with some other braves. On the way he was overtaken, shot,
and temporarily knocked out by three Gros Ventres. He came
to as they were standing over him, ready to take his scalp, so
he played dead. Instead, they noticed the several brass rings
on his right hand and, unable to pull them off, cut off the fin-
gers to remove the rings. Finger-That-Kills did not move during the operation, playing dead the whole time; however, he
got revenge on these people many times in later years. After
the incident, he went to Crow country, got the horses, and got
his squaw.

685   _____. "How Lindsay Turned Indian." Outing, 51, No. 3
       (Dec. 1907), 337-42.
       "Squaw" Owens tells Dad Lane the story of how old Lind-
say had turned Indian sixty-five years earlier. As a boy, Lindsay had lived in St. Louis. Fascinated by the West and Indians, he ran away. For a while he traveled with Pierre
Chouteau and his boatmen but, receiving poor treatment from
them at Fort Union, Lindsay ran away again. He followed a
broad trail of traveling Piegans and tried to join them, all the
while being chased by the boatmen. It was a cloudy day, but
suddenly a strange beam of sunlight encircled Lindsay. The
superstitious chief, Wounded Hoss, saved Lindsay from the
boatmen and adopted him. During his first exciting buffalo
hunt, Lindsay decided that Indian life was the life for him.

686   Sabin, Edwin L. "White Man's Pluck." Outing, 54, No. 4
       (Jul. 1890), 407-11.
       In 1876 Tichenor and his partner are buffalo hunting in
western Kansas. Tichenor dreams of his mother for three
nights straight, and each night in the dream she keeps repeating, "Do not stay here alone." Tichenor is not frightened,
but when his superstitious partner leaves, Tichenor is attacked
by Oglala Sioux Indians. Tichenor kills several Indians, but
suffers six bullet wounds. The Indians depart when snow begins to fall. After sleeping for a short time, Tichenor crawls
thirty miles through the snow to the nearest ranch.

687   Sacks, Clarence O. "Redskin Vengeance." Outing, 63, No. 5
       (Feb. 1914), 621-26.
       Old ex-scout Jasper Young tells the story of how the set-
tling of an Indian grudge thwarted the Ghost Dance movement
at Pine Ridge: Bull Head, who lived in Sitting Bull's camp,
owned a large silver medal which the powerful chief wanted.
Begrudgingly, Bull Head traded the medal for ten ponies. When
the ponies soon disappeared, an infuriated Bull Head left the
camp to join the Indian police. Two years later, as fear rose
among whites because of the Ghost Dance movement led by Sitting Bull, it was decided that the chief should be captured; Bull
Head, leading the Indian police, had the sweet revenge of killing Sitting Bull--but at the price of his own life.

688 Sandoz, Mari. "Birdman." Hostiles and Friendlies. Lincoln:
     Univ. of Nebraska Press, 1959, pp. 149-53. Originally pub-
     lished in the Omaha World Herald (Feb. 10, 1935).
        A prehistoric Indian boy called Birdman, whose assigned
     job it is to hunt birds, longs for a chance to prove his hunting
     prowess against buffalo. He gets it and succeeds.

689 _____. "Far-Looker." Hostiles and Friendlies. Lincoln:
     Univ. of Nebraska Press, 1959, pp. 223-224.
        A blind Indian youth, wandering at night, comes upon the
     camp of an enemy tribe planning to attack his village at dawn.
     The young brave drives off their ponies, so his name is changed
     from No Eyes to Far-Looker.

690 Saroyan, William. "Locomotive 38, the Ojibway." My Name
     Is Aram. New York: Harcourt, Brace, 1940, pp. 169-84.
        Locomotive 38 is a rich Ojibway Indian who owns some
     oil wells in Oklahoma. He seems to be wandering around the
     country with very little to do. When his donkey is killed by a
     trolley (in 1922) he buys a new Packard for three thousand dol-
     lars and gets fourteen-year-old Aram, an Armenian boy, to
     drive him around in it. The boy wants to go fishing, so Lo-
     comotive 38 goes along and watches him. Bored with the slow
     pace of the sport, Locomotive 38 drives off with his brother.

691 Sass, Herbert Ravenel. "Northwind." Hosses: An Anthology
     of Short Stories. Ed. Charles Wright Gray. Garden City,
     N.Y.: Garden City Publishing Co., 1927, pp. 191-214.
     Originally published in Herbert Sass's The Way of the Wild
     (Minton, Balch, 1925).
        Corane the Raven is a young Cherokee brave who decides
     that he must try to capture Northwind, a magnificent wild stal-
     lion. After a lengthy chase he manages to tie up the horse,
     but the hobbled animal eventually escapes down the river.

692 Sauber, H. H. "Hi Good and the 'Mill Creeks.'" Overland
     Monthly, n.s. 30 (1897), 122-27.
        In 1859 the twenty-two-year-old narrator moves to the
     California frontier to live with his uncle and two cousins, Henry
     and Tom. These are dangerous times because of a group of
     marauding Indians, several northern California tribes known as
     the "Mill Creeks." However, the area has the aid and protec-
     tion of Hi Good, a man devoted to the destruction of these In-
     dians. One day the Mill Creeks attack and kill a local man.
     There follows a wild night's ride to head off the renegades.
     With Hi Good as their ferocious leader, the settlers slaughter
     most of the Indians.

693 Scammon, C. M. "About the Stikine: How a Squaw Saved Her
     Husband." Overland Monthly, n.s. 15 (1890), 253-56. Re-
     printed in Overland Monthly, n.s. 32 (1898), 24-26.
        In 1865 the narrator, while on a voyage to the mouth of
     the Stikine River, meets a Canadian named LaBarge and his

faithful Indian wife, Panchita. Panchita tells how she once
saved her husband's life. While on a long trek through the
wilds with his wife and baby, LaBarge had come down with an
incapacitating fever; he was nursed back to health by his wife.
Later Panchita's father, a village chief, jokes about Panchita's
"two nursing babies. "

694 Schaefer, Jack. "Jacob. " The Plainsmen. Boston: Houghton
Mifflin, 1963, pp. 232-52.
In the late 1870s Jacob, a Nez Percé chief, and his tribe
live peacefully in their valley, but the white settlers think the
land is too good for Indians and begin moving in. When the
Indians fight back the troops come in, and finally two thousand
of them conquer the tribe and put them on a train to a reservation in Indian country. In a little scuffle at the railway sid-
ing, a ten-year-old boy keeps a drunken soldier from killing
Jacob and, in return, gets a pair of finely designed moccasins.

695 _____. "The Man Who Had No Thumbs. " Bar 5 Roundup
of Best Western Stories. Ed. Scott Meredith. New York:
Dutton, 1956, pp. 102-23.
A corrupt American bounty hunter, out with ten white
men and a score of Delaware Indians, is collecting Apache
scalps (including those of women and children) to sell to the
Mexican government for the bounty. His white scout (without
thumbs) whom he had kidnapped and betrayed, tricks him into
attacking an Apache village which is strongly fortified by Apaches expecting his attack. Later the Apaches and the scout
enjoy torturing the bounty hunter for four days until his death.

696 _____. "Out of the Past. " The Collected Stories of Jack
Schaefer. Boston: Houghton Mifflin, Riverside, 1966, pp.
288-98. Also published as "Three Days for Revenge" in
Bar 5 Roundup of Best Western Stories, ed. Scott Meredith
(New York: Dutton, 1956).
An Indian scout fighting Geronimo on the side of the cavalry risks his life to save that of a white soldier. Thirteen
years later that Indian is killed unjustly in a saloon by a red-
headed bartender, but the trial jury acquits the murderer.
Three years later the bartender is killed by the same soldier
whose life was saved by the Indian scout.

697 _____. "Sergeant Houck. " The Collected Stories of Jack
Schaefer. Boston: Houghton Mifflin, Riverside, 1966, pp.
48-71.
Sergeant Houck finds Cora, a white woman who has lived
three years among the Indians, and her two-year-old boy.
Houck's job is to return the woman to her husband (who doesn't
love her any more, can't father any children, and wants to send
her son away to a mission or some similar place). The sergeant, a strong, silent, granite kind of man, marries her.

698 Schultz, James Willard. "The Sacred Rock Vision. " St.

Nicholas Magazine, 63 (Jan. 1936), 9-11, 47, 51.
Little Bird and her brother belong to the Pikuni tribe of
the Blackfeet nation. One night during the summer, their father, Morning Eagle, has a vision of going to the Sacred Rock.
The chiefs of the tribe warn him of enemy danger and tell him
not to leave. But Morning Eagle packs and leaves with his
wife, Middle Singer, and the two children. The parents are
killed on the journey and the rich pack horses stolen. The
children survive with the help of their pet coyote's hunting skill,
and eventually are found by a friendly tribe.

699   Senarens, Luis P. "Frank Reade, Jr.'s Air Wonder Fights
      the Klamath Indians." Strange Signposts: An Anthology of
      the Fantastic. Ed. Sam Moskowitz and Roger Elwood. New
      York: Holt, Rinehart and Winston, 1966, pp. 118-29. Orig-
      inally published in Frank Reade Library (Oct. 5, 1894).
           Frank Reade, Jr., boy inventor, builds a kind of heli-
      copter air-ship and sets out with his companions (a black man
      and an Irishman) for the fur country of the Northwest. After
      visiting with American trappers who are resisting the monopoly
      of the Hudson Bay Company, he helps them to drive off a force
      of two thousand bloodthirsty savages led by a Hudson Bay em-
      ployee.

700   Sergeant, Elizabeth Shepley. "Good-by to the Superintendent."
      Harper's, 175 (1937), 347-53.
           Desiderio, an Indian youth (apparently from one of the
      New Mexico Pueblos), bids farewell to Mr. Pomfret, Superin-
      tendent of the Indian Boarding School. Desiderio, sad that his
      friend and father-figure is being transferred to another reser-
      vation, gives him a stone hunting talisman that had been his
      own father's. It appears that, because Indian youths cannot
      get jobs in town, Desiderio will now have to go back to farm-
      ing.

701   Serling, Rod. "Two Live Ghosts." Twilight Zone Revisited.
      New York: Grosset and Dunlap, 1964, pp. 3-20.
           Hank and Jeff, two trappers and prospectors, are unwit-
      tingly drawn into a fight with an enormous force of Sioux and
      Cheyenne Indians. They are struck down, but later get up and
      walk away. Later they overhear some soldiers describing their
      dead bodies at General Custer's ridge near the Little Bighorn
      River, and they realize they have been killed. Because they
      had earlier witnessed a ghostly exhibition at a large medicine
      tent, they are now "ghosts of the dead."

702   Shaw, Irwin. "The Indian in Depth of Night." Story, 18,
      No. 87 (Jan./Feb. 1941), 98-101.
           O'Malley walks home through Central Park, penniless,
      after a night of drinking whiskey. He is approached by a
      homosexual whom he turns away in a friendly manner. Then,
      a Creek Indian named Billy Elk (who claims to be a prize
      fighter) demands some money. With patience and friendliness,
      O'Malley convinces him that he has none.

703 Shinn, Charles H. "Old Man Chepo." Craftsman, 21, No. 6
     (Mar. 1912), 622-30.
         Old Man Chepo, a Mono Indian, gets apples from Shain
     (white) by saying that his wife, Susy, is sick--even though she
     is not. Shain gives Chepo some apple tree seedlings and offers
     to help plant them, but when Shain goes to Chepo's cabin, the
     Indian is gone. Many times Chepo tells small lies and half-
     truths to Shain in order to wheedle money and food, but there
     is something about the character that makes Shain and everyone
     else like him. When old Chepo dies, he is missed.

704 Shinn, M. W. "Cherokee Bob, the Original Jack Hambin."
     Overland Monthly, s. s. 16 (1890), 1-11.
         Mixed-blood Cherokee Bob is supposedly the model for
     Brete Harte's half-breed gentleman gambler, Jack Hamlin,
     sometimes known as Comanche Jack.

705 Shirreffs, Gordon D. "Lone Hunter of the Shoshones." Teen-
     Age Frontier Stories. Ed. A. L. Furman. New York:
     Lantern Press, 1958, pp. 197-213. Originally published in
     Boy's Life (1953).
         Little Spider is a young Shoshone brave who desperately
     wants to be selected for the Yellow Foreheads, the warrior
     society of his tribe. But he is taunted by the other braves be-
     cause he is lame and because he does squaw's work--taking
     care of his grandfather after all other members of his family
     die from a disease called Spotted Death. On a buffalo hunt,
     Little Spider is ridiculed by the rest of the tribe, but he saves
     the day when he stampedes part of the buffalo herd over a
     steep bank to their deaths when they try to get out of the can-
     yon. "Not one able bodied hunter had killed a buffalo, while
     he, a cripple, had supplied enough for the whole tribe."

706 Shoemake, Ben. (Shawnee/Quapaw/Osage/Cherokee). "Dear
     Friends." An American Indian Anthology. Ed. Benet Tved-
     ten. Marvin, S. D.: Blue Cloud Abbey, 1971, pp. 18-22.
         Ranny, an Indian, stays home most of the time now, but
     he prefers being outside watching the ducks on the pond, gather-
     ing firewood, sniffing the smoke from the chimney in the house,
     and thinking of old days, old friends, and the old wagon he
     used to go to the store in.

707 Shuey, Lillian H. "Calidonia of Red Cloud." Overland Monthly,
     n. s. 19 (1892), 239-46.
         A school marm, Estella Maye, tells a story about her
     stay near a mountain town named Walkerville. She meets and
     befriends a beautiful half-breed girl, Calidonia, recently mar-
     ried to a prominent man in town, Emmanuel Garcey, who is
     one-quarter Indian. (John Keyser is Calidonia's father and he
     loves his daughter very much; Calidonia's mother died when
     the child was born.) Calidonia, ashamed of her Indian blood,
     is about to run away with Three-Fingered Jack to a place where
     no one would know of her heritage, but her father stops them

(getting himself shot in the process). Estella intervenes and manages to convince all that the incident should be kept secret. Upon learning that John had loved Calidonia's Indian mother very much, Calidonia overcomes her shame and agrees to stay with Emmanuel.

708 _____ . "White Woman's Way. " Out West, 27, No. 6 (Dec. 1907), 520-22.
 An Indian girl named Sall goes to Wheatville for six months and comes back with pretty white-women's clothes. Though Straight Tom seems to like her a great deal, Sall marries the white man, Si Teevers, because she is interested in his thirty head of cattle. When Si goes away for a few days to get some money to pay off his gambling debts, Tom and Sall herd the cattle to Oregon and sell them. Si gets a divorce; Sall marries Tom.

709 Sienkiewicz, Henryk. "Sachem. " Western Septet: Seven Stories of the American West. Cheshire, Conn. : Cherry Hill Books, 1973, pp. 145-51. [This story, originally written in Polish (1883), was translated by Marion Moore Coleman.]
 The frontier town of Antelope, Texas, is built upon the ruins of a Black Snake Indian town which was destroyed fifteen years earlier by German immigrants who had come in the night and murdered all the Indians. One small boy escaped and later joined a traveling circus. He becomes Red Vulture, last Sachem of the Black Snakes, and a star tight rope performer. One night the circus comes to Antelope and the curious townspeople come to watch the Sachem perform. During his act, the Sachem sings an eloquent song, recites the cruelties of the whites, and vows that he, the last of his people, will exact vengeance. The townspeople, overwhelmed with guilt and terror, are relieved when the Sachem, instead of murdering them all, humbly passes a tin plate for donations.

710 Silko, Leslie. (Laguna Pueblo). "Bravura. " The Man to Send Rain Clouds: Contemporary Stories by American Indians. Ed. Kenneth Rosen. New York: Viking, 1974, pp. 149-54.
 Bravura, a young white college student and poet, leaves the university to "return to the simple life" by going to live and write in an Indian village west of Albuquerque. In his pitiful naiveté he pays too much to rent a house but justifies it by enjoying the clean air and the "simple warm-hearted souls who live here--that make me want to write about life. "

711 _____ . (Laguna Pueblo). "A Geronimo Story. " The Man to Send Rain Clouds: Contemporary Stories by American Indians. Ed. Kenneth Rosen. New York: Viking, 1974, pp. 128-44.
 Captain Pratt, a "squaw man," heads out with a group of Laguna Pueblo scouts to find Geronimo. They have been told that Geronimo had had a camp near a white town a couple of days' ride away. When the scouts arrive they discover what

they had already suspected--that Geronimo is nowhere around.
The camp had been made by a Mexican sheepherder.

712 _____. (Laguna Pueblo). "The Man to Send Rain Clouds."
The Man to Send Rain Clouds: Contemporary Stories by
American Indians. Ed. Kenneth Rosen. New York: Viking,
1974, pp. 3-8. Originally published in New Mexico Quarterly,
38, No. 4 and 39, No. 5 (Winter/Spring 1969) under the
name Leslie Chapman.
When old Teofilo dies his family prepares an Indian burial, bypassing the Catholic priest. Finally they do ask the
priest to sprinkle holy water on the grave--but only so that
Teofilo will not be thirsty, and so that he will have enough
moisture to be able to send rain clouds.

713 _____. (Laguna Pueblo). "Tony's Story." The Man to
Send Rain Clouds: Contemporary Stories by American Indians. Ed. Kenneth Rosen. New York: Viking, 1974, pp.
69-78. Reprinted in Redbook, 144, No. 3 (Jan. 1975),
75-76, 146-48.
A state policeman enjoys beating up Indians; he especially
singles out Leon and Tony, two young Pueblo Indians. Tony
gradually becomes convinced that the state policeman is a kind
of witch or evil spirit who must be killed and burned for the
welfare of the tribe. Shortly after Tony does shoot the policeman and burn his body, rain clouds form, marking the end of
a long drought.

714 _____. (Laguna Pueblo). "Uncle Tony's Goat." The Man
to Send Rain Clouds: Contemporary Stories by American
Indians. Ed. Kenneth Rosen. New York: Viking, 1974,
pp. 93-100.
A seven-year-old Pueblo boy tells of some experiences
with his uncle's favorite billy goat.

715 _____. (Laguna Pueblo). "Yellow Woman." The Man to
Send Rain Clouds: Contemporary Stories by American Indians. Ed. Kenneth Rosen. New York: Viking, 1974, pp.
33-45.
A young Pueblo wife and mother goes walking by the
river. There she sees, is drawn to, and is seduced by Silva,
(perhaps) a Navajo man. She returns home a few days later,
after Silva kills a white rancher who accuses him (quite ac-
curately) of stealing cattle.

716 Silverberg, Robert. "Sundance." The Best from Fantasy and
Science Fiction (19th Series). Ed. Edward L. Ferman.
Garden City, N.Y.: Doubleday, 1971, pp. 77-93.
Tom Two Ribbons is a Sioux biologist-spaceman a century
or two in the future. His job is to exterminate "Eaters" on
another planet to make room for humans who will migrate there.
(Eaters are strange little furry orange creatures with chicken-
legs and short arms; they eat oxygen-plants.) Tom Two Rib-

bons begins to feel guilty when he wonders whether exterminating these "pests" may not be like exterminating the buffalo and the Indians back in the nineteenth century. He feels even more guilty when he notices that the Eaters seem to have certain rituals and even a language. Finally Tom Two Ribbons undergoes memory-editing so that he will not feel guilty about what he is doing.

717 Simmons, Rose. "Old Angeline, the Princess of Seattle." Overland Monthly, n. s. 20 (1892), 506-12.
Angeline is a daughter of the late Chief Seattle. She falls in love with Martin, a brave of the tribe; however, her father had promised her to Chief Squanim of the Snoqualmies as a peace offering. Upon learning this, Angeline runs away into the night, sees a man near a canoe, and runs to him, assuming that it is Martin. But the man is Henri, a white fur trader who abducts her. She becomes his wife and has his child, Therese, who grows into a lovely young woman and who eventually marries a white man.

718 Simms, William Gilmore. "The Arm-Chair of Tustenuggee." The Wigwam and the Cabin. New York: Wiley and Putman, 1845 (First Series), pp. 120-48.
Conattee and Selonee, good friends, are handsome young braves of the Catawba people. Selonee is single, but Conattee is married to a shrewish, ugly squaw. On a hunting trip, the two Indians see a boar-wolf. Conattee wounds and then follows it, but disappears. Selonee searches for him for a few days and then sorrowfully returns to camp, where Chief Emathlor accuses him of murdering his friend. Just as he is about to be shot full of arrows, Macourah, Conattee's ugly wife, steps forward and claims Selonee as her new husband. Selonee, according to tribal custom, marries her, but soon runs away from the shrew, determined to find Conattee. All this time, Conattee has been trapped within a fallen, twisted old tree by the evil Grey Demon of Enoree, Tustenuggee. Only if someone takes his place can he escape. Macourah has followed Selonee and soon both come to the tree. Macourah becomes entrapped and Conattee is freed. Both braves return to the Catawba camp and eventually marry lovely women.

719 _____. "The Cherokee Embassage." Carl Werner, an Imaginative Story: With Other Tales of Imagination (Vol. 2). New York: George Adlard, 1838, pp. 175-208.
Cumming, together with an imposing party, approaches the Cherokee nation--twenty thousand strong--bearing gifts to seek alliance. He is met by several important chiefs. After the successful conference, Cumming takes seven Cherokee chiefs with him to London to meet King George and to sign a treaty of alliance. The terms of the treaty take advantage of the naive Cherokees, but the Indians and whites co-exist peacefully for a long time.

720 _____. "Jocassee." Carl Werner, An Imaginative Story:
With Other Tales of Imagination (Vol. 2). New York: George
Adlard, 1838; pp. 131-73. Reprinted in The Wigwam and
the Cabin (New York: Wiley and Putman, 1845, First Series), pp. 209-33.

In the early days, when the Cherokee nation is still vig-
orous, there are many sub-tribes, two of which are the Occonies (Brown Vipers) and the Estatoees (The Little Green Birds).
There is much bitterness between these two groups. A brave,
Nagoochie, of the Estatoees is hunting a buck on Occonie land;
he has the misfortune to break his leg, but is found and cared
for by an Occonie maiden, Jocassee. The two young Indians
fall in love and secretly become betrothed. Nagoochie distin-
guishes himself in a wolf hunt and claims Jocassee. Her enraged brother, Cheochee, sends the girl back to her own tribe.
The next day, members of the Occonies and Estatoees fight.
Cheochee gets an unfair advantage over Nagoochie, kills him,
and scalps him. When Jocassee sees her lover's scalp dangling
from her brother's neck, she throws herself into the river.

721 _____. "Oakatibbe, or the Choctaw Sampson." The Wigwam and the Cabin. New York: Wiley and Putman, 1845
(First Series), pp. 176-208.

Colonel Harris, a Mississippi plantation owner, hires a
number of Indians to pick his cotton crop along with his Negro
slaves. Most of the Indians are women and boys, but there is
one strong adult male named Slim Sampson. At check-in time,
Sampson and Loblolly Jack (the husband of one of the workers)
have a misunderstanding. Later that evening, at Lignon's grog
shop, Sampson and Jack, both drunk, get into a fight and Sampson kills Jack. When Sampson tells the colonel that Jack's
relatives will demand his life, Harris encourages Sampson to
run away. The Indian, however, returns the next day--because,
in his absence, the punishment would have befallen his kin. He
is executed.

722 _____. "Onea and Anyta." Carl Werner, An Imaginative
Story: With Other Tales of Imagination (Vol. 2). New
York: George Adlard, 1838, pp. 209-43.

When the Carolinians defeat the Yemassee Indians, the
few remaining Yemassees, led by Chief Echotee, leave to es-
tablish a new home in other lands. Years later, two young
Creek warriors, Onea and Hillaby, meet some maidens, de-
scendants of the Yemassee. Onea falls in love with Anyta and
Hillaby with Henamarsa. They meet secretly for many weeks,
fearing reprisal from the Yemassee warriors, who are enemies
of the Creeks. A marriage to one of her own tribe is arranged
for Anyta; Onea goes to the Yemassee camp to rescue his loved
one, but the two are caught. Creek warriors arrive before
Anyta and Onea can be executed, and the two tribes battle.
The ravaged Yemassees leave to find a new home, changing
their tribal name to Seminole, meaning "exiles" in their language.

723 _____ . "The Two Camps." The Wigwam and the Cabin.
New York: Wiley and Putman, 1845 (First Series), pp. 37-
70.

As a young man, David Nelson, with his wife and two
children (one of whom is six-year-old Lucy), settles in southern
North Carolina when the Cherokee nation is strong in that area.
Nelson, scouting one evening for evidence of Indian trouble,
suddenly notices in the distance an Indian camp and a strangely
familiar young white woman captive. But the dream or vision
then disappears. Returning to his cabin, he discovers a severely wounded Indian boy, takes him home, and nurses him
back to health. He learns that the boy is Lenatewa, the chief's
son. Weeks later, the Nelson cabin is surrounded by hostile
Indians, but the family is not harmed because of their kindness
to Lenatewa. Years later, Nelson comes upon a real scene
similar to the vision he had seen earlier. To his dismay, he
sees that the captive is his daughter, Lucy. Lenatewa helps
her to escape. Later, Nelson learns that Lucy and Lenatewa
are in love; however, before a marriage can take place, Lenatewa is killed by his enemies. Lucy never marries.

724 Skinner, Constance Lindsay. "Becky's Christmas Turkey."
Indians, Indians, Indians. Ed. Phyllis R. Fenner. New
York: Franklin Watts, 1950, pp. 140-54. Originally published in Becky Landers, Frontier Warrior (Macmillan,
1926).

Becky Landers is the "man of the house" now that her
father is dead and her brother has been captured by Kentucky
Indians. Out to shoot a Christmas turkey, she accidentally
flushes out some Indians about to ambush George Rogers Clark.

725 Smith, J. Gordon. "The Outcast." Overland Monthly, n. s.
46 (1905), 117-22.

Bryce, a prospector, and his companion, Hakwa, a half-
breed Siwash, find a sick old Opitsat man near a lake. They
learn that his name is Skundo, that twenty years earlier he
had been unfairly banished from his tribe, and that he planned
to return and plead to be taken back into the tribe. Bryce,
touched by the old man's story, agrees to accompany him back
to the Opitsats. Skundo becomes delirious and dies. Bryce
delivers the body and demands that it be accepted.

726 Snelling, William Joseph. "The Captive." Tales of the Northwest: Or, Sketches of Indian Life and Character. Boston:
Hilliard, Gray, Little, and Wilkins, 1830, pp. 1-20. The
original edition (1830) appeared anonymously. Reprinted in
1936, with an introduction by John T. Flanagan (Minneapolis:
Univ. of Minneapolis Press), pp. 7-23.

An Iowa Indian named Washtay Wawkeeah leads two white
fur traders to his tribe. For no other reason than that he had
never killed a man before, he murders the two men while they
are sleeping. Until the villain can be brought to justice, the
soldiers take as captive an eighty-year-old chief from his tribe.

The old Indian becomes a favorite around the fort. Finally
Washtay Wawkeeah is brought in, tried, and immediately shot.
"This is the way to live in peace with Indians. An eye for an
eye, and a tooth for a tooth, is their own law."

727 _____. "Charles Hess." Tales of the Northwest: Or,
Sketches of Indian Life and Character. Boston: Hilliard,
Gray, Little, and Wilkins, 1830, pp. 66-83. The original
edition (1830) appeared anonymously. Reprinted in 1936,
with an introduction by John T. Flanagan (Minneapolis: Univ.
of Minneapolis Press), pp. 62-76.
Charles Hess is a white man who had been raised by Indians. He marries a Chippewa girl and they have six children.
After he is dismissed as a clerk in the fur industry, he fends
for himself and his family in the wilderness. When Charles
is out hunting one day a band of Dakotas attack his family, killing his wife and five of his six children. The sixth, his eldest
daughter, is carried off by a Dakota man to become his wife.
Charles eventually goes unarmed to the Dakota camp and se-
cures his daughter's release.

728 _____. "The Devoted." Tales of the Northwest: Or,
Sketches of Indian Life and Character. Boston: Hilliard,
Gray, Little, and Wilkins, 1830, pp. 39-51. The original
edition (1830) appeared anonymously. Reprinted in 1936,
with an introduction by John T. Flanagan (Minneapolis: Univ.
of Minneapolis Press), pp. 39-49.
Two young Dakota men kill two soldiers. To avoid bringing hardship on their tribe, one of the young Indians and the
father of the other one turn themselves in to the soldiers at
the fort. The father is ultimately released; the other is sent
to St. Louis for trial. He is advised to plead not guilty and,
since there is no witness against him, the Indian is acquitted.
Eventually he is murdered by John Moredock, the famous "Indian hater."

729 _____. "The Hohays." Tales of the Northwest: Or,
Sketches of Indian Life and Character. Boston: Hilliard,
Gray, Little, and Wilkins, 1830, pp. 21-38. The original
edition (1830) appeared anonymously. Reprinted in 1936,
with an introduction by John T. Flanagan (Minneapolis: Univ.
of Minneapolis Press), pp. 24-38.
The Dakota Weeteeko treats his wife (Khotah Way) very
badly, so she has an affair with Nahpay Tunkah, a man from
another family. The angry and jealous Weeteeko vows to kill
them both, but he attacks too rashly and is instead killed by
Nahpay Tunkah. A long and terrible feud between the two fam-
ilies ensues--one which eventually involves, and splits, the Dakota tribe. The losers finally leave Dakota country; these are
the Hohays, or Assiniboins.

730 _____. "La Butte des Morts." Tales of the Northwest:
Or, Sketches of Indian Life and Character. Boston: Hil-

liard, Gray, Little, and Wilkins, 1830, pp. 213-22. The original edition (1830) appeared anonymously. Reprinted in 1936, with an introduction by John T. Flanagan (Minneapolis: Univ. of Minneapolis Press), pp. 183-90.

Some rebellious Sac Indians, occupying what came to be called the Hillock of the Dead, incur the displeasure of French fur traders by stopping boats and demanding tribute. Jean St. Denis Moran decides to put a stop to this practice. Setting off with three hundred soldiers and several boatloads of liquor, he first uses the liquor to win some Menominis as his allies, and then sees that the Sacs "capture" a boatload of liquor. When the Sacs are all drunk, the combined French/Menomini force attacks the village and kills every man, woman, and child there.

731 _____. "The Lover's Leap." Tales of the Northwest: Or, Sketches of Indian Life and Character. Boston: Hilliard, Gray, Little, and Wilkins, 1830, pp. 263-78. The original edition (1830) appeared anonymously. Reprinted in 1936, with an introduction by John T. Flanagan (Minneapolis: Univ. of Minneapolis Press), pp. 224-36.

Weenoona, a Dakota maiden, is unusually attractive. She loves Chakhopee Dootah, but her father will not consent to a marriage. She spurns all of her many other suitors, including Raymond, the French fur trader who offers to pay a substantial sum for her. When her father insists that she marry Raymond, Weenoona leaps to her death from a cliff.

732 _____. "Payton Skah." Tales of the Northwest: Or, Sketches of Indian Life and Character. Boston: Hilliard, Gray, Little, and Wilkins, 1830, pp. 52-65. The original edition (1830) appeared anonymously. Reprinted in 1936, with an introduction by John T. Flanagan (Minneapolis: Univ. of Minneapolis Press), pp. 50-61.

Payton Skah is a noble Dakota hero. When his first wife is seized and presumably murdered by enemy Mandans he is saddened and enraged, but is eventually prevailed upon by his mother to take a second wife. When he finds her to be unfaithful, he gives her to her lover as a wife, then goes to the enemy Mandan camp to be killed. There his bravery and kindness save his life. He is reunited with his first wife and makes peace between the two tribes.

733 _____. "Pinchon." Tales of the Northwest: Or, Sketches of Indian Life and Character. Boston: Hilliard, Gray, Little, and Wilkins, 1830, pp. 223-62. The original edition (1830) appeared anonymously. Reprinted in 1936, with an introduction by John T. Flanagan (Minneapolis: Univ. of Minneapolis Press), pp. 191-223.

Pinchon is a tough and clever Canadian fur trader whose exploits are recounted: he frightens off a whole village of Winnebagos; he wins a footrace with some Dakotas; he flamboyantly tricks some Dakotas into giving him their furs; he and his friend

(Joseph Le Duc) outwit several bands of Dakotas, and then go to live among them to get their furs, marry their women, and so on. Pinchon is finally killed in a duel by Le Duc.

734 _____. "Weenokhenchah Wandeeteekah." Tales of the Northwest: Or, Sketches of Indian Life and Character. Boston: Hilliard, Gray, Little, and Wilkins, 1830, pp. 197-212. The original edition (1830) appeared anonymously. Reprinted in 1936, with an introduction by John T. Flanagan (Minneapolis Press), pp. 170-82.

Toskatnay is a Dakota "dandy," much enamored of all the women because of his light, long hair and his foppish ways. Weenokhenchah Wandeeteekah one day saves his life by killing a mad wolf about to attack him, so (out of gratitude) he marries her. They have a child. When the ambitious Toskatnay decides that to become chief he must have more wives and brings home a new wife, Weenokhenchah Wandeeteekah takes their child, runs out to a canoe, and carries the child to death with her over the falls.

735 Sorensen, Virginia. "The Grandson." Arizona Quarterly, 6, No. 2 (Summer 1950), 101-11.

Adan, a young Yaqui brave, talks to his old grandfather, Achai, who is disturbed because the boy has sold his grandmother's cane to some "gringos." Adan had done so to get money for modern improvements, but, his grandfather disapproves. Each is frustrated at the reasoning of the other. Finally, the grandfather suggests that the cane money be used to purchase a new image of the Virgin Mary for the church. This, he explains, will gain the favor both of the mayor and of the father of Micaela, Adan's betrothed. Adan thinks over the proposition; when he sees Micaela, Adan agrees to follow his grandfather's wishes.

736 Spencer, Grace Evelyn. "Golden Eyes." Overland Monthly, n.s. 56 (1910), 509-12.

Golden Eyes, a young girl, is riding her horse in the desert when she finds a young man lying unconscious in the sand. She brings him back to the Piute camp and nurses him back to health. After some time the white man, Lyle Brooks, sadly leaves the Indian camp. He and Golden Eyes have fallen in love, but he does not feel that he can marry an Indian. Once at home, Lyle's mother tries to interest him in nice young women. She introduces him to the striking Miss Olive Rivers, who seems strangely familiar. Lyle overhears a conversation at the men's club concerning Miss Rivers's past. Apparently she had, as a young girl, been captured by Indians and had grown up in a Piute camp. It was then that Lyle knew why Olive was familiar--she was Golden Eyes, and not an Indian after all. They decide to marry.

737 Spero, Anne Kalfus. "A Son of Comptche." Sunset, 14 (Dec. 1904), 146-49.

Squealing Will is a lazy, good-for-nothing, booze-loving Indian who robs a stage so that he can take a pretty maiden to the carnival. He is thrown into jail.

738   Sperry, Armstrong. "Buffalo and Injuns." Indians, Indians, Indians. Ed. Phyllis R. Fenner. New York: Franklin Watts, 1950, pp. 155-71. Originally published in Wagons Westward (John C. Winston Co., 1936).
    Three Pawnees attack two whites who are away from camp on a buffalo hunt. The whites kill one, wound one, and drive the third one off.

739   Stafford, Jean. "A Summer Day." The Collected Stories of Jean Stafford. New York: Farrar, Straus, and Giroux, 1944, pp. 345-59. Originally published in New Yorker (1944), and reprinted in the same magazine in 1968.
    Jim Littlefield, a Cherokee orphan, is sent to an Indian boarding school by train. He is picked up by some Indian officials in a government car. There is an epidemic at the school, and many of the children have died. Jim wants to escape, but decides to wait.

740   Steinbeck, John. "Flight." The Long Valley. New York: Viking, 1938, pp. 45-70.
    Pepe Torres appears to be half-Mexican and half-Indian. He kills a man in a knife fight, runs to the mountains, and is finally shot.

741   _____. "The Leaders of the People." The Long Valley. New York: Viking, 1938, pp. 283-303.
    A tiresome old man seems to live only to tell the story of how he led a wagon train of people across the plains, fighting Indians, hunger, etc. Now that the Indians are gone there is, as the old man says, "no place to go" anymore.

742   Stockwell, Lillian. "The Great Spirit Rock." Overland Monthly, n. s. 46 (1905), 307-10.
    In the Russian River Valley north of San Francisco stands the Great Spirit Rock. In its shadow live some Indians, among them a maiden named Wichita and a brave named Klama. They marry and have a son, Onawa. Klama goes away on a trading trip to the south, and does not return with the rest of the travelers. Rumors reach Wichita that he has stayed with the beautiful Leawa, daughter of a chief. Wichita's heart is broken, so, with the baby in her arms, she flings herself off the Great Spirit Rock. After a month, Klama returns with a beautiful garment for Wichita; he had only been waiting for Leawa to finish making it. Grief-stricken at the sad news, he leaves his homeland and travels for the rest of his life, returning to the Great Spirit Rock only to die.

743   Stout, Herbert Arthur. "The Vengeance of the Wild." Overland Monthly, n. s. 50 (1907), 487-92.

Joe Curran, a half-breed, notices four panthers--two cubs, and their parents--feasting on a freshly killed deer. He mercilessly kills the two cubs for their soft fur, and the parents get away. Joe and his dog head for an abandoned cabin. Once in the cabin, he notices the two adult panthers prowling outside. Eventually, Joe and his dog are killed by the panthers.

744 Strobridge, Idah Meacham. "According to One's Standpoint." The Loom of the Desert. Los Angeles: Baumgart, 1907, pp. 98-106.

"Old George," a Piute Indian, begs nickels from passengers at the train station. A young "eastern" couple (holding a stereotyped view of the Indians as "degenerate") speculates that the old "creature" has never experienced the more subtle joys of life--that the Indians "go through life now in docile stupidity, without anything rousing them." The narrator then explodes the myth, detailing the "true" story of Old George: love, marriage and four children; jealousy and the "other woman"; hatred and revenge when he returns to his wife; and the tragedy of injury to himself and death of loved ones.

745 _____. "The Blue-Eyed Chief." Land of Sunshine, 13, No. 3 (Aug. 1900), 174-78. Reprinted in The Loom of the Desert (Los Angeles: Baumgart, 1907), pp. 90-97.

A slow-moving wagon headed for California is attacked by Indians. They capture a blue-eyed baby boy and take him to the Indian camp; the boy's older sister (eight years old) escapes. Much later the two meet again and she persuades him to go "home" with her to the "city by the sea," but within a few days he returns to his squaw and children, preferring to live among Indians.

746 _____. "An Old Squaw." The Loom of the Desert. Los Angeles: Baumgart, 1907, pp. 23-29.

A useless old Piute woman is starved to death by her family and left for the coyotes to eat.

747 Stuart, C. D. "The Sheriff's Deputy." Sunset, 11 (Sep. 1903), 455-59.

A Pima Indian is in jail for killing a white man, one who was apparently about to violate an Indian maiden. A mob comes to lynch him, but a brave young deputy sheriff saves the day, and drives off the mob just as the rope is about to tighten.

748 Stuart, Jessie. "The Great Cherokee Bill." A Jesse Stuart Reader. New York: McGraw-Hill, 1963, pp. 108-20.

Cherokee Bill is a three-quarter blood Cherokee who makes his living entertaining high school students at their assembly programs. He is strong, sharp with a whip, and a crack shot with a rifle.

749 Sullivan, E. A. "Kan-gi-shun-ca." Prairie Schooner, 7, No. 4 (Fall 1933), 166-71.

Kan-gi-shun-ca (Crow Dog), a Sioux in the Indian Mounted
Police at the Rosebud Agency in the Territory of Dakota, returns home to learn that Spotted Tail, Chief of the Brulés, had
tried to take his (Crow Dog's) wife to his (Spotted Tail's) village
and, failing, had promised to return for her the next day. An
angry Crow Dog confronts Spotted Tail and kills him in self-
defense; however, Crow Dog is arrested, tried, and convicted
in a white man's court. He requests leave to return home to
settle his affairs, promising to come back in November to be
hung. The request is granted. Crow Dog returns and waits
until January for his hanging, at which time the case is thrown
out of court because it is learned that the federal court cannot
try an Indian offense against an Indian in Indian country.

750   Swarthout, G. "Attack on the Mountain." The Saturday Evening
       Post, 232, No. 1 (Jul. 4, 1959), 24, 65-66.
       Sergeant Ammon Swing of the 24th Infantry is in charge of
three privates and a corporal at the Bill Williams Mountain Station. Their job is to be on the lookout for Apaches and to relay messages. The boring tasks are only occasionally relieved
by trips to a nearby settlement for water and rations. Sergeant
Swing there meets Martha Cox, a spinster of about his own age.
He is interested, but fears that a man in mid-forties is too old
for marriage. One day the men discover a newly-built Apache
dwelling. They are suspicious at first, but then grow lax and
respond to the Apaches' friendliness. They are attacked by
Apache braves, and all except Sergeant Swing are killed. When
Martha Cox arrives to investigate, the wounded sergeant can
think of only one way to relay a message--use Martha's petti-
coat as a signaling device. An embarrassed Miss Cox demands
and receives a proposal of marriage.

751   Sylvester, Alice Pierce. "The Trade." Sunset, 32 (Feb.
       1914), 395-97.
       Wescott is annoyed by an Indian who wants to buy his dog.
To get rid of him, Wescott says, "I'll trade the dog for the
baby." The Indian takes him up on it and the trade is made
--until the squaw comes to recover her child, and the dog slips
its collar.

752   Tapahonso, Luci. (Navajo). "The Snakeman." Sun Tracks,
       Vol. 4 (1978), 11-12.
       Every night a Navajo girl who attends a boarding school
slips out the window and goes down the fire escape to talk with
her mother in the cemetery. Her mother had died years earlier, when the little girl was six. While the girl makes her
nightly trips, the other girls huddle in the dark to tell ghost
stories, or speculate about the man in the attic who might
throw "evil powder" on them, or whisper about the snakeman
who steals jewelry and wears a silver bracelet that can para-
lyze people.

753   Tassin, A. G. "A New Year's Eve in New Mexico." Over-
       land Monthly, n.s. 15 (1890), 54-63.

At the foot of the Burro Mountains is a small military post, the look-out station against Apache renegades. Sergeant Buford is in charge of five privates, one of whom is fat, jolly, Irish, Timothy Timrod. Nearby lives a settler named Smith who has a sixteen-year-old daughter (Polly) in whom both Timrod and Sergeant Buford are interested. At the close of a New Year's Eve celebration, the cabin is attacked by Chiricahua Apaches under the leadership of Ju; however, the 6th U.S. Cavalry arrives in time to save the settlers. Only Buford is killed in the fight. Timrod later marries Polly.

754 _____. "Noltche." Overland Monthly, n. s. 13, No. 76 (Apr. 1889), 353-63.

The quartermaster of Fort Mojave is friendly with an old Indian woman named Noltche (also called Confidence) and her son, Lying Jim. Noltche and Lying Jim continually beg for supplies from the quartermaster. When Lying Jim, who practices tribal medicine, loses a patient, the deceased's relatives want to kill him; but the quartermaster saves Jim by giving money to the relatives as retribution. This costs the quartermaster nearly a whole month's pay. Fortunately for the quartermaster's bankroll, he is transferred to another post; however, one day Lying Jim shows up. The quartermaster is at first dismayed, but Jim protects him from some bandits and saves his life. Lying Jim is thereafter known as Honest Jim.

755 Tate, Douglas. "Ghost Men of Coronado." Teen-Age Frontier Stories. Ed. A. L. Furman. New York: Lantern Press, 1958, pp. 25-40. Originally published in Boy's Life (1953).

In 1541 Mahtocheega (Mandan) and Burning Foot (Comanche) set out after the "ghost men"--"pale bloodless creatures with hard shells" (whites wearing breast plates) who ride "elk-dogs" (horses), to find the Comanche's captured son, Shonka, and to prove Mahtocheega's manhood. In their encounter with Coronado and his Spanish explorers, the Indians are able to free Shonka, and Burning Foot gives Mahtocheega his new warrior's name, Mahto Hopeneche, meaning "The Medicine Bear."

756 Tate, J. W. "Across the Plains." Overland Monthly, n. s. 22 (1893), 300-03.

When a group of white fortune hunters crosses the plains to the California gold mines in 1850, the "unscrupulous" Shoshone Indians steal cattle from the white camp. The white men stage a surprise attack against the large Shoshone camp and drive off some cattle. Although the fighting soon becomes too much for the small group of white men, most of them escape. The narrator loses his horse, but is able to make it back to camp, most of the way on foot.

757 Temple, Ronald. "The Carbines." Sunset, 32 (May 1914), 1009-15.

Bannister, an ex-army man, has become a Zuni "squaw man," kept in the power of his Zuni woman by her doles of

liquor and his own weakness. He steals some new army carbines and takes them to the Zuni bandit, T'sumalo, but finally
refuses to reveal how they work.

758 Tenn, William. "Eastward Ho!" The Best from Fantasy and
Science Fiction (9th Series). Ed. Robert P. Mills. Garden
City, N.Y.: Doubleday, 1960, pp. 95-112.
    The Indians have taken control of the country. Under
Chief Three Hydrogen Bombs and his son, Makes Much Radi-
ation, the Indians (especially the Sioux and the Seminoles) con-
solidate their power and eventually drive the whites back to
the sea. The last remnants of this vanishing race set sail in
their navy (three sailing vessels) for Europe where they hope
to discover "a new and hopeful world--a world of freedom."

759 Terry, Marshall. "The Real." Southwest Review, 56, No. 4
(Autumn 1971), 329-37.
    Holcomb, an aging disillusioned businessman, is vacation-
ing at Laguna Madres on the Gulf of Mexico. One night he
goes to a rundown fishing strip called Indian Bay and, with
the proprietress, sees a huge white shark--a rare occurrence
for those waters. The proprietress is a filthy old Indian woman
named Victoria Elena Keno. Holcomb tells her that he is a
magazine writer and wishes to stay around to photograph the
catching of the shark; actually he is, for some reason, fascinated with the gruff old woman. He learns from her changing
stories that she is either from Oklahoma or Arizona, and is
either a full-blooded Apache or a half-breed Kiowa. Holcomb
remains for ten days, but then must return to Dallas. The
shark is not seen again.

760 Thanet, Octave. "His Duty." Harper's, 93 (Sep. 1896), 612-
21.
    Amos Wickliff is a special agent employed to arrest David
Harned, who is wanted for murder. Harned pleads for mercy,
swearing that he murdered in the heat of passion. That night
there is an Indian attack led by Red Horse and some hostile
Indians. Wickliff spikes their whiskey with cyanide and some
of them die inside the door. Red Horse attempts to kill the
special agent but Harned shoots the Indian. Wickliff refuses
to bring Harned back because he owes his life to the "wanted"
man.

761 Thomas, Chauncey. "Manitou." Golden Book Magazine, 8,
No. 45 (Sep. 1928), 341-48.
    The Utes, who call themselves "The Dwellers of the Sky,"
once killed and buried Spanish gold-seekers in the rich gold
mine they (the Spaniards) had dug in Berthound Pass. The Indians then hid the entrance because they did not want any more
white fortune hunters. It has remained hidden for generations
and is unknown to the whites when they demand that the Utes
leave their tribal lands. White Eagle, a medicine man of the
Utes, returns to Berthound Pass, a traditional place of wor-

ship, one last time before his departure. There he meets Mason, a white gold-seeker. White Eagle does not want the mine ever to be found by whites; however, lightning starts a forest fire, and the Indian leads Mason to the secret entrance of the mine, the only place of safety from the raging fire. Mason spots the gold, but because he has been temporarily blinded by the fire, he is unable to memorize the way to the mine on the return trip.

762 Thompson, Thomas. "Memento." With Guidons Flying: Tales of the U.S. Cavalry in the Old West. Garden City, N.Y.: Doubleday, 1970, pp. 177-97. Originally published in Zane Grey's Western Magazine (1951).

Jim Willie, seventeen, is an Apache who has been raised by a kind Quaker family. He loves his adopted family, especially the teenage daughter, Mollie, but he realizes that it would not be good for her to love an Indian. When the Apache cook introduces Jim Willie to his Apache relatives, he feels torn between his two worlds; he is loyal to his white family, and also to his Apache heritage. He is forced to choose between them when he kills a greedy white man who is trying to kill Molly's father. Knowing that the white man's law will punish him for this, Jim Willie leaves to live with the Apaches.

763 Thunen, Frank. "The Burning at Bald Rock." Overland Monthly, n.s. 56 (1910), 576-81.

Thompson and two friends (all white) go to Bald Rock to observe a Digger burning--a cremation at which material goods are sacrificed to the flames. There they see John Chinaman, a noted "master of ceremonies" for Digger burnings, and also Captain Bill, a chief of a local Digger clan. Knowing that the Indians gamble at these affairs, Thompson has secretly brought along some liquor in the hopes that he can get the Indians drunk and win some money. Thompson, however, loses both his money and his liquor, but the white men get away unharmed.

764 Tilden, Kate T. "His Story." Overland Monthly, n.s. 33 (1899), 447-48.

In 1862 the narrator's son (Artie) and two neighbor girls go berry-picking in the mountains. Artie returns, hysterical and wounded, relating how the two girls had been killed by Indians and how he'd been shot with an arrow while escaping. The small settlement is then besieged by "human wolves" throughout the night, but the Indians leave by morning. The bodies of the girls are never found.

765 Tomlinson, Norma. "The Pretty Surprise." Stanford Short Stories, 1957. Ed. Wallace Stegner and Richard Scowcroft. Stanford: Stanford Univ. Press, 1957, pp. 65-80. Originally published in Pacific Spectator (1956).

Victoria, a young Pueblo woman, is caught up in the details of making a home for her little sister now that their father is dead. She decides she must take a trip out past Bernalillo to get clay; she wants to show her sister how to work with it, so that the girl will learn more than she can in the white school. With fifty cents she gets from letting a white tourist take her picture, Victoria buys her sister a spotted butterfly-- one reminiscent of one of the old dances.

766   Track, Soge.   (Sioux/Taos Pueblo).   "The Clearing in the
        Valley. "   The American Indian Reader: Literature.   San
        Francisco: Indian Historian Press, 1973, pp.   63-78.
        On a trip into the woods to gather firewood for the winter, the narrator, a little girl, comes upon an old man in a hidden valley. He tells her the story of four young men who were once sent out to save the pueblo from ruin. Hearing the story, she knows that some day she will be needed to help her people: "We will love one another and there will be peace. " The next day she learns that Old Man has died, so she goes up to the fifth story of the pueblo to take his place as watcher.

767   Traill, Mrs.   "The Indian Maiden's Grave. "   Canadian Maga-
        zine, 4 (1894), 280-82.
        In an inlet in Canada there is an island called Polly Cow's Island, named after a maiden who died of a broken heart. Her father, Captain Jack, had refused to give her to the suitor that she loved, Red Cloud. So Red Cloud left the camp and Polly Cow steadily lost her health, died, and was buried on the is-land.

768   Train, Arthur.   "And Lesser Breeds Without the Law. "   Mr.
        Tutt Comes Home.   New York: Scribner's, 1941, pp. 187-
        220.
        A rich, fat, ugly Pueblo half-breed named Spotted Dog lusts after young Dawn Flower, a full-blooded Pueblo. Be-cause the old man is rich, Dawn Flower's mother agrees to let him marry her daughter, but only after he gives her the deed to some valuable land. After the Christian ceremony there is an Indian one, but the young Casique who performs it (and who also wants to marry Dawn Flower) hears a voice from the Pueblo gods forbidding the marriage because Spotted Dog is not a pure-blood. As a result Dawn Flower refuses to marry Spotted Dog, so Spotted Dog reclaims the land. Mr. Tutt, a visiting New York lawyer, helps Dawn Flower to regain the property--doing so in a brilliant courtroom performance. At the end it is discovered that Spotted Dog had murdered his previous (fifth) wife.

769   Treacy, Mildred F.   "Owl in the Sunlight. "   Western Human-
        ities Review, 12, No. 2 (Spring 1958), 121-30.
        Tucos, a Chiricahua Apache, and Fruit-Gatherer, his old step-mother-in-law, prepare the body of Snarling Wolf for bur-ial. He and his new horse have died as a result of a fall while returning to camp with Broken Tail and his new horse. Tucos, Fruit-Gatherer, and Broken Tail--all fearful of the dead--bury Snarling Wolf in a box canyon. Broken Tail's horse

is restless on the way home and the Indian confesses, after
seeing and hearing an owl in daylight--a bad omen--that the
horse is really Snarling Wolf's, and that it was his own horse
that had died. Tucos returns to the canyon with the horse and
kills it to appease the spirit of Snarling Wolf.

770   Troy, Lillian Mary.   " 'Vaneety, ' the Cherokee Maid. "   Over-
      land Monthly, n. s. 54 (1909), 351-55.
            Brisbane, who has been on a railroad survey trip with
      Murray and Nelson, is hiding in the brush on a river bank
      awaiting an approaching canoe which he assumes contains the
      Apache group that had earlier killed his companions. Instead,
      its occupant is a young, beautiful Cherokee girl, an escaped
      captive of the Apaches, who helps Brisbane also to escape the
      Apaches. Brisbane discovers that the Cherokee girl speaks
      English because her mother had been white, and that their
      common white heritage is the reason she has helped him. Bris-
      bane talks the girl into going back to the white world with him.

771   Ulyatt, Kenneth. "Ghost Riders of the Sioux. " The Usurping
      Ghost and Other Encounters and Experiences. Ed. Susan
      Dickinson. New York: Dutton, 1971, pp. 115-42.
            Eleven-year-old Ben lives on a ranch near the Black
      Hills. One evening in 1889 he is frightened by what appear
      to be ghosts in the woods. He tells his father about the ghosts,
      and soon the entire white community is enraged. They feel
      threatened by these ghosts who are really Sioux Indians dancing
      their Ghost Dance. Soldiers come and kill many of the Indians
      --men, women, and children--at Wounded Knee. Ben's white
      neighbors are relieved that the danger is past.

772   Underwood, Earl. "The Chase of the Little Gray Wolf. "
      Overland Monthly, n. s. 54 (1909), 449-54.
            Corporal O'Dowd and his trusty scout, Running Lizard,
      lead E Troop on the trail of Little Gray Wolf and his renegade
      band. After following their bloody trail for some time, the
      white men encircle the Apaches in a bowl-shaped canyon. The
      surprise attack is a success for the white troops. Corporal
      O'Dowd stabs Little Gray Wolf in the heart after a tough strug-
      gle.

773   Updike, John. "The Indian. " The Music School: Short Sto-
      ries. New York: Knopf, 1966, pp. 9-17.
            A lone Indian sits and wanders around Tarbox, a New
      England town. He is looked upon as "lazy" and generally
      worthless by the townspeople.

774   Van Deusen, A. M. "Hoss Fat. " Sunset, 52, No. 4 (Apr.
      1924), 24-26, 64.
            The narrator, a white man, talks with Minnie, a three-
      hundred-pound Piute washerwoman as she does his laundry.
      Minnie has been married many times and always has tales to
      relate concerning one husband or another. She tells about Hoss

Fat, who had been married to Mary, another Piute woman, before marrying Minnie: One winter he was forced into taking a job cutting wood--or starve. Mary was then very unhappy because, according to Piute tradition, he was doing woman's work. She refused to eat and became ill. She finally relented when Hoss Fat brought home a baby burro he had killed, but Mary soon died anyway. Being ignorant about Christian teaching, Hoss Fat thought Mary would come back to life; disappointed that she did not, he married Minnie. One day, prospector Malapi Pete sought retribution for his baby burro--the one Hoss Fat had killed to feed Mary--and brought Hoss Fat to court. After a humorous trial, Hoss Fat was free, but he left Minnie after having had a realistic dream about his first wife.

775 _____. "Love Medicine." Sunset, 53, No. 5 (Nov. 1924), 24-27, 81.

Minnie, a three-hundred-pound Piute washerwoman, tells this tale to her white male employer: She had once had a worthless husband named Mike--tricked into marrying him and taking care of his old, blind mother when he had told her she reminded him of a slender willow. Mike's wise mother was a joy to Minnie, but Mike--with his selfish schemes--was not. Once he talked Minnie into giving him a hundred dollars so that he could learn to be a medicine man. Mike's medicine did not work on his mother when she became ill; instead, the old woman died. For a while, Mike was a successful medicine man, but when he became ill his self-ministrations did not work.

776 _____. "The Marriages of Minnie." Sunset, 53, No. 5 (May 1923), 12-13, 105-09.

Minnie, a three-hundred-pound Piute washerwoman, tells a white man about her marital experiences: She was the veteran of many marriages, and her husbands were always critical and fault-finding. Minnie could not tolerate this because she considered herself an excellent wife. After the first seven or eight marriages, she learned that beating her husbands would help to quiet or subdue them. She concludes that a woman's life is happier and more peaceful without a husband.

777 Van Doren, Mark. "The Long Shadow." Collected Stories, Vol. II. New York: Hill and Wang, 1965, pp. 233-41.

Elias, a Cherokee youth, falls in love with a white girl, Harriet, who lives near his mission boarding school in Connecticut. Despite intense disapproval in her family, she marries Elias and returns with him to Georgia. There he builds her a good house and they have two children. After ten years, however, President Andrew Jackson decrees that the Cherokees should be moved to Indian territory west of the Mississippi. Elias favors moving, but the other Cherokees do not, so they kill him. Harriet goes back to her brother in Connecticut.

778 Vann, Dorothy Vidler. "Natani, a Prairie-Dog Chief." Young Readers' Indian Stories. New York: Lantern Press, 1951, pp. 91-107.

Kee, a young Navajo sheepherder, wants a pet dog. Dogs eat too much, though, so he decides to find a prairie dog for a pet instead. By accident he snares an albino prairie dog and brings it home, but his grandfather is horrified because the albino is considered to be a sacred chief of the prairie dogs, and tradition dictates that it must be returned immediately. In the end, Kee finally gets his real dog.

779 _____. "Ten Horses." Arizona Quarterly, 15, No. 4 (Winter 1959), 314-27.

Nedesbah, a Navajo, wants to marry Tom Manygoats, a handsome young man she has met at the mission school where she is training to become a nurse. Her father, however, has sold her to an old medicine man for ten horses. She tricks the old man by slipping some sleeping pills into his coffee. Thought to be a "witch," she finally gets to marry the man she wants.

780 Van Waters, Miriam. "The Coming of the Sea Wind." Overland Monthly, n. s. 45 (1905), 355-57.

Margaret Hill finds an Indian girl, Killamah, with a sick baby and takes them home. They nurse the baby back to health and then Margaret hears Killamah's story: The girl's mother was a half-breed and her father was a Nehalem Indian. She had been happy until she was sixteen. At that time, her mother ran off with a white man and, subsequently her father married a white woman. This woman was cruel to Killamah, who soon ran away. Returning later, she learned that her father was dead. She sought help at a Nehalem camp, but was driven out; however, the chief's son, Sea Cliff, saved her, took her to his cabin, and loved her. They had a baby, Sea Wind. One day, Sea Cliff was injured and taken to a hospital; since then, Killamah had been trying to find him. As Killamah finishes telling the story, Sea Cliff paddles up in his canoe looking for her.

781 Vassault, F. I. "Patsy's Potlach." Overland Monthly, n. s. 19 (1892), 461-64.

Shupald, the old chief of the Skokomish, gives a potlach after many years of saving. A considerable amount of his earnings had come from doing menial labor at a lumber mill, where he was known as "Patsy." At the festivities Shupald distributes many yards of calico and two thousand dollars in silver. Although now penniless, Patsy and his wife (Aunt Sally) are very pleased with their newly acquired esteem.

782 Vestal, Stanley. "Dakota Courtship." Southwest Review, 24, No. 2 (Jan. 1939), 148-63. Also published in Roundup Time: A Collection of Southwestern Writing, ed. George S. Perry (New York: McGraw-Hill, 1943), pp. 70-84. [Stanley Vestal, an authority on the Plains Indians, also writes under the name of W. S. Campbell.]

Joe Lone Bear (a young Dakota male) and his grandparents visit the home of Lillie Fineweather's grandfather, Chief

Hardtack. Lillie and her family are Crow, and the Crow and
Dakota tribes have always been traditional enemies. Joe and
Lillie had met at the Indian boarding school and wish to marry.
The grandparents argue at length about the young couple's plans,
all the while trading insults. Joe and Lillie begin to fight too,
but soon stop, realizing the futility of it all. They decide to
confront their grandparents with their wish not to let the traditional tribal enmity prevent their happiness. The argument
then shifts to what the names of the great-grandchildren should
be. Joe and Lillie decide the names can be neither Crow nor
Dakota--they must be animal names. Joe suggests "Mickey
Mouse" if it is a boy; Lillie's choice for a girl is "Minnie
Mouse."

783   . "Warpath." Hoof Trails and Wagon Tracks. Ed.
    Don Ward. New York: Dodd, Mead, 1957, pp. 85-102.
    Originally entitled "Son of the Prairie Raiders" (1936).
        Long Orphan, a young Cheyenne, is ridiculed and mis-
    treated by No Heart (the Cheyenne war chief) on the youth's
    first war-raid against the Crows. Long Orphan distinguishes
    himself in bravery and fighting ability, displacing No Heart as
    the war hero of the raid.

784 Vide, V. V. "The Flight of the Catawba Chief." American
    Tableaux No. 1: Sketches of Aboriginal Life. New York:
    Bucland and Sumner, 1846, pp. 193-206.
        Minaree, the beautiful daughter of the chief of the Wateree
    (a branch of the Catawbas) has a strange sense of foreboding
    about her husband's hunting trip. Indeed, as he is shooting a
    deer, her husband realizes that Seneca Indians (enemies of the
    Catawbas) are on his trail. He is captured--but only at the
    expense of seven Seneca warriors. He is taken to the Seneca
    camp and is sentenced to be tortured to death, but he escapes.
    He kills five warriors of the search party following him, takes
    their scalps, and stops for the scalps of the first seven Indians
    he had killed. The other Senecas are now too frightened to
    follow. Minaree is ecstatic at her husband's return.

785   . "Monica--The Itean Captive." American Tableaux
    No. 1: Sketches of Aboriginal Life. New York: Bucland
    and Sumner, 1846, pp. 209-24.
        Monica, an Itean maiden absorbed in grief over her infant
    brother's death, drifts for many miles in a canoe. Upon land-
    ing, she is captured by Pawnee warriors (enemies of her tribe),
    and it is decided that she should be a victim in the annual hu-
    man sacrifice for the crops. However, Monica is rescued by
    Petalesharro, son of Chief Latalashaw, and she returns to her
    people. Later, in Washington, D. C., Petalesharro is com-
    mended for this brave rescue.

786   . "Tula, or the Hermitess of Athapasca." American
    Tableaux No. 1: Sketches of Aboriginal Life. New York:
    Bucland and Sumner, 1846, pp. 227-50.

Old Kaf-ne-wa-go, a Chippewa warrior, is the father of Ish-ta-le-ah, a strong brave, and Tula, a beautiful maid. Tula marries O-ken-ah-ga, the chief's son, and they live with Tula's parents. One night some Athapascan attackers enter Kaf-ne-wa-go's wigwam and kill everyone except Tula and her baby. These two are taken captive and soon the baby is killed too. After many days, Tula escapes during a storm, wanders for many miles, and finally builds a cozy shelter--intending to spend the rest of her life in seclusion. However, some English traders and their Ottawa guides find Tula's encampment. She agrees to go with them, but refuses to marry any of them. They come upon a camp in which Tula happily discovers her brother, Ish-ta-le-ah.

787 Walters, Anna Lee. (Pawnee/Otoe). "Chapter 1." The Man to Send Rain Clouds: Contemporary Stories by American Indians. Ed. Kenneth Rosen. New York: Viking, 1974, pp. 82-92. [As the short story's title suggests, this apparently is Chapter 1 of a novel-in-progress.]
Natanii is a seven-year-old Navajo boy whose people are attacked (in 1863) by U.S. soldiers in the Canyon de Chelly. He survives by hiding in the junipers.

788 Warman, Cy. "The Bell of Athabaska." Weiga of Temagami and Other Indian Tales. Toronto: McLeod and Allen, 1908, pp. 128-44.
Belle, a lovely Cree maiden, falls in love with "Smith the Silent," the young white surveyor who is "too busy to get married and too poor to support a wife." Jacques, the Siwash Indian (one-quarter white) courts Belle, but she rejects him, just as her "white god" had rejected her.

789 _____. "The Bishop of Price." Frontier Stories. New York: Scribner's, 1898, pp. 81-89.
Indians bother some white gold-seekers, taking their whiskey and then sending them back home.

790 _____. "The Brakeman and the Squaw." Frontier Stories. New York: Scribner's, 1898, pp. 137-46.
McGuire is a conductor on the branch railroad line being built from Maysville to the booming camp at Monarch. Though the Indians in the area are generally peaceful, one day the head brakeman is captured by Indians. McGuire goes to Maysville and returns with a posse, but a squaw (for whom McGuire had done a few favors) offers to lead the men to the captive. The brakeman is rescued without bloodshed.

791 _____. "Chekko and Uncle Ben." Weiga of Temagami and Other Indian Tales. Toronto: McLeod and Allen, 1908, pp. 145-75.
Two white men set up a plan to swindle twelve thousand dollars from a banker. One of them poses as Chekko, an Indian who distrusts white men but who knows the whereabouts of a fabulous mine.

792   _____. "A Couple o' Captains." Frontier Stories. New York: Scribner's, 1898, pp. 235-46.
Tom and Gene are both cavalry captains fighting Indian wars--particularly against the Sioux. When the fighting ends the men seek other employment. Though close friends, they go separate ways: Gene into law practice, Tom with the Burlington Railroad.

793   _____. "The Cross of the Cree." Weiga of Temagami and Other Indian Tales. Toronto: McLeod and Allen, 1908, pp. 54-67.
Carmel is a young Cree maiden who loves Koto, a poor but honest Indian. Accordingly, she refuses to marry Gaybird, an Indian who is rich enough to pay her father a horse in exchange for her hand. In the end she poisons herself.

794   _____. "Half-Breeds." Frontier Stories. New York: Scribner's, 1898, pp. 121-25.
This story bears out the author's theory that "after firewater, French blood is the worst thing that can be mixed up with Indians." The four half-breed sons of a French Canadian make trouble for the white settlers, and are punished.

795   _____. "The Heathen." Weiga of Temagami and Other Indian Tales. Toronto: McLeod and Allen, 1908, pp. 106-13.
A Cree, Old Charley, is the most useful Indian employed by the Hudson Bay Company. When asked why he never became a Christian, he answers that in a time of famine he had asked the Christian God for food, and got nothing. Then he had asked the Cree god, and soon a deer stood before him. Ever since, he has not been hungry.

796   _____. "Hoskaninni." Frontier Stories. New York: Scribner's, 1898, pp. 149-57.
Hoskaninni is a Navajo chief who sells a Navajo silver mine to a white man, only to have his decision overturned by a council of tribal leaders.

797   _____. "Injun Fin'um Paper Talk." Frontier Stories. New York: Scribner's, 1898, pp. 19-33.
In the valley of San Juan (located where Colorado, Utah, and Nevada meet) a band of renegade Ute robbers is led by Old Hatch, an evil desperado who is a mixture of "Ute, Mexican, Hot Tommolla, and white man." Old Hatch threatens his men, saying that if he is ever killed by one of them he will come back and tear out all their eyes and tongues. When Old Hatch is finally killed by a member of the band, local cowboys devise a plan; they put a note in the eye socket of Old Hatch's skull which reads, "One more sleep an' Old Hatch come back and put out your eyes, an' pull out...." When the robbers read the note, they leave the San Juan Valley permanently.

798 _____. "In the Hospital." Frontier Stories. New York: Scribner's, 1898, pp. 69-77.
Frank Wilson is in the hospital recovering from a broken leg suffered in a railroad accident. While delirious with fever, he relates a tale from an earlier period when he was a construction engineer for the Kansas Pacific: Indians trapped a conductor and murdered him by throwing rocks and shooting arrows. Wilson and some other men arrived too late to save the conductor, so from that day on he had no "Christian sympathy" for his red brothers.

799 _____. "The Little Bird and the Blacksmith." Weiga of Temagami and Other Indian Tales. Toronto: McLeod and Allen, 1908, pp. 83-90.
A small French/Cree half-breed boy loses his companion, a little bird. Later he finds him nesting in the coat pocket of a friend, the blacksmith.

800 _____. "Little Cayuse." Frontier Stories. New York: Scribner's, 1898, pp. 171-94.
Little Cayuse is a Pawnee boy who, at age three, is sold by a Sioux to a white man at the Pony Express station. The white man raises the Pawnee child, who is eventually instrumental in defending the station against several Sioux attacks. Some years later he is kidnapped back by the Sioux, but after a year he escapes and returns, eluding a wolf pack.

801 _____. "Sabo." Weiga of Temagami and Other Indian Tales. Toronto: McLeod and Allen, 1908, pp. 92-103.
Sabo, son of an Indian woman and a half-French father, is generally lazy and good-for-nothing, preferring to play his mouth-harp rather than to work. He marries Lorine, also part-Indian, but she soon wants a divorce. Sabo drives away Chippewa Charley, a rival for his wife's love.

802 _____. "A Scalp for a Scalp." Frontier Stories. New York: Scribner's, 1898, pp. 37-47.
A small group of Pawnee scouts is attacked by a much larger force of Sioux. The story focuses on a single combat between two equally ferocious Indians. Each finally simultaneously scalps the other, and then both plunge together into the river.

803 _____. "Slaying the Wild Bull." Frontier Stories. New York: Scribner's, 1898, pp. 51-57.
As the railroad crew watches, two Sioux Indians duel an old buffalo bull. The Sioux make it a kind of game, perhaps even a ritual, using arrows rather than their rifles.

804 _____. "Tickaboo." Frontier Stories. New York: Scribner's, 1898, pp. 159-67.
Shirtz, one of two white Mormon boys raised by Ute Chief Tickaboo, begs his mentor to show them the lost Josephine

Mine. The chief finally agrees, so the three set out to find it. On the last night before reaching their destination, the chief grows fearful because (as a joke) Shirtz's companion has put gun powder into Tickaboo's pipe and the pipe explodes. Tickaboo considers this a bad omen; Shirtz never learns the mine's location.

805 _____. "Valley Tan." Frontier Stories. New York: Scribner's, 1898, pp. 61-67.

Two federal agents, on their way to arrest the operators of an illegal still, watch two drunken Indians, a Ute and a Piute, murder each other. (The Ute is a half-breed, and is one of the proprietors of the still. Half-breeds, we are told, have "enough 'white blood' to make them ambitious, and enough red to make them kill a man for a new saddle.")

806 _____. "The Wahsatch Band of Bandits." Frontier Stories. New York: Scribner's, 1898, pp. 197-207.

A group of bandits ("The Wahsatch Band of Bandits") is led by a half-breed. An Indian and his band offer to destroy the robbers, but they all get drunk and fail. Later the half-breed, after several unsuccessful attempts to rob trains, is deposed as leader of the bandits.

807 _____. "Wantawanda." Frontier Stories. New York: Scribner's, 1898, pp. 209-33.

About 1830 an English captain named Stuart comes to America looking for adventure. Soon after arrival he is saved from death by a Crow maiden, Wantawanda. Stuart and Fitzpatrick, a trapper, engage in various confrontations with friendly Cheyenne and Sioux Indians against a small enemy Crow band. A planned massacre of the white men by Crows is thwarted when Wantawanda warns Stuart.

808 _____. "Weiga of Temagami." Weiga of Temagami and Other Indian Tales. Toronto: McLeod and Allen, 1908, pp. 15-28.

An Algonquin Indian youth comes into the hunting ground of Meniseno, an old Ojibway. The Algonquin, believing he has a terminal illness, wants only to die in peace, but Meniseno is angry at this intrusion into his land. Weiga, Meniseno's daughter, incurs her father's wrath by befriending the newcomer. Meniseno tries to kill the sick man, but the Algonquin's domesticated moose protects his master. Finally the old man dies; and the Algonquin recovers from his illness and marries Weiga.

809 _____. "The Welcome of the Wild." Weiga of Temagami and Other Indian Tales. Toronto: McLeod and Allen, 1908, pp. 11, 31-51.

Bannihan's Mormon wife runs off to become an actress. Soon thereafter, Bird, a Cree maiden who is a "guileless child of the wild," offers to become his wife. He refuses, but later

reconsiders. Motivated partly by a desire to convert her to
Christianity, he finally does marry her. She is so happy that
she throws herself into his arms and lies "softly sobbing on
his broad breast precisely as a white woman might sob."

810   Weadock, Jack. "A Pair of Red-Topped Boots." Roundup
      Time: A Collection of Southwestern Writing. Ed. George
      S. Perry. New York: McGraw-Hill, 1943, pp. 64-69.
         Ignacio Flores, a Papago sub-chief, murders a bad white
      man named Texas Jack. He turns himself in to the sheriff.
      There is due process, more or less, and though everyone likes
      the Indian and knows they would have done the same in his
      shoes, the jury sentences him to be hanged. Ignacio's friend, the
      sheriff, tearfully officiates at the hanging.

811   _____. "A Rebel Rides." Dust of the Desert: Plain Tales
      of the Desert and the Border. New York: D. Appleton-
      Century, 1936, pp. 161-72.
         While some two hundred of Cochise's Apaches lay siege
      to Tubac, a Texan sneaks out for a night ride to Tucson for
      help. He returns with twenty-five men, and the Apaches are
      driven off.

812   _____. "The Scalp-Hunters." Dust of the Desert: Plain
      Tales of the Desert and the Border. New York: D. Appleton-
      Century, 1936, pp. 189-99.
         Unidentified southwestern Indians and Mexicans impose
      desert justice against some cheating white scalp-hunting gang-
      sters by attacking a town.

813   _____. "When Wolf and Gray Wolf Meet." Dust of the
      Desert: Plain Tales of the Desert and the Border. New
      York: D. Appleton-Century, 1936, pp. 37-46.
         Captain John Jeffords, in charge of getting the mails
      through Apache country, is losing most of his riders to Apache
      raiders. He decides he must strike a bargain with Cochise
      directly, so he rides alone into the Apache camp in the Chiri-
      cahuas. Cochise respects the white man's bravery and decides
      that he can trust Jeffords. They make a pact.

814   Webb, Walter Prescott. "The Singing Snakes of the Karankawas."
      Mid-Country: Writings from the Heart of America. Ed.
      Lowry C. Wimberly. Lincoln: Univ. of Nebraska Press,
      1945, pp. 232-35. Originally published in Southwest Review.
         Mitch Talley, a white man, befriends old Joseph, the
      last of the Karankawa Indians, and in return the old Indian
      shows Mitch how he calls together fifty snakes and gets them
      to sing. The singing snakes become a kind of choir, complete
      with soprano, alto, tenor, and bass.

815   Weeks, Raymond. "The Cheyenne Lodge." The Hound-tuner
      of Callaway. New York: Columbia Univ. Press, 1927,
      pp. 179-82.

A detachment of soldiers in the late 1860s comes upon the funeral lodge and bier of a Cheyenne man. Frozen to death, kneeling on the ground before it, is his wife.

816   Weiler, P. Garrett. "Cut-Hand." South Dakota Review, 6, No. 2 (Summer, 1968), 14-24.
Billy Gipson, a young Comanche, had been born of rich parents (oil wells) in Texas. He has received an M. A. from the University of Texas and has been trained in Indian ways and lore at his mother's knee. Billy is torn between being Indian and being white; he is frustrated, unable to prove himself in traditional Indian manners. When Billy starts working on a ranch, one of his fellow workers is an old Crow Indian named Joe Eagle. Billy suffers from a cut hand which has become infected, but he does not have it treated. When Joe and Billy are working at an isolated part of the ranch, Billy becomes quite ill and goes outside one night to die. Joe decides to bury the troubled young man according to Indian tradition. Billy has at last done something as an Indian; he has died as an Indian.

817   Wellman, Manly Wade. "A Star for a Warrior." The Golden 13. Ed. Ellery Queen. New York: World, 1970, pp. 3-21. Originally published in American Mercury (1946).
A young Indian policeman, David Return, solves his first case, the murder of a pretty young Indian woman anthropologist. She had been visiting the Tsichah (an imaginary tribe much like the Cheyenne) in order to record some of their secret ceremonial songs. She was murdered, David discovers, by one of the young medicine men who refused to cooperate with the woman in her research.

818   Wharton, Ann. "The Disappearing Sun: A Story of the Battle of San Jacinto." Southwest Review, 21, No. 4 (Jul. 1936), 400-07.
A young Cherokee man, Tahlequah, son of a medicine man, is a captive in Santa Anna's camp. While the Mexicans sleep, Tahlequah criticizes Santa Anna and his men in his thoughts for their ignorance of "proper" Indian ways. Only the alert Tahlequah is aware of the Texas army's rapid approach. The young boy unsuccessfully tries to escape the Mexican camp; he is shot by a Texan as he shouts, "Me no Goliad. Me no Alamo."

819   Wheelwright, Richard. "Mudhead." Arizona Quarterly, 26, No. 4 (Winter 1970), 325-33.
Albert Lololoma, a Hopi of Old Oraibi, with traditional early rearing, has spent some years among the whites going to school. He has also spent two years at the Institute of American Arts in Santa Fe learning painting and sculpture, and some time at the Indian school at Phoenix learning to be an electrician. Since his return to the reservation, his savings have dwindled and it has been difficult for him to make

a living despite his training. He lovingly looks at the family Kachina masks and makes a decision to sell a mudhead mask. Albert walks to a deserted section of Old Oraibi, awaits two anthropologists, and sells the mask.

820   Whitaker, Herman. "Sheep: A Story of Natural Selection." Sunset, 40, No. 3 (Mar. 1918), 35-37, 58, 60-63.
      The narrator, a young professor, is guided to New Mexican pueblos by John Dee, a wool trader. John is quite hesitant about the subject of marriage--even though he is quite taken by a young and beautiful widow, Nellie Bridges, who lives with her Zuni cook and employs two white sheepherders, Hank and Dave. It is not until the two bumbling sheepherders and the suave and rich rancher, Nye Taylor, all ask to marry Nellie that John is finally moved to confess his love for her. He learns that she loves him too.

821   _____. "A Tale of the Pasquia Past." Overland Monthly, n. s. 36 (1900), 123-28.
      In an abandoned cabin, three men (one an Indian) discover the skeletons of Strong John West, a white man, and Zaar, his half-breed lover. They find John's ledger telling of his tragic love and death at the hands of Indians angry at him for taking her.

822   White, James L. "The Deer." South Dakota Review, 9, No. 1 (Spring 1971), 58-65.
      Simon (Indian) with his white friend, Stephan, returns to Old Laguna for a deer hunt. Simon's mother sees them off, but Simon's Navajo wife does not participate in or care to learn the Laguna traditions. At first the camped men are nervous about a white man's presence because they believe it may ruin the hunt; however, Stephan manages to gain acceptance. During the night an owl hoots--a bad omen--but the next morning Simon kills a deer anyway, and for a short time revels in and is revitalized by the old Laguna ways.

823   Whitlock, Will T. "The Circumflex." Overland Monthly, n. s. 33 (1899), 348-54.
      Chaota (a young Sioux) is home for vacation following three years at a Chicago medical school--after having been sent there by an army major who had raised him. Chaota talks with Mishawaka (his love since childhood) and, though he still loves her, is slightly ashamed of her Indian ways. Sensing this, Mishawaka secretly runs away to attend school at a fort one hundred miles away in order to learn white ways and make Chaota proud of her. Three years later, at a fort ball celebrating Chaota's (now Dr. Wainwright's) completion of medical school, a young girl enters the room to play the piano. It is Mishawaka. Their love is rekindled.

824   Whitman, Carl, Jr. "Composite Portrait of an Indian: John Big Skunk." Journal of American Indian Education, 5, No. 2 (Jan. 1966), 17-24.

John Big Skunk arrives home after a week's drunken celebration with a number of his friends. He is hesitant about seeing his wife. John is always losing his land, money, or other
possessions because of his generosity and his love of celebrat-
ing. Once he made short work of ninety thousand dollars that
he received from an oil lease. Now John's financial situation
is so bad that his wife and ten children must live with his in-
laws. But John's wife loves him and, after her initial annoyance subsides, she is glad that he has come home.

825 Whitman, Walt. "The Half-Breed, A Tale of the Western
Frontier." Early Poems and Fiction. Ed. Thomas L.
Brasher. New York: New York Univ. Press, 1963, pp.
257-91. Originally entitled "Arrow-Tip" when first published
in The Aristidean (Mar. 1845).
Arrow-Tip is an Indian chief who gets into a scuffle with
Peter Brown, a blacksmith, and nearly kills him. The townspeople, thinking Brown is dead, summarily hang Arrow-Tip,
but only because Boddo (the deformed, hunchback son of a Catholic priest and an Indian woman), wanting revenge against Arrow-Tip for a private quarrel, refuses to convey the message
that Brown is still alive.

826 Whittaker, Herman. "White Man's Food." Overland Monthly,
41 (1903), 300-07.
Bob Young tricks some Cree Indians into trading ten
horses for some worthless "chop" (horse food), telling them it
is flour. Later he is captured in Riel's rebellion, and for fifteen days is fed nothing by his captors except the foul-tasting
chop.

827 Wiebe, Rudy. "Where Is the Voice Coming From?" Fourteen
Stories High. Ed. David Helwig and Tom Marshall. n. p. :
Oberon Press, 1971, pp. 112-21.
A small Canadian museum exhibits pictures of Almighty
Voice, an escaped Cree prisoner, who in 1896 made a last
stand in the hills nearby. He killed several of the many police-
men surrounding him, and eventually died there himself. Other
Indians took his body away, but now a piece of his skull is on
display in the museum.

828 Wilkins, Mary E. "Silence." Harper's, 87 (Jul. 1893), 233-
50. Reprinted in Silence and Other Stories (New York:
Harper, 1898).
Silence is a young woman who one day sees red in all
that she looks at. She feels that there will be an Indian attack.
That night her fear is realized and the town is almost destroyed.
Many people are killed, and Silence's fiancé is captured. A
rescue party is sent but her lover is not returned. She calls
for him every day, but he does not come. When he finally
does return she does not initially recognize him.

829 Williams, Albert, Jr. "The Cremated Digger." Overland
Monthly, n. s. 19 (1892), 289-301.

Zeb Winslow and Jim Calkins are partners in a gold claim at Grizzly Gulch in California. When the claim starts to dry up Jim leaves and heads East without telling anyone his destination; Zeb hires some Digger Indians to continue working the claim. "Stovepipe" (a Digger) dies unexpectedly and his fellow Indians begin a cremation ceremony, but Zeb stops them and the body is buried instead. Zeb's friend (Dr. Lane) steals the skull from the grave, and much later the headless body is found and believed to be Jim's. Zeb is brought to trial for the "murder" but Dr. Lane proves his friend's innocence by producing the Digger skull.

830   Williams, Edward Huntington, M. D. "Old Mac's White Lie."
       Outing, 54, No. 4 (Jul. 1909), 434-41.
       In the northern wilderness, a Hudson Bay Company factor sends Jack Martin on the "long trail" into the backwoods without weapons or supplies, with the nearest village a three-weeks' walk away. This is Jack's "punishment" for trapping in forbidden territory. Most men similarly treated die; however, a year later, much to everyone's surprise, Jack returns to the settlement. The cruel factor sends him on the "long trail" again with the half-breed, Black Pierre, following. These men never return, and the factor also disappears. Twenty years later, Mac, who had been a boy in the northern settlement at the time of the incidents, sees Jack Martin and learns what had happened. Having narrowly survived the first "long trail," Jack had vowed to get even with the factor. Anticipating a second punishment, Jack had cached weapons and supplies in the woods. These he used to force Black Pierre and the factor into taking their own "long trail." To relieve Jack's guilt, Mac lies--telling him that the two had been found and rescued.

831   Williams, Ted C. (Iroquois). "Bedbug." The Reservation.
       Syracuse, N. Y.: Syracuse Univ. Press, 1976, pp. 45-49.
       A twelve-year-old Tuscarora boy, Bedbug, comes crying to the narrator because his house has burned down and he cannot find his mother. Since it is Bedbug's birthday, a party is given for him. The next day the boy visits another family and they have a second birthday party for him. The day after that, Bedbug's mother finds him and she wants to celebrate his birthday still another time.

832   _____. (Iroquois). "Cassandra." The Reservation. Syra-
       cuse, N. Y.: Syracuse Univ. Press, 1976, pp. 57-68.
       Cassandra, an old Tuscarora woman, is the grandmother of Less Laughing, a teenager. Cassandra wants the boy to become a doctor or a lawyer, but Less Laughing is interested only in farming. When Cassandra catches her grandson alone with his pretty young school teacher, Cassandra changes her mind and no longer forces him to get an education. She also hires a local witch to put a spell on the school teacher.

833   _____. (Iroquois). "The Cucumber Tree." The Reserva-

tion. Syracuse, N. Y. : Syracuse Univ. Press, 1976, pp. 91-94.

At night Naw'HRET-HRET, a Tuscarora man, shoots a drunk trespasser for urinating on his prized cucumber tree. Then Naw'HRET-HRET's wife, OO'doos, accidentally shoots her husband.

834 _____. (Iroquois). "Father." The Reservation. Syracuse, N. Y. : Syracuse Univ. Press, 1976, pp. 15-35.

The narrator's father is a well-known Tuscarora medicine man who cures many sick people, both Indian and white, but refuses to sell medicines to some white visitors who are eager to buy his cure for cancer.

835 _____. (Iroquois). "The Feast." The Reservation. Syracuse, N. Y. : Syracuse Univ. Press, 1976, pp. 141-79.

The New Year's Feast is a happy time on the Tuscarora reservation. One of the highlights is a hunting contest between the young (unmarried) men and the old men. Each side tries to outdo the other, and, whenever they can, to humiliate the other side by trickery.

836 _____. (Iroquois). "Hogart." The Reservation. Syracuse, N. Y. : Syracuse Univ. Press, 1976, pp. 103-08.

Hogart is a white man who lives among the Tuscaroras and tries very hard to be like them. He never succeeds, however, at becoming an Indian: His skin burns instead of getting tan; his hair turns white; he can't learn to shoot straight; he can't stomach an Indian soup made of tree frogs. Even when he dies, he is buried off the reservation.

837 _____. (Iroquois). "The House That Song Built." The Reservation. Syracuse, N. Y. : Syracuse Univ. Press, 1976, pp. 95-102.

A Tuscarora man, Song, and his wife, Big Melon, love to sing for people. When their son, Glare, is killed in an automobile accident, however, Big Melon goes crazy and runs away with their deaf and dumb daughter, Melon. Heeengs, a medicine woman, fortunately finds and cures them both, then returns with them to live in Song's house--which is shaped like a number seven and attached to four trees.

838 _____. (Iroquois). "Many Lips and Lala La." The Reservation. Syracuse, N. Y. : Syracuse Univ. Press, 1976, pp. 69-89.

A Tuscarora man, Many Lips, has for many years treated his wife, Lala La, like a servant. He has been completely unaware of her loneliness and unhappiness. She never complains, but one afternoon she quietly pushes him over the edge of a cliff.

839 _____. (Iroquois). "Mrs. Shoe's Gang." The Reservation. Syracuse, N. Y. : Syracuse Univ. Press, 1976, pp. 37-44.

Mrs. Shoe lives with other members of the Beaver Clan (Tuscarora) in an old log house shaped like a shoe. There are so many people (including numerous children) living in that small house that they divide up into two groups--the day crew and the night crew--which take turns eating and sleeping in the house and scavenging around the reservation.

840   _____. (Iroquois). "Old Claudie and Bullet." The Reservation. Syracuse, N.Y.: Syracuse Univ. Press, 1976, pp. 117-23.

An old Tuscarora man, Old Claudie, is a poor drunk who works as a farm hand for a shrewd, rich Indian farmer named Bullet. Old Claudie has a party to mourn the death of his old friend, Groover (another drunk), and accidentally sets fire to Bullet's house. The house and barn burn down.

841   _____. (Iroquois). "The Picnic Snake." The Reservation. Syracuse, N.Y.: Syracuse Univ. Press, 1976, pp. 51-56.

The narrator, a Tuscarora boy, takes a green snake to a big picnic on the reservation. When the preacher sees the boys betting money on whether that snake can climb up a string, he angrily kills the snake. The boys know that it is always bad luck to kill a snake. Sure enough, a little later the preacher breaks his thumb during a ball game, and a huge thundercloud brings a bad storm.

842   _____. (Iroquois). "The Reservoir." The Reservation. Syracuse, N.Y.: Syracuse Univ. Press, 1976, pp. 181-204.

The government decides to build a reservoir which will flood part of the Tuscarora Indian Reservation. The Tuscaroras who oppose this reservoir (but whose opinions make no difference) try many clever, often humorous, usually non-violent tactics to discourage the surveyors and engineers and bulldozers that invade their reservation.

843   _____. (Iroquois). "The Sultan." The Reservation. Syracuse, N.Y.: Syracuse Univ. Press, 1976, pp. 109-16.

The Sultan is a young Tuscarora man who always wears a pair of second-hand shoes, the toes of which curl up at the end because they are too long for him. His doctor has told the Sultan that he has only a year to live, so he digs his own grave (he wants to be buried standing up) and leads a carefree life. Exactly one year after his conversation with his doctor, he climbs into his grave and drinks himself to death.

844   _____. (Iroquois). "The Tellers." The Reservation. Syracuse, N.Y.: Syracuse Univ. Press, 1976, pp. 215-54.

The narrator, a young Tuscarora boy, repeats many of the stories that he has heard from some of the old men and women, "The Tellers," around the reservation. He regrets, however, to think that these good talkers--like Star Silver, Old Sly, SETHcloss, Cap Peters-Hi-Velocity, and Heee'engs-- won't be around by the time he grows up. Then he realizes that by that time he himself will be "A Teller."

845 _____ . (Iroquois). "Thraangkie and You-swee(t)-dad."
The Reservation. Syracuse, N.Y.: Syracuse Univ. Press,
1976, pp. 125-40.
You-swee(t)-dad, an old Tuscarora who has not become
a Christian, has a long argument with Thraangkie, a Christian
Tuscarora. The narrator, a Tuscarora boy, listens with great
interest, first being swayed by the one speaker, then by the
other.

846 _____ . (Iroquois). "The Trailers." The Reservation.
Syracuse, N.Y.: Syracuse Univ. Press, 1976, pp. 205-13.
The many differences of opinion on the Tuscarora reservation sometimes lead to trouble. The trailer park controversy
is a good example. Some Tuscaroras let the white construction workers park trailers on their land while the dam is being
built; other Indians oppose this idea of letting whites live on
their reservation, despite the money it brings them. Nevertheless, the trailers come by the hundreds, and when the dam
is finished, the workers linger on. The Indians still do not
agree, but finally the whites are pressured into removing the
trailers from the reservation.

847 _____ . (Iroquois). "When I Was Little." The Reservation.
Syracuse, N.Y.: Syracuse Univ. Press, 1976, pp. 1-13.
The narrator tells about his parents, Mischew and Steel-
plant, and how they courted each other. He also remembers
the time his ninety-two-year-old grandmother, Geese-a-geese,
fell out of a cherry tree and broke her hip. These are some
of the narrator's earliest memories about his life on the Tuscarora reservation in New York.

848 Wilmot, Robert Patrick. "Fast Gun." The Saturday Evening
Post Reader of Western Stories. Ed. E. N. Brandt. Garden
City, N.Y.: Doubleday, 1960, pp. 269-83.
Matt Howard stumbles into town without his "britches"
and with a Chiricahua Apache arrow in his chest. In the course
of the story he beats up the town bully, marries a lovely virgin, and has his life saved by Billy the Kid, who shoots up
Howard's three attackers (only the Mojave half-breed escaping
with his life).

849 Wilner, Herbert. "Dovisch Among the Savages." The Saturday
Evening Post, 238, No. 12 (Jun. 19, 1965), 58-60, 62-68,
70, 72. Reprinted as "Dovisch in the Wilderness" in The
Best American Short Stories, 1966, ed. Martha Foley and
David Burnett (Boston: Houghton Mifflin, 1966), pp. 328-57.
Dovisch, Professor of American Literature, drives from
California to Pyramid Lake (on the Piute reservation) for a
four-day solitary vacation. When he gets into his car to re-
turn for a Monday morning lecture, he finds that it will not
start. He walks miles to a shack, where a Piute Indian named
Mike sullenly offers to help him--for a fifteen dollar fee. Un-
able to get the car started, Mike does additional damage before

towing it to a gas station. An oil company executive comes along and rescues Dovisch, who gets home in time to tell his students about the experience.

850 Wilson, Bourdon. "The Last Cartridge." Sunset, 24 (Apr. 1910), 372-76.
    Masters has come West to find gold. He finally strikes it rich in Apache country, only to be attacked by Apaches. He is wounded, grows delirious, and uses all his bullets except one (which he is saving for himself), but the cavalry arrives in time to save his life.

851 _____. "Ockinsaw: A Narrative of the Chiricahua Apaches." Sunset, 10 (Feb. 10, 1903), 290-94.
    A dude from Arkansas (named, appropriately, Ockinsaw) signs on as a cook for a small group of railway surveyors, who enjoy playing tricks and scaring him with snakes and tales of Indians. When the Apaches really do attack, however, Ockinsaw saves their lives.

852 Wilson, Calvin Dill. "Their Law." Overland Monthly, n. s. 45 (1905), 514-16.
    A white man talks to two Indians, Red Fox and Black Bear, to find out why they are in prison. He learns that they had killed their chief, Chief Mogul. Though they had broken white man's law, they had kept Indian law; Chief Mogul had felt himself going mad, and had ordered his own death for the protection of his people. Red Fox and Black Bear had bravely volunteered to do the deed, and now they are being punished for following their own tribal tradition.

853 Wilson, Harry. "Travelers in All Seasons." South Dakota Review, 1, No. 2 (May 1964), 33-40.
    Voljos, whose mother was an Indian, runs a small gift store with some crafts from the reservation. The end of the season is approaching and the snows will soon come. Voljos notices a young, tall, blond boy (the only guest at Mrs. Kelsey's hotel) and invites him into the shop. The two have a brief conversation and Voljos learns that the boy is just traveling, without much direction.

854 Wilson, Joseph S. "Seneca Captive." Teen-Age Frontier Stories. Ed. A. L. Furman. New York: Lantern Press, 1958, pp. 180-96. Originally published in Boy's Life (1956).
    Ben, a sixteen-year-old white boy, sets out to find his mother, who was captured by Senecas while he was away fighting with General Herkimer at Oriskany in 1777. Ben becomes a "blue-eyed 'Indian' like the renegade white men who live like Indians and fight their own people" and, disguised as such, gains the confidence of a few Mohawks who help rescue the woman.

855 Winchell, Ernestine. "Soldaddy." Out West, 27, No. 5, (Nov. 1907), 439-46.

Soldaddy (a corruption of the Spanish "Soledad") is a lazy, old, freeloading Indian who refuses to work, but who is nevertheless kind and considerate. He lives by charity and begging. Soldaddy is finally a "hero" when he works--successfully--to save some white women and children from a forest fire.

856 _____. "Suanee." Out West, 27, No. 6 (Dec. 1907), 514-19.

Tom Willis (white) asks Old Mary (Indian) to help his wife Elizabeth with the laundry. She agrees to help. One day, after doing the wash, Old Mary tells Elizabeth about her past: When young, she had been called Suanee and had married a tribesman named José. Their first baby died, but she had been happy in those days. Then they went to a white lumber camp so José could work; there, Mac, a white lumberman, started paying attention to Suanee. She had Mac's baby, and José began to drink all the time. This baby also died, but she had another by Mac. José continued to drink. Mac finally went away. The second of Mac's babies lived but, after some years, José died. Mary is now a grief-stricken old squaw.

857 Winslow, Thyra Samter. "Indian Blood." My Own, My Native Land. Garden City, N. Y.: Doubleday, Doran, 1935, pp. 195-201.

Ralph Austin, an Oklahoma Indian who has done well in high school, goes off to college. After the family money runs out, he takes a job at an Indian Education Exhibition in Chicago, but finally returns to Oklahoma to start a haberdasher's shop.

858 Wister, Owen. "Balaam and Pedro." Harper's, 88 (Dec. 1893), 52-57.

Balaam meets a man named Shorty, who carries a message instructing Balaam to return the borrowed horses in his possession to the owner--a judge. Meanwhile, Balaam buys a horse (called Pedro) from Shorty. Although he at one time had suffered a broken leg, Pedro is a good horse. While chasing a runaway horse, Pedro saves Balaam's life by evading Indians who had planned an ambush.

859 _____. "The General's Bluff." Red Men and White. New York: Harper, 1896, pp. 82-114.

General Crook successfully "captures" three hundred Indians with a force of forty soldiers.

860 _____. "The Gift Horse." The Saturday Evening Post Reader of Western Stories. Ed. E. N. Brandt. Garden City, N. Y.: Doubleday, 1960, pp. 284-305.

Old Washakie, chief of the Shoshone, gives the narrator a map to a little-known spring. (The rest of the story does not concern Indians.)

861 _____. "A Kinsman of Red Cloud." The Jimmyjohn Boss. New York: Harper, 1900, pp. 67-99.

In the early 1870s Scout Jarvis Cutler has dinner at the

post with Captain Brent and Lieutenants Baldwin and Powell after having accepted a position as wagon master for the White River expedition. He then goes to play poker with his friends, Loomis and Kelly, and the French/Sioux half-breed, Toussaint, whose mother was Red Cloud's sister. Toussaint cheats, and a fight follows in which the half-breed kills Loomis and Kelly. Cutler goes after him, and puts him in jail. Toussaint is convicted and sentenced to be hanged, but he escapes. With the help of Two Knives, Cutler again finds Toussaint, this time in Sioux disguise. Red Cloud threatens war but, after talking with Toussaint, agrees that the white men should have him. Eventually Toussaint hangs.

862 _____. "Little Big Horn Medicine." Harper's, 89 (Jun. 1894), 118-32. Reprinted in Red Man and White (New York: Harper, 1896), pp. 3-35.
   Cheschapah is a Crow Indian who claims to be the greatest medicine man because he is able to make cold water boil. Little known to his fellow Crows, he does this by using chemicals bought from the Indian agent, Kinney. The cavalry is sent to break up an unauthorized meeting of the Crows with the Sioux, and as the Sioux are being led away Cheschapah tries to stop the cavalry. A skirmish is avoided when Cheschapah's father (Old Pounded Meat) intervenes. But Cheschapah plans even greater magic--the Crows prepare to fight the white man. Finally, Cheschapah leads an attack in which he is killed and his companion (Two Whistles) commits suicide.

863 _____. "Napoleon Shave-Tail." The Jimmyjohn Boss. New York: Harper, 1900, pp. 137-57.
   Pompous young Officer Augustus Albumblatt arrives at Fort Brown, where he relates stories of his German military education, his faith in books, and his "practical experience" in fighting. After receiving a telegram from the Crow Agency in Montana, Captain Duane sends Albumblatt to the Fort Brown Indian settlement to capture Ute Jack (who has killed a Crow Indian). Nothing in Albumblatt's book training has prepared him for this duty. After some time he does manage to kill Ute Jack, but in doing so he loses a valuable sergeant. Albumblatt is not so pompous after this experience.

864 _____. "The Patronage of High Bear." Cosmopolitan, 30, No. 3 (Jan. 1901), 250-59.
   Horace Pericles Bryam, better known as "Horacles," is a clerk in a Montana reservation store. He is an unpleasant man who has gotten this job through an influential uncle in Washington. When the agent leaves on an alleged trip to St. Paul, he asks his friend, Scipio le Moyne (Indian/French), to keep an eye on the store. Actually, the agent goes to Washington to check on rumors that a new store--with Horacles in charge--is scheduled to open next to his. Scipio is disturbed when he learnes that Horacles is, indeed, soon opening a new store, and feels badly that this is to occur while the agent is

away. Scipio shrewdly spreads the word among the Indians that
Horacles is a "heap-big" medicine man. Horacles fulfills this
image on opening day of his store by doing magic tricks; but
when Scipio encourages Horacles to display his false teeth, the
Indians are permanently scared away from the new store.

865 _____. "The Promised Land." Harper's, 88 (Apr. 1894),
781-96.
The Callams (an immigrant family) are crossing the country, heading through Iowa, where they meet Wild Goose Jake
and his assistant, Andy Leander. Jake agrees to ferry them
across the Okanagon River. After the raft is built, some Indians break into Jake's shack and steal some whiskey. (Jake
is involved in bootlegging whiskey to the Indians.) Some days
later, Jake gets into an argument with the Indians and they kill
Andy. In the ensuing battle most of the Indians are killed, too,
but one manages to shoot Jake, who dies just as the sheriff
arrives to arrest him.

866 _____. "Specimen Jones." Harper's, 89 (Jul. 1894), 204-
16. Reprinted in Red Men and White (New York: Harper,
1896), pp. 36-63.
A young tenderfoot (Cumnor) enters a saloon in Arizona.
The lad has plans to travel through the Flora Pass in which a
man was found dead, apparently killed by Apaches. For some
reason Specimen Jones has compassion for the boy, and he
catches up to Cumnor. On the way they find the burning wagons of some Mexicans. Jones's gun is empty; Cumnor's foot
is bleeding, so he takes off his boots and chases the Indians
while they are dancing. The Indians flee, and the two white
men decide to enlist at Fort Grant.

867 Wolfe, Bernard. "Mr. Economos and the Sand Painters."
Move Up Dress Up Drink Up Burn Up. Garden City, N.Y.:
Doubleday, 1968, pp. 96-125. Originally published under
the title "The Hard Times of a Hollywood Squaw Man," and
under the author's pseudonym "Andrew Foxe," in Cavalier
(1966).
Farley Munters, in Hollywood making a movie, has an
affair with Dorotheen, who is three-eighths Osage. Later he
hires Angelica, an Otoe, to do his housekeeping. After a series of comic misadventures (in one of which the two Indian girls
learn that Apaches once did sand painting and, therefore, try
to recapture their cultural heritage by doing salt painting) Farley returns to his wife in Kew Gardens. Soon he finds himself
making up an elaborate story to explain a letter from Mr. Economos, owner of a Los Angeles laundry, about a claim for
lost laundry that Dorotheen had made using the name of Mrs.
Munters.

868 Wood, Kerry. "The Boy and the Buffalos." Young Readers'
Indian Stories. New York: Lantern Press, 1951, pp. 159-
74.

Jim Ochiese, a Chippewa chief, likes to tell a story of his youth: When he was four years old, he had wandered off and had become lost. Two buffalo cows became his foster parents. He drank their milk and slept near their warm bodies at night. Two years later he was found again by members of his tribe out on a buffalo hunt.

869 _____. "Justice on the Trap Trail." Young Readers' Indian Stories. New York: Lantern Press, 1951, pp. 38-58.
A half-breed Indian is caught stealing pelts from the traps of some Cree trappers. The Crees demand his death, but Chief Mia-Kun has promised to uphold the laws of Canada, which demand that the guilty man be tried and sentenced. Instead of either alternative, however, the wise chief makes the thief run along a path in which bear traps are supposedly concealed, thus allowing the fear-crazed coward to escape into the forest.

870 _____. "The Runaway Boy." Young Readers' Indian Stories. New York: Lantern Press, 1951, pp. 59-73.
Samson Beaver, a Stoney Indian boy, tires of boarding school and runs away. After many days and nights on the month-old trail of his family, he finally joins them.

871 Woodbridge, Bradford. "Santa Teresa." Overland Monthly, n. s. 28 (1896), 422-26.
Teresa, a young Mexican orphan, has a memorable religious experience after which she leaves her village. She is captured by a band of Yaquis but, through her amazing power of healing, gains control over them and leads them in battles against their Mexican enemies. When she and six Yaquis are captured and are about to be executed, Teresa shouts a death wish to the assassins--who mysteriously fall to the ground. The rest of the soldiers flee in fear; Teresa and her Yaquis go free.

872 _____. "A Tragedy of Pit River." Overland Monthly, n. s. 29 (1897), 640-42.
An old white man tells a story: He and his partner ("Red") once had a problem with Pit River Indians who interfered with their mail and express business. The two white men baked two hundred loaves of bread loaded with strychnine which, through a ruse, was delivered to the Indians. The Indians, their numbers greatly reduced by deaths from the poisoning, moved away.

873 Woolf, Douglas. "Slayer of the Alien Gods." Southwest Review, 42, No. 3 (Summer 1957), 177-84.
George Whitlock (Navajo) comes home to tell his wife, Nancy, that he must serve as radio operator during a fire fight in the mountains. All the while George and Jimmie Charlie drive to the fire site, George explains the blaze in terms of Navajo myth.

874 Wright, Harry Robinson. "The Trailers." Outing, 46, No. 2 (May 1905), 234-37.

Private Damer, stationed with a small force at Guadalope Canyon, begins his daily search for signs of Geronimo and his Apaches with two Indian scouts, Big Head and Pretty. Separated from his Indian guides, Damer determines that the two scouts have discovered an Apache trail and that one has attacked the other. He finds Pretty, calmly attacks him, and forces his confession. While dragging the dead Big Head out from the bushes, Pretty is suddenly bitten by a rattlesnake. He demands a knife, cuts away at his palm, then swiftly attacks Damer. The poison, however, kills Pretty before he can kill the white man.

875 Wyatt, Edgar. "Kit Carson's Navajo Trail." Young Readers' Indian Stories. New York: Lantern Press, 1951, pp. 23-37.

Kit Carson enters Canyon de Chelly in 1863 and conquers some eight thousand Navajos with a troop of only four hundred soldiers. Later he helps them to return to their homeland from the New Mexico reservation.

876 Wyatt, Lawrence. "Everybody Else and Indians." The Falcon, 14, No. 6 (Spring 1973), 19-37.

Amicus Gatcomb, a poet, is spiritually dry--having gone over to the "administration" in helping to put down a student riot in his school. He finds himself impotent, both poetically and sexually. Amicus goes to Alaska on a lecture tour, and meets his image-to-be in Kleinemann, a vice-president Amicus grows to hate because he sees himself in the man. John Bigrock (Indian) helps lead him into the underground passages for a party where, with the help of a guide in the maze, he finds and "uses" Kleinemann's daughter--and finds himself pure and potent again. He dresses as an Indian, and Bigrock helps him to sneak out of the airport; as the plane starts down the runway, Kleinemann's pistol fires at Amicus from the boarding gate.

877 Yarbro, Chelsea Quinn. "The Ghosts at Iron River." Men and Malice: An Anthology of Mystery and Suspense. Ed. Dean Dickensheet. Garden City, N.Y.: Doubleday, 1973, pp. 126-47. Reprinted in Best Detective Stories of the Year, 1974, ed. Allen J. Hubin (New York: E. P. Dutton, 1974), pp. 11-42.

James Raven Feathers, a young anthropology professor at McGill University, is an Iron River Indian who is helping his people move peacefully to a new location so that the Canadian government can build a hydroelectric dam on the tribal grounds. The Iron River group is willing to relocate only if their dead ancestors will be dug up and relocated with them. While Raven Feathers is overseeing this removal of bones, he accidentally discovers the skeleton of a white anthropologist who

disappeared years earlier while writing a book about the Iron
River Indians. Along with the skeleton is evidence indicating
that the anthropologist had been murdered, probably by a rival
white anthropologist who subsequently published a condescending
book about the Iron River Indians.

878   Zitkala-Sa. (Sioux). "The Soft-Hearted Sioux." Harper's,
        102 (Mar. 1901), 505-08.
        A young Indian converts to Christianity despite his par-
ents' urging that he be a brave. He leaves and returns dressed
as a white man holding a Bible, much to his parents' disgust.
When the food supply runs out, he is ordered to find more; he
does so, but a man steals the food from him. In a struggle
the thief is killed. Returning home, the young Indian learns
that his father is dead; he is arrested and hanged for murder.

879   _____. (Sioux). "The Trial Path." Harper's 103 (Oct.
        1901), 741-44.
        An old Indian woman tells her granddaughter a tale: Two
good friends had fought each other over her--one killing the
other. To test the survivor the girl's father had the young
man ride a pony, stipulating that if he fell off he was to be
killed. The boy was able to remain astride and was allowed
to marry the girl. Later, when the woman's husband died,
his pony was killed so that it might accompany the Indian to
the afterworld. The old woman's story falls on deaf ears,
however, because the little girl has fallen asleep, unable to
hear the sacred knowledge.

880   Zogbaum, Rufus Fairchild. "Trooper George Pays His Debt."
        Outing, 47, No. 4 (Jan. 1906), 481-85.
        Sergeant Taylor and Mr. Kent discuss the troops, Kent
confiding to Taylor that he doesn't care for the "nigger" troops.
But Sergeant Taylor relates how Colonel Matt's black batallion
once saved four troops from decimation in an Indian skirmish.

INDIAN TRIBES INDEX

The Indian tribes represented in the short stories of this bibliography are listed below in alphabetical order.

Three tribes--Apache, Sioux (Dakota), and Pueblo--deserve particular attention because each group is made up of various subgroups. There are a dozen sub-groups of the Apache tribe, the ones most commonly named in short fiction being Jicarilla and Chiricahua; similarly, the Sioux tribe has more than a dozen sub-divisions, the most common of which is Oglala. Stories naming only the general classification "Apache" or "Sioux" are, of course, indexed accordingly; however, stories which specify a sub-tribe are additionally indexed as such. For example, if a story is about Jicarilla Apaches it will be listed twice--under APACHE, and under JICARILLA. Therefore, a scholar seeking all stories about Apaches need only check under the single listing APACHE; another scholar seeking only stories specifically mentioning "Jicarilla" Apaches has immediate access to the limited list without having to check all stories in the APACHE category.

The New Mexico Pueblo Indians are treated differently, for the purposes of this index, because they are more closely related to one another than are the Apache or the Sioux groups. In this index, then, we have not attempted to list Pueblo villages separately. Even if the Laguna Pueblo Indians are mentioned, for example, the story is indexed under PUEBLO only.

ABNAKI 75, 147, 365, 452
ACHOMAWI 198
ALGONQUIN 43, 185, 223, 808
APACHE 12, 14, 42, 46, 51, 61, 74, 101, 123, 169, 205, 208,
    217, 225, 229, 242, 246, 263, 264, 304, 305, 306, 342, 351,
    353, 363, 367, 369, 370, 396, 455, 456, 459, 462, 466, 481,
    485, 500, 504, 518, 558, 569, 572, 615, 621, 647, 651, 655,
    656, 657, 682, 695, 696, 750, 753, 759, 762, 769, 770, 772,
    811, 813, 848, 850, 851, 866, 867, 874
ARAPAHO 209, 248, 287, 545
ASAROKEE 653
ASSINIBOIN 135, 570, 627, 729
ATHAPASCA 786

BAGOG 681

BANNOCK 253, 673
BLACKFEET 78, 98, 102, 204, 271, 272, 319, 322, 330, 334, 352, 386, 419, 427, 684, 698
BLACK SNAKE 432, 709
BRULE 749

CADDO 379, 542
CAHUILLA 505, 599
CALIFORNIA 25, 28, 258, 403, 404, 405, 406, 407, 408, 409, 410, 411, 412, 413, 414, 415, 416, 417, 636, 692
CATAWBA 718, 784
CAYUSE 146
CHEMEHUEVI 172
CHEROKEE 60, 70, 128, 168, 186, 267, 360, 361, 378, 691, 704, 719, 720, 723, 739, 748, 770, 777, 818
CHEYENNE 3, 4, 141, 245, 268, 278, 279, 281, 284, 290, 293, 294, 336, 349, 388, 467, 518, 545, 620, 652, 658, 701, 783, 807, 815, 817
CHICKASAW 235, 236, 237, 238, 239, 240
CHINOOK 494, 632
CHIPPEWA 135, 154, 317, 319, 335, 345, 347, 422, 727, 786, 868
CHIRICAHUA 51, 246, 353, 656, 769, 851
CHOCTAW 9, 133, 378, 500, 721
CHUMASH 256, 602
CHURUCTA 603
COMANCHE 2, 83, 127, 231, 307, 324, 499, 500, 506, 507, 523, 539, 626, 651, 655, 704, 755, 816
COOS 157
COOSUCK 381
COUTEAUX JAUNES 580
CREE 254, 319, 371, 372, 422, 580, 600, 788, 793, 795, 799, 809, 826, 827, 869
CREEK 134, 702, 722
CROW 98, 143, 197, 224, 319, 328, 330, 350, 380, 388, 393, 591, 659, 678, 684, 782, 783, 807, 816, 862, 863
CROWFOOT 435, 441

DAKOTA see SIOUX
DEERFOOT 577
DELAWARE 315, 639, 695
DIGGER 212, 338, 339, 364, 411, 417, 763, 829

EEL RIVER 332
ESKIMO 29, 262, 469, 517

FLATHEAD 397

GRAY EAGLE 441
GREAT SLAVE 317, 319
GROS VENTRE 684

HAVASUPAI 1
HOHAY 729
HOPI 16, 17, 18, 19, 22, 171, 193, 282, 342, 611, 675, 819

HUNKPAPA 224, 247
HURON 315, 421, 422, 513

IOWA 726
IRON RIVER 877
IROQUOIS 69, 309, 348, 421, 660
ISHMAELITISH 482
ITEA 785

JICARILLA 42, 74, 242, 459

KARANKAWA 814
KENNEBEC 674
KIOWA 60, 283, 325, 521, 522, 523, 524, 525, 526, 527, 528,
     529, 530, 531, 532, 533, 534, 535, 536, 538, 539, 541, 543,
     544, 545, 546, 547, 548, 550, 551, 552, 553, 554, 555, 759
KLAMATH 341, 699
KUTENAIS 322

LAKOTA 623
LIPAN 225

MANDAN 732, 755
MENOMINI 730
MESCALERO 225, 246, 306
MINGO 125
MODOC 58, 198, 669
MOHAWK 191, 227, 232, 308, 310, 854
MOHICAN 184
MOJAVE 178, 425, 848
MONO 596, 703

NAVAJO 16, 31, 38, 42, 44, 55, 62, 85, 86, 87, 88, 89, 90, 91,
     92, 93, 94, 95, 96, 137, 160, 163, 164, 166, 170, 171, 200,
     213, 214, 215, 216, 217, 218, 226, 227, 277, 301, 304, 312,
     313, 316, 366, 373, 375, 426, 453, 454, 457, 460, 461, 472,
     509, 562, 563, 619, 631, 633, 675, 677, 715, 739, 752, 778,
     779, 787, 796, 820, 822, 873, 875
NEHALEM 155, 156, 157, 158, 780
NEZ PERCE 73, 269, 476, 576, 694
NIPISSING 421
NOKI 318
NOPAH 314, 318
NULATO 492

OGLALA 248, 261, 620, 686
OJIBWAY 129, 130, 131, 132, 153, 221, 347, 354, 355, 557, 564,
     635, 690, 808
OMAHA 584, 585, 586, 588, 589, 590, 594
ONEIDA 84
OPITSAT 725
OSAGE 500, 582, 867
OTOE 586, 867
OTTAWA 786

PAPAGO   47, 48, 64, 65, 66, 401, 609, 810
PAWNEE   76, 298, 323, 451, 465, 479, 589, 738, 785, 800, 802
PENACOOK   144
PEQUOT   184, 513
PIEGAN   322, 659, 683, 685
PIKUNI   698
PIMA   747
PIT RIVER   872
PIUTE   5, 33, 35, 36, 40, 41, 49, 53, 176, 177, 196, 247, 270,
    316, 545, 672, 736, 744, 746, 774, 775, 776, 805, 849
PONCA   584
POPELOUTECHOM   259
POTAWATOMI   149, 182, 331
PUEBLO   22, 32, 46, 122, 126, 159, 169, 199, 200, 201, 202, 218,
    362, 374, 458, 481, 507, 509, 561, 573, 611, 612, 613, 615,
    617, 640, 642, 645, 647, 700, 711, 713, 714, 715, 765, 766,
    768, 820, 822
PUYALLUP   483

QUECHUA   203

ROANOKE   442

SAC   167, 607, 730
SAGHARAWITE   50
SALISHAN   427, 428, 429, 430, 431, 432, 433, 434, 435, 436, 438,
    439, 440, 443, 444, 445, 446, 447, 448, 449, 450
SANTEE   135
SARANAC   514
SEMINOLE   667, 722, 758
SENECA   119, 194, 227, 309, 402, 784, 854
SHAWNEE   7, 71, 72, 233, 424, 448
SHEBOYAH   314
SHEHANG   450
SHOSHONE   34, 49, 160, 176, 195, 326, 352, 545, 565, 705, 756,
    860
SHUSWAP   63
SIOUX (DAKOTA)   76, 97, 135, 138, 151, 165, 179, 180, 181, 219,
    221, 222, 224, 247, 248, 261, 276, 280, 286, 288, 289, 291,
    292, 295, 334, 336, 349, 389, 398, 451, 468, 479, 480, 520,
    540, 545, 564, 579, 586, 591, 608, 620, 622, 627, 630, 652,
    686, 696, 701, 705, 716, 727, 728, 729, 731, 732, 733, 734,
    749, 758, 771, 782, 792, 800, 802, 803, 807, 823, 861, 862,
    878
SISSETON   280
SIWASH   110, 111, 112, 115, 117, 118, 359, 491, 496, 497, 725,
    788, 865
SKOKOMISH   781
SNAKE   597, 668
SNOQUALMI   717
SPOKANE   397
STIKINE   693
STONEY   400, 870
SUISUNE   410, 603

TAHUAHUCA 655
TETON 292
TEWA 374
TOLTEC 679
TONKAWA 124
TONTO 396
TOPOYTO 603
TSICHAH 817
TULARE 403, 414
TUSCARORA 831, 832, 833, 834, 835, 836, 837, 838, 839, 840, 841, 842, 843, 844, 845, 846, 847

ULO 641
UMATILLA 376
UTAWA 625
UTE 54, 316, 508, 523, 530, 644, 646, 649, 761, 797, 804, 805, 863

WAHULA CREEK 559
WAXAHACHIE 9
WINDEGO 511
WINNEBAGO 56, 386, 733
WYLACKIE 103, 104, 105, 106, 107, 108, 109, 113, 114, 116

YAKIMA 155, 227
YANKTON 222
YANKTONAI 295
YAQUI 572, 735, 871
YELLOW KNIFE 317, 319
YEMASSEE 722
YOKIO 669
YOLO 603
YOSEMITE 193
YUKON 490, 498
YUMA 643

ZUNI 18, 275, 757, 820

SUBJECT KEY WORDS INDEX

Some of the "key words" listed below are self-explanatory; those requiring clarification are primarily of two types--combination categories, and categories that take on special meaning in terms of relationships between fictional characters.

Expediency, for the most part, determined our combinations of subject matter for the first type. For example, "religion" is a system of attitudes, beliefs, and practices; "mission" is a place; "missionary" is a person. Yet they tend to overlap when considered as subject matter in fiction and, therefore, have been combined as RELIGION/MISSION/MISSIONARY in our index. "Hunting" and "trapping" are, indeed, different activities, but both place the participating characters out-of-doors in a "human-versus-animal" situation. Our HUNTING/TRAPPING designation covers all related activity. Our other combination categories can be demonstrated to share similar characteristic relationships.

The second type separates rather than combines. Three subjects--capture, revenge, and romance--are abundant in short fiction about Indians. But "capture" stories vary depending upon who is captured and who is the capturer; likewise, a story about "romance" is uniquely dependent upon which of the lovers is Indian and which is non-Indian. Thus we have broken down these three categories according to "who-does-what-to-whom" in the case of CAPTURE and REVENGE, and according to race and sex of characters in the case of ROMANCE. Specific relationships are noted following each category; these appear as "I" (Indian) and "NI" (non-Indian) separated by a diagonal mark. For the purposes of this index a half-breed, or a character with any Indian blood, is considered Indian.

In "capture" and "revenge" stories, the first listed is the aggressor against the second; for example, REVENGE NI/I indicates stories in which a non-Indian seeks revenge against the Indian. In "romance" stories, the first listed designates the male character, the second is female; thus, the category ROMANCE I/NI includes stories of romantic involvement between Indian men and non-Indian women.

AGRICULTURE (incl. other land use) 18, 33, 77, 85, 103, 127, 159, 188, 199, 200, 210, 216, 233, 273, 275, 280, 283, 287, 309, 343, 357, 373, 379, 421, 465, 466, 468, 483, 521, 551,

576, 592, 600, 619, 627, 637, 694, 700, 703, 715, 721, 785, 832, 833, 840

ANIMAL 2, 3, 5, 12, 14, 29, 39, 40, 55, 60, 72, 76, 77, 78, 79, 80, 81, 82, 83, 91, 93, 96, 98, 99, 100, 104, 105, 106, 107, 113, 115, 116, 123, 130, 134, 137, 138, 140, 142, 146, 163, 167, 169, 202, 203, 204, 209, 213, 215, 217, 220, 222, 226, 229, 233, 234, 235, 240, 242, 246, 255, 261, 262, 264, 278, 280, 283, 289, 290, 296, 298, 306, 307, 313, 316, 317, 319, 321, 322, 323, 325, 327, 334, 336, 342, 344, 348, 362, 373, 380, 381, 382, 392, 404, 405, 409, 412, 418, 419, 427, 431, 434, 437, 438, 443, 447, 452, 454, 456, 471, 476, 477, 478, 482, 486, 500, 502, 505, 507, 509, 511, 516, 517, 519, 520, 525, 528, 532, 535, 536, 541, 545, 548, 550, 551, 552, 555, 560, 563, 564, 574, 578, 583, 586, 588, 590, 597, 600, 610, 615, 627, 636, 637, 651, 653, 654, 661, 662, 664, 668, 670, 672, 673, 676, 680, 682, 683, 684, 685, 686, 687, 688, 689, 690, 691, 698, 705, 708, 714, 715, 716, 718, 720, 724, 734, 736, 738, 743, 746, 751, 755, 756, 759, 769, 774, 778, 779, 784, 793, 795, 799, 800, 803, 808, 814, 820, 826, 841, 851, 858, 868, 879

ARSON 114, 135, 177, 233, 242, 318, 411, 420, 424, 447, 451, 609, 670, 828, 831, 840, 866

ATTACK/BATTLE 2, 3, 5, 6, 7, 8, 11, 14, 16, 25, 32, 33, 37, 41, 50, 58, 61, 76, 83, 84, 98, 99, 101, 110, 112, 116, 118, 119, 121, 124, 135, 136, 138, 141, 146, 150, 151, 153, 159, 162, 165, 167, 179, 181, 183, 184, 185, 187, 188, 189, 192, 194, 202, 204, 205, 208, 215, 219, 224, 225, 229, 230, 231, 234, 239, 247, 248, 250, 255, 256, 261, 264, 268, 269, 270, 272, 274, 276, 278, 285, 290, 293, 299, 302, 303, 304, 309, 314, 315, 316, 318, 319, 323, 324, 331, 332, 334, 336, 337, 338, 340, 342, 349, 351, 353, 359, 365, 367, 370, 372, 384, 388, 389, 393, 398, 405, 413, 414, 415, 416, 418, 420, 421, 424, 425, 431, 432, 442, 444, 447, 448, 451, 459, 462, 466, 470, 486, 487, 493, 494, 498, 500, 504, 506, 507, 508, 509, 514, 518, 523, 527, 528, 530, 537, 541, 554, 569, 577, 579, 586, 591, 597, 598, 602, 606, 608, 609, 613, 620, 621, 624, 634, 635, 639, 640, 650, 651, 655, 658, 659, 665, 668, 671, 673, 681, 682, 684, 686, 687, 689, 692, 694, 695, 698, 699, 709, 713, 720, 721, 722, 724, 727, 729, 730, 733, 738, 741, 745, 747, 749, 750, 753, 754, 755, 756, 758, 760, 762, 764, 770, 771, 772, 783, 786, 787, 792, 798, 800, 802, 805, 807, 811, 812, 813, 818, 826, 827, 828, 848, 850, 851, 854, 858, 862, 863, 865, 866, 871, 874, 875, 876, 880

CAPTURE--I/I 14, 56, 110, 112, 319, 322, 414, 431, 441, 448, 449, 498, 523, 589, 651, 687, 727, 732, 770, 784, 785, 786, 800

CAPTURE--I/NI 6, 7, 27, 71, 72, 111, 112, 116, 119, 124, 135, 136, 149, 153, 186, 188, 230, 241, 245, 246, 257, 264, 303,

316, 318, 330, 338, 347, 381, 387, 389, 390, 391, 393, 419,
421, 443, 454, 466, 483, 489, 506, 541, 554, 568, 596, 603,
628, 639, 650, 652, 660, 671, 672, 697, 723, 724, 736, 745,
790, 826, 828, 854, 869, 871

CAPTURE--NI/I 116, 184, 202, 246, 250, 256, 259, 272, 276,
293, 305, 306, 316, 324, 341, 369, 396, 418, 494, 602, 607,
655, 658, 717, 726, 755, 818, 827, 859, 863, 875

CAPTURE--NI/NI 325, 360, 390, 568, 695, 697

CULTURAL MISUNDERSTANDING 3, 9, 10, 14, 19, 34, 38, 54,
58, 62, 64, 65, 66, 68, 73, 74, 85, 88, 89, 92, 94, 97, 102,
121, 132, 153, 160, 168, 171, 173, 175, 176, 177, 178, 179,
180, 181, 182, 184, 194, 201, 206, 211, 214, 215, 216, 226,
227, 232, 239, 242, 244, 249, 251, 262, 263, 266, 272, 276,
277, 282, 284, 287, 289, 297, 300, 309, 316, 318, 338, 350,
352, 356, 373, 374, 376, 377, 383, 386, 387, 390, 392, 393, 411,
421, 429, 446, 453, 455, 457, 458, 460, 469, 472, 475, 479,
484, 489, 490, 494, 506, 512, 515, 519, 521, 522, 531, 542,
544, 547, 549, 551, 557, 558, 561, 562, 563, 564, 565, 566,
570, 573, 581, 582, 585, 593, 600, 615, 616, 617, 618, 623,
627, 630, 633, 638, 639, 679, 690, 698, 707, 709, 710, 735,
741, 744, 749, 751, 763, 771, 774, 777, 798, 804, 817, 818,
822, 832, 834, 845, 846, 852, 877

DRUNKEN INDIAN 21, 59, 63, 66, 74, 97, 115, 119, 128, 159,
166, 188, 195, 204, 207, 226, 252, 315, 333, 334, 360, 392,
404, 418, 426, 453, 474, 476, 480, 486, 502, 503, 555, 572,
579, 619, 622, 627, 630, 642, 667, 721, 730, 737, 760, 763,
789, 805, 806, 824, 833, 840, 843, 856

EDUCATIONAL DISORIENTATION/I-NI INNER CONFLICT 10, 17,
19, 20, 22, 29, 34, 41, 46, 47, 54, 56, 63, 73, 85, 87, 89,
91, 94, 95, 97, 102, 134, 144, 145, 160, 164, 166, 168, 173,
175, 177, 179, 180, 184, 186, 194, 196, 211, 226, 242, 243,
244, 248, 249, 252, 262, 263, 277, 282, 283, 295, 297, 301,
302, 304, 308, 309, 316, 318, 325, 341, 350, 363, 370, 372,
374, 375, 376, 378, 379, 382, 383, 386, 387, 388, 390, 391,
393, 395, 397, 411, 413, 453, 455, 456, 457, 475, 481, 484,
490, 512, 517, 519, 520, 521, 522, 531, 540, 544, 545, 547,
548, 549, 551, 559, 562, 563, 565, 568, 570, 575, 581, 582,
593, 595, 596, 613, 616, 617, 619, 623, 627, 628, 630, 633,
635, 636, 639, 641, 642, 646, 647, 677, 690, 700, 706, 707,
716, 735, 736, 739, 741, 745, 752, 757, 762, 765, 770, 777,
800, 801, 805, 809, 816, 819, 822, 823, 832, 836, 843, 845,
846, 857, 870, 878

EDUCATIONAL EXPERIENCE 1, 6, 10, 12, 13, 16, 17, 19, 22,
31, 39, 43, 45, 54, 56, 58, 60, 66, 67, 69, 70, 71, 72, 73,
75, 84, 87, 88, 89, 91, 93, 94, 95, 97, 102, 103, 105, 110,
111, 112, 115, 117, 118, 120, 131, 143, 146, 148, 151, 159
160, 166, 168, 178, 179, 180, 182, 184, 193, 196, 198, 199,

201, 204, 206, 207, 209, 210, 211, 214, 216, 220, 222, 223,
226, 227, 232, 235, 237, 238, 240, 243, 244, 248, 262, 264,
265, 269, 272, 276, 279, 280, 281, 282, 285, 287, 294, 304,
309, 311, 312, 313, 315, 316, 325, 327, 329, 335, 336, 343,
347, 350, 355, 358, 361, 363, 370, 376, 377, 379, 380, 382,
386, 387, 388, 390, 391, 392, 395, 399, 406, 407, 409, 414,
415, 424, 426, 445, 452, 455, 456, 458, 460, 464, 466, 467,
468, 469, 472, 473, 481, 484, 485, 492, 493, 496, 504, 506,
510, 512, 515, 519, 521, 522, 525, 531, 535, 536, 537, 538,
539, 540, 545, 546, 549, 551, 553, 556, 557, 561, 562, 563,
573, 574, 575, 600, 602, 611, 619, 623, 628, 631, 636, 638,
639, 642, 643, 660, 661, 662, 667, 676, 677, 685, 691, 700,
707, 709, 710, 719, 735, 739, 745, 748, 752, 754, 755, 759,
761, 763, 765, 766, 779, 782, 800, 804, 813, 814, 822, 823,
832, 836, 844, 845, 849, 852, 857, 863, 864, 867, 876, 879

EXPLOITATION   9, 18, 21, 23, 73, 77, 78, 103, 105, 109, 133,
137, 142, 153, 160, 173, 215, 230, 238, 243, 249, 251, 273,
283, 286, 318, 329, 339, 343, 345, 360, 378, 386, 400, 401,
422, 423, 424, 429, 456, 458, 460, 482, 491, 492, 498, 552,
577, 579, 600, 616, 619, 633, 638, 641, 662, 667, 694, 699,
703, 708, 709, 710, 719, 730, 731, 733, 735, 754, 761, 763,
765, 768, 793, 796, 817, 819, 824, 842, 846, 849, 864, 877

FORTUNE HUNTER   15, 21, 23, 49, 72, 88, 103, 105, 117, 120,
169, 170, 172, 205, 222, 228, 255, 280, 286, 299, 338, 339,
346, 361, 395, 400, 401, 403, 423, 454, 463, 464, 476, 487,
492, 494, 496, 672, 690, 695, 699, 701, 708, 725, 733, 756,
761, 763, 774, 789, 791, 796, 829, 850

HALF-BREED   10, 26, 34, 40, 42, 46, 48, 54, 60, 89, 99, 124,
127, 128, 131, 132, 133, 134, 145, 174, 190, 192, 202, 228,
235, 237, 238, 239, 240, 242, 247, 253, 254, 255, 258, 259,
260, 271, 295, 316, 317, 336, 339, 341, 347, 348, 350, 354,
372, 376, 379, 387, 388, 390, 408, 428, 439, 471, 483, 489,
496, 500, 501, 520, 539, 558, 560, 565, 581, 582, 609, 624,
635, 640, 641, 653, 654, 662, 663, 664, 665, 666, 669, 672,
675, 679, 693, 704, 707, 717, 725, 727, 740, 743, 745, 748,
759, 768, 770, 777, 780, 788, 794, 797, 799, 801, 805, 806,
821, 825, 830, 848, 853, 856, 861, 864, 867, 869

HUMOR   4, 9, 20, 28, 32, 43, 46, 48, 51, 65, 68, 70, 84, 89,
92, 96, 103, 104, 105, 106, 107, 108, 109, 113, 114, 116, 143,
146, 171, 175, 200, 206, 214, 216, 242, 251, 265, 266, 279,
291, 307, 320, 326, 327, 333, 338, 340, 343, 344, 354, 366,
369, 370, 398, 455, 465, 475, 476, 479, 496, 541, 593, 634,
638, 653, 659, 661, 662, 663, 667, 693, 703, 708, 719, 750,
751, 758, 774, 775, 776, 782, 797, 799, 804, 820, 824, 826,
831, 832, 833, 836, 839, 841, 842, 843, 851, 864, 867, 876

HUNTING/TRAPPING   50, 76, 77, 78, 79, 81, 82, 93, 99, 100,
104, 107, 110, 111, 113, 130, 135, 138, 148, 163, 183, 203,
213, 215, 217, 220, 222, 235, 240, 247, 249, 264, 272, 293,

298, 307, 317, 319, 321, 326, 330, 342, 348, 355, 362, 380,
382, 384, 409, 418, 419, 422, 423, 434, 451, 452, 460, 477,
494, 497, 509, 511, 519, 520, 535, 560, 564, 574, 576, 578,
580, 583, 590, 593, 607, 660, 661, 664, 665, 680, 683, 686,
688, 691, 699, 700, 701, 705, 717, 718, 720, 724, 726, 727,
730, 733, 738, 743, 778, 784, 795, 807, 808, 822, 830, 835,
868, 869

INDIAN ANTAGONIST   2, 4, 5, 8, 11, 14, 16, 25, 27, 72, 76, 101,
119, 123, 125, 134, 136, 141, 143, 146, 149, 151, 153, 162,
188, 189, 190, 202, 205, 208, 219, 225, 229, 231, 233, 234,
241, 245, 263, 268, 269, 270, 271, 274, 276, 302, 303, 305,
330, 332, 337, 348, 349, 351, 360, 365, 381, 389, 393, 396,
397, 398, 405, 411, 414, 415, 416, 420, 421, 425, 431, 462,
470, 487, 489, 490, 491, 492, 494, 501, 504, 506, 507, 508,
518, 527, 528, 554, 566, 569, 572, 586, 588, 591, 597, 598,
606, 620, 621, 625, 634, 650, 655, 656, 658, 665, 668, 669,
671, 673, 682, 683, 684, 686, 687, 692, 698, 701, 708, 715,
716, 723, 724, 727, 738, 740, 741, 746, 750, 753, 756, 758,
760, 764, 772, 792, 794, 797, 798, 800, 802, 805, 806, 811,
825, 828, 848, 850, 851, 858, 861, 862, 863, 866, 872, 880

INDIAN CULTURE/HERITAGE/TRIBAL TRADITION   1, 3, 12, 15,
16, 17, 18, 19, 20, 22, 29, 33, 35, 38, 43, 45, 46, 50, 52,
53, 54, 56, 57, 62, 64, 66, 67, 75, 76, 84, 86, 88, 89, 90,
91, 93, 94, 97, 100, 102, 116, 118, 122, 124, 126, 129, 130,
131, 132, 135, 155, 156, 157, 159, 160, 163, 166, 169, 170,
171, 174, 177, 178, 180, 181, 183, 184, 185, 186, 193, 194,
197, 198, 199, 200, 201, 202, 207, 214, 216, 218, 220, 223,
224, 226, 227, 228, 232, 236, 237, 240, 241, 244, 249, 252,
254, 256, 262, 273, 275, 277, 279, 280, 282, 284, 287, 288,
289, 295, 298, 300, 301, 303, 304, 307, 308, 309, 312, 314,
316, 318, 320, 321, 323, 330, 335, 336, 338, 346, 350, 352,
361, 363, 364, 372, 373, 374, 375, 377, 379, 380, 382, 383,
386, 387, 388, 390, 391, 392, 393, 394, 399, 418, 429, 432,
433, 435, 436, 441, 443, 444, 446, 448, 455, 456, 457, 458,
461, 462, 463, 464, 469, 472, 473, 475, 482, 483, 484, 485,
489, 490, 491, 493, 498, 499, 509, 512, 513, 514, 515, 516,
521, 524, 525, 527, 529, 530, 531, 532, 533, 534, 536, 537,
538, 539, 540, 542, 543, 545, 546, 547, 548, 549, 550, 551,
553, 556, 559, 561, 562, 563, 564, 565, 567, 570, 573, 574,
580, 583, 584, 585, 587, 588, 589, 590, 592, 594, 600, 601,
605, 608, 609, 615, 616, 617, 619, 623, 626, 627, 630, 633,
638, 644, 645, 646, 647, 648, 649, 651, 653, 663, 664, 667,
675, 678, 679, 685, 688, 689, 698, 705, 706, 707, 709, 710,
712, 714, 717, 718, 720, 721, 722, 723, 725, 726, 727, 728,
729, 730, 731, 732, 733, 734, 735, 741, 744, 746, 748, 759,
761, 763, 765, 766, 767, 768, 769, 771, 774, 775, 776, 778,
779, 781, 782, 783, 785, 793, 795, 796, 803, 808, 814, 815,
816, 817, 819, 822, 827, 829, 831, 834, 835, 836, 837, 839,
843, 844, 845, 847, 849, 852, 853, 856, 866, 867, 869, 870,
873, 877, 879

INDIAN GUIDE/SCOUT   3, 12, 49, 58, 69, 79, 99, 120, 124, 139,
    144, 161, 213, 248, 250, 263, 278, 281, 317, 325, 327, 329,
    331, 349, 367, 370, 372, 382, 400, 422, 452, 454, 460, 497,
    535, 557, 608, 624, 632, 654, 657, 661, 674, 677, 696, 711,
    772, 786, 790, 802, 874, 876

INDIAN SUPERSTITION   11, 29, 35, 37, 42, 43, 45, 50, 53, 55,
    57, 66, 79, 80, 85, 86, 90, 100, 118, 134, 139, 140, 156,
    157, 163, 164, 169, 170, 174, 177, 191, 202, 216, 228, 229,
    241, 250, 252, 272, 284, 289, 290, 295, 296, 309, 314, 317,
    318, 320, 338, 347, 352, 361, 368, 383, 393, 397, 399, 425,
    432, 433, 440, 442, 443, 447, 448, 450, 458, 459, 461, 474,
    492, 494, 504, 513, 514, 526, 532, 536, 537, 545, 547, 562,
    567, 573, 578, 580, 583, 584, 585, 586, 589, 590, 592, 601,
    612, 622, 632, 640, 641, 647, 648, 652, 653, 664, 676, 678,
    679, 685, 698, 712, 713, 718, 752, 755, 766, 769, 774, 775,
    778, 779, 795, 797, 804, 822, 832, 841, 862, 864, 871, 873,
    879

INTER-RACIAL FRIENDSHIP   6, 7, 12, 13, 26, 38, 40, 41, 49,
    58, 59, 68, 69, 74, 76, 77, 78, 79, 80, 95, 97, 98, 99, 102,
    110, 111, 112, 115, 116, 118, 120, 121, 127, 135, 139, 143,
    144, 145, 147, 148, 154, 159, 161, 166, 167, 170, 171, 176,
    180, 181, 182, 184, 186, 193, 197, 198, 202, 204, 207, 209,
    210, 213, 214, 215, 216, 217, 221, 222, 226, 228, 232, 235,
    237, 240, 243, 244, 246, 247, 251, 255, 259, 261, 264, 265,
    267, 272, 274, 276, 280, 281, 286, 290, 292, 293, 294, 298,
    304, 307, 309, 312, 313, 315, 316, 318, 319, 325, 328, 329,
    330, 334, 336, 339, 341, 344, 347, 356, 359, 360, 363, 367,
    368, 370, 371, 372, 375, 377, 388, 393, 395, 397, 400, 402,
    406, 407, 409, 412, 414, 417, 422, 428, 429, 430, 431, 433,
    434, 436, 443, 445, 446, 450, 452, 458, 461, 464, 466, 467,
    473, 475, 477, 482, 487, 490, 493, 494, 497, 500, 505, 510,
    511, 512, 516, 519, 521, 526, 544, 549, 551, 552, 557, 560,
    573, 575, 577, 578, 587, 599, 600, 605, 606, 623, 624, 627,
    629, 637, 651, 654, 655, 657, 659, 660, 661, 664, 672, 674,
    675, 676, 677, 680, 681, 683, 685, 690, 694, 696, 700, 703,
    707, 711, 719, 721, 723, 725, 726, 727, 731, 745, 754, 759,
    761, 762, 763, 770, 772, 774, 776, 780, 786, 790, 795, 796,
    800, 804, 807, 810, 813, 814, 820, 822, 829, 834, 836, 854,
    855, 856, 860, 864, 867, 871, 874, 875, 876, 880

KILLING   2, 3, 5, 7, 14, 24, 25, 29, 33, 50, 58, 60, 61, 63, 73,
    76, 83, 91, 98, 99, 101, 115, 118, 119, 122, 124, 125, 126,
    136, 137, 140, 150, 156, 163, 165, 167, 176, 179, 181, 184,
    185, 186, 187, 190, 192, 194, 195, 196, 202, 203, 204, 205,
    208, 212, 215, 218, 224, 228, 234, 239, 240, 249, 250, 253,
    255, 256, 263, 264, 269, 270, 271, 274, 276, 278, 282, 288,
    302, 303, 304, 306, 309, 314, 315, 322, 330, 331, 337, 338,
    340, 341, 348, 349, 352, 353, 356, 360, 362, 363, 364, 367,
    368, 372, 378, 379, 384, 385, 387, 393, 394, 397, 403, 416,
    418, 421, 424, 438, 439, 441, 445, 454, 457, 459, 462, 464,
    466, 471, 478, 482, 483, 486, 490, 491, 492, 494, 495, 497,

500, 501, 506, 507, 508, 509, 511, 523, 527, 528, 530, 554,
557, 560, 566, 569, 572, 573, 579, 582, 584, 586, 587, 588,
589, 591, 594, 595, 596, 598, 602, 606, 609, 612, 614, 617,
620, 621, 625, 627, 629, 632, 635, 639, 640, 641, 643, 644,
646, 650, 654, 655, 656, 657, 658, 665, 668, 669, 671, 675,
677, 680, 681, 684, 686, 687, 692, 695, 696, 698, 701, 709,
713, 715, 716, 720, 721, 722, 723, 724, 726, 727, 728, 729,
730, 731, 733, 734, 738, 740, 742, 743, 744, 746, 747, 749,
750, 753, 756, 760, 761, 762, 764, 768, 770, 771, 772, 777,
784, 786, 793, 797, 798, 802, 805, 807, 810, 813, 815, 817,
818, 821, 825, 827, 828, 829, 830, 837, 838, 848, 852, 861,
862, 863, 865, 866, 871, 872, 874, 877, 878, 879

LAZY INDIAN 9, 20, 59, 68, 88, 94, 103, 104, 105, 106, 107,
108, 109, 113, 114, 116, 183, 200, 207, 251, 279, 345, 354,
357, 369, 385, 404, 426, 505, 559, 561, 627, 633, 690, 702,
703, 737, 754, 773, 775, 801, 824, 849, 855

LEGAL/BUREAUCRATIC CONFLICT 9, 14, 19, 20, 48, 61, 64,
76, 77, 96, 104, 108, 109, 110, 111, 168, 173, 176, 177, 179
180, 181, 190, 194, 196, 214, 227, 233, 237, 238, 249, 262,
271, 277, 280, 281, 282, 283, 291, 293, 343, 373, 385, 393, 465,
472, 475, 476, 491, 502, 521, 551, 570, 577, 604, 613, 614,
627, 656, 666, 667, 670, 680, 696, 719, 726, 728, 737, 739,
747, 749, 762, 768, 774, 777, 810, 829, 842, 846, 852, 869,
878

MEDICINE/MEDICINE MAN 29, 43, 45, 53, 57, 66, 75, 85, 93,
122, 139, 140, 156, 158, 170, 194, 198, 202, 216, 223, 244,
252, 272, 284, 289, 295, 298, 314, 323, 356, 360, 371, 377,
382, 388, 399, 430, 448, 450, 458, 459, 465, 483, 492, 493,
494, 520, 533, 536, 543, 547, 564, 567, 580, 583, 585, 588,
592, 621, 628, 640, 647, 653, 664, 672, 678, 679, 693, 701,
736, 752, 754, 755, 761, 775, 779, 816, 817, 818, 823, 832,
834, 837, 843, 862, 864, 870

MILITARY CONFRONTATION 8, 11, 28, 32, 56, 58, 61, 69, 71,
83, 101, 141, 150, 151, 165, 178, 184, 187, 189, 245, 256,
268, 269, 274, 276, 282, 283, 305, 324, 325, 336, 349, 353,
365, 367, 368, 369, 370, 389, 396, 402, 424, 487, 504, 518,
569, 597, 599, 602, 609, 621, 634, 652, 654, 658, 665, 674,
682, 694, 696, 726, 728, 730, 750, 753, 771, 787, 792, 813,
815, 818, 850, 859, 862, 863, 874, 875, 880

MINING (incl. search for all precious gems and metals) 15, 30,
49, 86, 109, 120, 172, 192, 205, 255, 286, 299, 400, 401, 404,
494, 496, 635, 672, 676, 756, 761, 789, 791, 796, 804, 829,
850

NON-INDIAN ANTAGONIST 3, 15, 21, 22, 23, 37, 61, 73, 77, 83,
87, 88, 91, 138, 142, 167, 169, 170, 173, 176, 179, 181, 182,
196, 201, 213, 214, 215, 216, 227, 239, 248, 250, 253, 256,
261, 280, 282, 283, 293, 299, 306, 309, 315, 317, 324, 331,

343, 353, 378, 386, 424, 429, 472, 473, 479, 500, 512, 551,
577, 579, 602, 607, 629, 657, 666, 670, 681, 685, 694, 695,
696, 699, 713, 719, 733, 755, 771, 787, 791, 810, 812, 830,
842, 846, 864, 865, 877

OUTCAST 14, 18, 38, 41, 43, 46, 54, 59, 63, 85, 91, 94, 103,
104, 105, 106, 107, 108, 109, 113, 114, 116, 131, 134, 180,
186, 202, 211, 213, 219, 226, 228, 249, 271, 285, 290, 295,
297, 314, 316, 338, 339, 341, 350, 379, 380, 390, 394, 395,
413, 430, 439, 441, 457, 482, 484, 490, 499, 503, 509, 510,
514, 549, 555, 558, 569, 572, 581, 582, 586, 590, 594, 595,
607, 613, 614, 633, 636, 640, 642, 643, 656, 702, 705, 725,
732, 742, 746, 762, 767, 779, 780, 788, 793, 808, 824, 830,
836, 840, 855, 878

RELIGION/MISSION/MISSIONARY 1, 6, 11, 21, 23, 25, 26, 27,
28, 38, 45, 46, 63, 75, 79, 92, 97, 101, 120, 140, 152, 156,
159, 163, 174, 177, 180, 187, 194, 199, 201, 206, 207, 210,
216, 219, 221, 223, 232, 244, 255, 256, 258, 259, 260, 273,
282, 289, 298, 308, 309, 312, 315, 316, 318, 335, 338, 359,
361, 363, 372, 394, 397, 399, 403, 404, 405, 406, 407, 408,
409, 410, 411, 412, 413, 414, 415, 416, 417, 421, 429, 432,
439, 440, 448, 458, 465, 474, 481, 484, 485, 489, 490, 494,
496, 498, 512, 515, 521, 522, 526, 539, 543, 545, 548, 560,
565, 566, 569, 573, 585, 595, 602, 605, 606, 616, 622, 623,
635, 638, 643, 647, 659, 664, 676, 678, 679, 687, 698, 712,
735, 761, 763, 768, 769, 771, 774, 777, 778, 785, 795, 798,
803, 809, 817, 825, 829, 841, 845, 871, 878

RESERVATION 1, 2, 3, 4, 9, 12, 13, 59, 61, 68, 83, 87, 127,
138, 167, 173, 177, 193, 204, 229, 244, 252, 261, 263, 277,
282, 284, 294, 301, 302, 308, 318, 338, 343, 350, 369, 375,
386, 396, 426, 455, 475, 476, 480, 482, 483, 521, 522, 525,
531, 562, 563, 570, 577, 611, 614, 630, 635, 651, 657, 670,
694, 700, 777, 819, 831, 832, 833, 834, 835, 836, 837, 838,
839, 840, 841, 842, 843, 845, 846, 847, 849, 853, 864, 865,
875

REVENGE--I/I 6, 14, 44, 51, 53, 107, 114, 118, 134, 135, 155,
156, 158, 176, 185, 192, 218, 219, 224, 228, 288, 314, 364,
379, 385, 394, 441, 474, 475, 490, 497, 498, 499, 509, 511,
514, 520, 523, 526, 580, 584, 592, 594, 595, 609, 635, 641,
645, 646, 649, 662, 675, 684, 687, 689, 717, 718, 720, 721,
722, 723, 725, 729, 731, 732, 734, 742, 744, 749, 754, 777,
779, 783, 784, 785, 786, 788, 793, 797, 801, 802, 806, 808,
825, 833, 838, 869, 874

REVENGE--I/NI 3, 14, 37, 83, 98, 103, 145, 148, 153, 165, 181,
184, 188, 190, 192, 194, 195, 196, 202, 206, 214, 215, 216,
230, 242, 249, 250, 263, 264, 276, 278, 289, 290, 293, 303,
318, 325, 338, 343, 347, 360, 384, 393, 424, 457, 458, 459,
477, 489, 491, 492, 494, 506, 519, 557, 570, 577, 578, 587,
593, 602, 606, 614, 629, 632, 642, 644, 665, 667, 670, 672,

680, 681, 694, 695, 709, 713, 715, 733, 755, 761, 762, 763, 807, 812, 817, 821, 826, 832, 842, 846, 850, 862, 864, 865, 867, 874

REVENGE--NI/I 2, 5, 101, 136, 141, 142, 162, 184, 204, 233, 234, 239, 245, 270, 306, 315, 324, 331, 338, 396, 424, 459, 477, 501, 508, 566, 569, 577, 579, 613, 666, 669, 681, 686, 692, 694, 726, 728, 730, 738, 740, 743, 747, 756, 757, 758, 770, 772, 774, 790, 794, 797, 798, 804, 810, 811, 830, 848, 854, 861, 872, 874

REVENGE--NI/NI 150, 213, 309, 383, 479, 488, 604, 639, 685, 695, 696, 699, 830, 871, 876, 877

ROMANCE--I/I 13, 17, 19, 20, 28, 31, 36, 38, 42, 44, 46, 47, 49, 51, 52, 54, 55, 67, 86, 87, 90, 95, 96, 122, 129, 130, 131, 132, 137, 140, 145, 155, 156, 157, 158, 160, 164, 171, 172, 176, 183, 185, 200, 210, 218, 224, 236, 237, 250, 254, 256, 258, 260, 262, 271, 274, 279, 285, 300, 301, 308, 314, 322, 327, 352, 361, 364, 366, 372, 373, 374, 375, 384, 385, 394, 397, 427, 430, 432, 435, 437, 440, 441, 442, 444, 447, 448, 449, 450, 454, 457, 475, 482, 483, 486, 490, 498, 499, 500, 502, 520, 521, 529, 530, 534, 548, 556, 559, 576, 580, 584, 586, 587, 588, 589, 594, 596, 602, 606, 609, 635, 636, 641, 645, 646, 648, 649, 663, 669, 684, 707, 708, 715, 717, 718, 720, 722, 729, 731, 732, 734, 735, 737, 742, 744, 749, 767, 768, 774, 775, 776, 779, 780, 782, 784, 786, 788, 793, 801, 808, 815, 823, 824, 832, 838, 847, 856, 879

ROMANCE--I/NI 54, 62, 124, 154, 184, 197, 218, 237, 257, 296, 303, 310, 318, 327, 367, 387, 390, 410, 455, 456, 459, 460, 471, 489, 506, 515, 549, 558, 566, 568, 577, 587, 603, 619, 677, 723, 762, 777, 780, 788

ROMANCE--NI/I 26, 30, 34, 40, 42, 47, 48, 49, 55, 58, 73, 80, 95, 120, 142, 145, 147, 148, 152, 156, 160, 165, 172, 184, 190, 192, 202, 203, 228, 230, 236, 247, 253, 292, 326, 341, 347, 350, 355, 358, 384, 388, 391, 400, 428, 439, 443, 457, 488, 493, 495, 496, 500, 517, 581, 593, 596, 600, 604, 605, 606, 609, 636, 639, 640, 642, 643, 646, 675, 679, 681, 693, 708, 717, 727, 731, 733, 745, 757, 770, 780, 788, 809, 820, 821, 856, 867

ROMANCE--NI/NI 1, 24, 25, 40, 48, 62, 71, 80, 119, 124, 148, 149, 150, 171, 184, 190, 210, 230, 231, 233, 270, 310, 315, 337, 338, 346, 353, 367, 383, 388, 398, 400, 460, 462, 496, 516, 568, 571, 621, 624, 650, 671, 697, 736, 750, 753, 809, 828, 848, 876

SCALP HUNTER 2, 101, 150, 184, 202, 263, 302, 315, 338, 340, 360, 396, 490, 507, 632, 684, 695, 720, 784, 802, 812

SCIENCE FICTION/FANTASY 11, 35, 43, 55, 57, 75, 79, 80, 100,

118, 134, 139, 153, 156, 163, 164, 227, 232, 250, 255, 309, 320, 321, 322, 323, 361, 363, 382, 383, 418, 432, 448, 463, 464, 465, 474, 513, 514, 536, 550, 567, 578, 608, 615, 622, 634, 641, 648, 653, 664, 667, 675, 685, 686, 699, 701, 716, 718, 723, 752, 758, 771, 814, 871

STAGECOACH/WAGON/WAGON TRAIN   24, 30, 91, 136, 143, 208, 212, 225, 234, 248, 255, 268, 296, 327, 328, 337, 351, 389, 420, 425, 431, 462, 500, 668, 673, 737, 741, 745, 861, 865, 866

THEFT   2, 3, 4, 5, 9, 13, 14, 24, 35, 37, 60, 81, 82, 91, 98, 99, 104, 106, 107, 108, 109, 111, 112, 113, 115, 117, 123, 143, 170, 196, 205, 206, 209, 228, 242, 246, 247, 248, 255, 261, 265, 272, 278, 290, 298, 299, 316, 325, 328, 338, 344, 345, 348, 369, 398, 403, 404, 410, 413, 445, 446, 454, 458, 477, 480, 487, 492, 494, 497, 500, 502, 510, 528, 597, 609, 627, 637, 659, 662, 670, 680, 684, 687, 698, 702, 708, 715, 733, 737, 754, 756, 757, 774, 789, 791, 797, 806, 829, 865, 869, 878

TORTURE   72, 101, 122, 125, 135, 167, 202, 203, 242, 263, 264, 271, 293, 314, 316, 338, 421, 435, 441, 443, 446, 492, 500, 595, 606, 607, 609, 634, 640, 642, 660, 672, 684, 695, 784, 798

TRADING/TRADING POST   12, 40, 72, 78, 82, 86, 157, 186, 216, 217, 262, 271, 277, 293, 316, 317, 318, 419, 422, 423, 446, 457, 461, 467, 474, 492, 552, 563, 578, 588, 605, 633, 662, 665, 683, 687, 717, 726, 730, 731, 733, 742, 786, 820, 826, 830, 862, 864